THE ENVIRONMENTAL LEGACY OF THE
UC NATURAL RESERVE SYSTEM

THE ENVIRONMENTAL LEGACY
OF THE UC NATURAL RESERVE SYSTEM

EDITED BY PEGGY L. FIEDLER, SUSAN GEE RUMSEY, AND KATHLEEN M. WONG

UNIVERSITY OF CALIFORNIA PRESS

Berkeley   Los Angeles   London

THE PUBLISHER GRATEFULLY ACKNOWLEDGES THE GENEROUS CONTRI-
BUTION TO THIS BOOK PROVIDED BY THE UNIVERSITY OF CALIFORNIA
NATURAL RESERVE SYSTEM.

University of California Press, one of the most distinguished university
presses in the United States, enriches lives around the world by advancing
scholarship in the humanities, social sciences, and natural sciences. Its
activities are supported by the UC Press Foundation and by philanthropic
contributions from individuals and institutions. For more information, visit
www.ucpress.edu.

University of California Press
Berkeley and Los Angeles, California

University of California Press, Ltd.
London, England

© 2013 by The Regents of the University of California

Library of Congress Cataloging-in-Publication Data

The environmental legacy of the UC natural reserve system / edited by Peggy
L. Fiedler, Susan Gee Rumsey, and Kathleen M. Wong.
    p.   cm.
  Includes bibliographical references and index.
  ISBN 978-0-520-27200-2 (cloth : alk. paper)
  1. Natural areas—California.   2. University of California Natural Reserve
System—History.   3. University of California (System)—Faculty.
4. Environmental protection—California.   5. Ecology—Study and teaching—
California.   6. Natural history—Study and teaching—California.   I. Fiedler,
Peggy Lee.   II. Rumsey, Susan Gee.   III. Wong, Kathleen M. (Kathleen
Michelle)
  QH76.5.C2E59   2013
  333.73'1609794—dc23   2012014651

Manufactured in China
19 18 17 16 15 14 13
10 9 8 7 6 5 4 3 2 1

Cover image: South Fork Eel River, Angelo Coast Range Reserve.
Photo by Christopher Woodcock.

For Kenneth S. Norris, Mildred E. Mathias,
Wilbur W. Mayhew, and the NRS community of managers,
students, and scholars, past, present, and future

In every walk with Nature one receives far more than he seeks.

JOHN MUIR, *letter dated Salt Lake, July 1877*

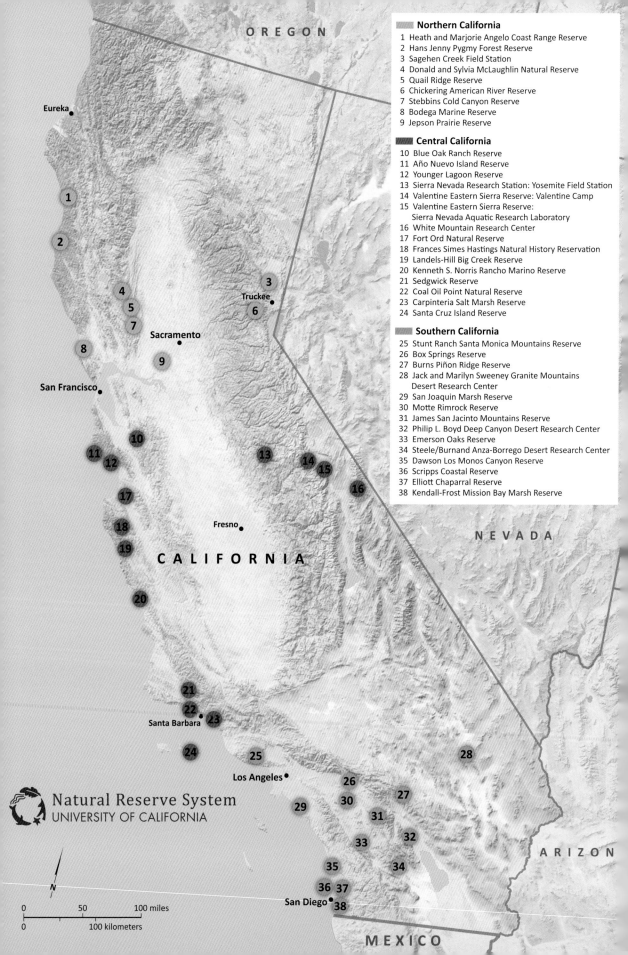

OREGON

Eureka

Northern California
1 Heath and Marjorie Angelo Coast Range Reserve
2 Hans Jenny Pygmy Forest Reserve
3 Sagehen Creek Field Station
4 Donald and Sylvia McLaughlin Natural Reserve
5 Quail Ridge Reserve
6 Chickering American River Reserve
7 Stebbins Cold Canyon Reserve
8 Bodega Marine Reserve
9 Jepson Prairie Reserve

Central California
10 Blue Oak Ranch Reserve
11 Año Nuevo Island Reserve
12 Younger Lagoon Reserve
13 Sierra Nevada Research Station: Yosemite Field Station
14 Valentine Eastern Sierra Reserve: Valentine Camp
15 Valentine Eastern Sierra Reserve:
   Sierra Nevada Aquatic Research Laboratory
16 White Mountain Research Center
17 Fort Ord Natural Reserve
18 Frances Simes Hastings Natural History Reservation
19 Landels-Hill Big Creek Reserve
20 Kenneth S. Norris Rancho Marino Reserve
21 Sedgwick Reserve
22 Coal Oil Point Natural Reserve
23 Carpinteria Salt Marsh Reserve
24 Santa Cruz Island Reserve

Southern California
25 Stunt Ranch Santa Monica Mountains Reserve
26 Box Springs Reserve
27 Burns Piñon Ridge Reserve
28 Jack and Marilyn Sweeney Granite Mountains
   Desert Research Center
29 San Joaquin Marsh Reserve
30 Motte Rimrock Reserve
31 James San Jacinto Mountains Reserve
32 Philip L. Boyd Deep Canyon Desert Research Center
33 Emerson Oaks Reserve
34 Steele/Burnand Anza-Borrego Desert Research Center
35 Dawson Los Monos Canyon Reserve
36 Scripps Coastal Reserve
37 Elliott Chaparral Reserve
38 Kendall-Frost Mission Bay Marsh Reserve

Truckee

Sacramento

San Francisco

Fresno

CALIFORNIA

NEVADA

Santa Barbara

Los Angeles

Natural Reserve System
UNIVERSITY OF CALIFORNIA

ARIZONA

San Diego

N

0   50   100 miles
0   100 kilometers

MEXICO

CONTENTS

PREFACE

The strength of any program within the University of California is measured in two ways: first, its contributions to research and teaching, and second, the degree to which these contributions are unique and important in fundamental ways. The UC Natural Reserve System (NRS) achieves highly by both measures and is indeed unique in the world.

Because of the stewardship, dedication, and effectiveness of its staff, the reserve system has for close to half a century made it possible for students and faculty to advance public understanding of natural environments and their complex functioning. NRS managers and stewards accomplish miracles daily. They keep the reserves running on a shoestring, look after the researchers and students, and voluntarily seek ways to contribute to the public good. Their dedication is exceptional and, in the face of an overwhelming workload, they remain creative and enterprising.

During the past 150 years, widespread disregard for the integrity of the natural world has resulted in a level of disruption with frightening implications for the future. In this situation, the value of the research and teaching that the NRS enables has become widely evident. The NRS is an irreplaceable resource, and whatever stresses the University endures, the NRS will survive and prosper.

Alexander N. Glazer
Director, Natural Reserve System, 1997–2009

ACKNOWLEDGMENTS

We wish to thank the managers of the NRS reserves who provided the raw material for each reserve description and gave generously of their time to help us ensure accuracy, interest, and quality. These kind managers include Paul Aigner, James M. André, Andrew J. Brooks, Virginia (Shorty) Boucher, William Bretz, Jeff Brown, Don Canestro, Steve Davenport, Daniel Dawson, Faerthen Felix, Carol Felixson, Becca Fenwick, Ken Halama, Michael P. Hamilton, Isabelle Kay, Catherine E. Koehler, Tasha La Doux, Lyndal Laughrin, Allan Muth, Suzanne Olyarnik, Mark Readdie, Cristina Sandoval, Peter Steel, and Mark Stromberg. Special thanks go to reserve managers Kate McCurdy, author of the Sedgwick Reserve chapter, and Peter Bowler, author of the San Joaquin Marsh chapter.

Equally generous were the visual artists, scientists, and nonprofit organizations who provided artwork and photographs as well as the generous permission to reproduce their work. They include Adventure Risk Challenge; Debbie Aldridge, courtesy of UC Davis; Ansel Adams, courtesy of the UC Riverside Museum of Photography; Daniel Anderson; Lisa Anderson; James M. André; Mike Baird; Michael Benard; Jerry Booth; Peter Bowler; Chris Brown; Marie-Thérèse Brown; Kevin Browne; Don Canestro; Mark A. Chappell; Norden H. (Dan) Cheatham; Ammon Corl; Daniel P. Costa; Don Croll; Lyndsay Dawkins; Donna Dewhurst; Nick DiCroce; the Estate of Richard Diebenkorn in cooperation with the Santa Cruz Island Foundation, particularly Peggy Dahl and Marla Daily; Gage Dayton; Tara de Silva; Max Eissler; Deborah Elliott-Fisk; Baotran Ellner; Jeff Falyn; Becca Fenwick; Wayne R. Ferren Jr.; Mark Fisher; Steven M. Freers; Dennis Galloway, courtesy of UC Berkeley; Jan Goerrissen; Joyce Gross; David J. Gubernick; Jennifer Gurecki; Michael P. Hamilton; Holli Harmon; Tree and J. Hensdill; Ann Howald; Stephen Ingram; Isabelle Kay; Kim Kratz; Tom Killion; Catherine E. Koehler; Kim Kratz; Jonathan Lamb; Kevin Lafferty; Lyndal Laughrin; Minette Layne; David Lee; Daniel Liberti; Steve Lonhart; Bruce Lyon; Dave Menke; Sean McStay; Peter Morning, courtesy of Mammoth Mountain; Pat Morris; Museum of Vertebrate Zoology, UC Berkeley; Violet Nakayama; the Norris Family; Vide Ohlin; Robert W. Patterson; Jessica Peak; Bruce Perry; Hank Pitcher; John T. Rotenberry; Galen Rowell, courtesy of Barbara Laughon of Mountain Light Photography; Cristina Sandoval; Leslie Saul-Gershenz; Jacqueline Sones; Will James Sooter; Michael Sulis; Stephen Ting; Tim Torell, courtesy of the Nevada Department of Wildlife; the University and Jepson Herbaria, UC Berkeley; the US Fish and Wildlife Service; the US Postal Service; John W. Wall; Larry Wan; Lobsang Wangdu; Catherine M. Watters; Jeffery T. Wilcox; and Alan and Elaine Wilson. In particular, we wish to thank Christopher Woodcock, an exceptionally gifted photographer, who so freely gave his magnificent photographs of each reserve to grace these pages.

Additional contributors to the text include NRS systemwide staff, faculty, and NRS campus coordinators whose earlier writings and analyses we drew upon, sometimes heavily. We thank Peter Alagona, Jerry Booth, Elaine Miller Bond, Peter Bowler, Jeffrey Clary, Peter G. Connors, Daniel P. Costa, Don Croll, Gage Dayton, Michael Dorward, Carol Felixson, Ava Ferguson, Wayne R. Ferren Jr., Alexander N. Glazer, Sarah Steinberg Gustafson, Margaret L. Herring, Elizabeth Howard, Pam Huntley, Violet Nakayama, Chen Yin Noah, Frank Powell, Liza Riddle, Philip W. Rundel, J. Roger Samuelsen, Jacqueline Sones, John Smiley, Sue Swarbrick, Tim Stephens, and Jeffery T. Wilcox. We remain grateful to all for allowing us to repackage their words and for their patience with us as we continued to ask favor after favor.

People who have provided inspiration and unflagging encouragement include not only the founders of the NRS but also Peter Bowler, Ann Bromfield, Beth Burnside, Norden H. (Dan) Cheatham, Philippe Cohen, Daniel P. Costa, Paul K. Dayton, Trish Holden, Claudia Luke, John Rotenberry, and H. Bradley Shaffer. In addition, we would like to recognize the great kindness of Phyllis Faber, who helped to bring the idea of this book to the attention of the University of California Press. Chuck Crumly, Kate Hoffman, and Lynn Meinhardt, also of the University of California Press, worked hard to conjure this unusual compendium of text and images, and each deserves heartfelt thanks for shepherding this book into publication.

INSPIRATION AND VISION

ORIGINS OF THE UC NATURAL RESERVE SYSTEM

Kenneth S. Norris

In 1948, Ken Norris was a graduate student in the laboratory of zoologist Ray Cowles at the Los Angeles campus of the University of California. For his dissertation, he decided to study the heat-tolerant desert iguana (*Dipsosaurus dorsalis*) of the Coachella Valley. Norris spent weeks in the dunes at the edge of Palm Springs observing these reptiles in their natural habitat. The experience sparked a lifelong quest to secure wildlands for teaching and research. The following are excerpts from his last book, *Mountain Time* (2010), published posthumously.

·   ·   ·

At one point in the spring, I had noticed half a dozen lath stakes pounded into the shoulder of the road down by the green-banded telephone pole, with unintelligible black writing scrawled on them. I hope whoever it is doesn't clean away all the *Dicoria* bushes that the iguanas love so much, I thought, assuming that a road crew was at work. But the coming events were to be much worse than that!

On my next trip to the Coachella Desert, I was appalled to encounter a wide swath of planed-down desert—over half of my study area was vacant sand. Bulldozers had lumbered north off the road and flattened a long tract of hummock dunes. Creosote bushes lay in ragged, forlorn heaps on the bare sand. A large motor hotel soon sprang up on the cleared place. The Coachella Valley had begun its precipitous plunge into a world of golf courses, housing tracts, and condos. And it has not stopped yet.

When the bulldozers planed down that strip of dunes, my graduate research program was stopped cold. I was just beginning to know all the players out there in the dunes, their life patterns, their associates. It was no use continuing on that piece of desert. Soon traffic, pavement, visiting children, pets, and all the rest would rip apart the society of animals I had chosen to observe. How far into the dunes the effects would go was anybody's guess. I was dismayed, cast adrift.

The catastrophe of the desert iguana study plot shook loose in me a clear and somber vision of the future of wildland America. No question about it, the rapidly urbanizing United States would soon be a place where the natural land and its life would be embattled nearly everywhere.

As a graduate student, I listened many times to Doc Cowles's somber assessment

Land developers ended Ken Norris's research project on desert iguanas when they bulldozed the iguana's habitat to build a motel. The experience spurred Norris to organize what is now the UC Natural Reserve System. (Mark Fisher)

of the future, especially about the disappearance of natural environments. He had watched, with obvious pain, as the wild places that supported his teaching and research disappeared. Several times, he had tried to convince the University to accept large tracts of wildland offered to him for these purposes; officialdom had always refused.

So when Doc Cowles retired in the early 1960s and I replaced him on the staff at UCLA, one of the very first things I tried to solve after substituting my junk for his in the office desk was this reluctance of the University about what seemed so obviously important to us. My conclusion was that there were nine UC campuses, and if the Regents approved a reserve for one, the other campuses would jump in, wanting their own lands.

So as a brand-new assistant professor with no obvious inhibitions about what was and was not possible—I had no idea—I decided that the solution was a statewide plan, one with limits that administrators could hang their budgetary hats on. Plan it all at once for the whole state, I thought. And so I began an effort that still engages me.

I started by going to my ichthyology mentor, Dr. Boyd Walker, who seemed to know the byzantine University ropes. Good choice.

Boyd said that, first and foremost, I needed a very senior, very august committee to steer the effort, and it must come from all campuses. High-level academics can be used to impress high-level administrators. Oh, good idea! I never would have thought of that.

Granite boulders and views of the San Bernardino Mountains characterize Burns Piñon Ridge
Reserve. (Christopher Woodcock)

Then we needed a local committee that could draw up plans for the consideration of
the more celestial group. We had to lay out what we wanted, and why, and where. Good
idea, Boyd. I never would have thought of that.

Then somebody had to do the spadework. That proved to be me.

And so we did those things, and I found, right away, that there were scientists and
teachers throughout California who saw the same future as I and who wanted to help.
In time, I found that these same concerns were shared by thoughtful people throughout
the state—businessmen, ranchers, people locked in cities, old families who saw their
land going away, politicians, and especially new-minted students.

Thus we began. University President Clark Kerr liked the idea and knew just how to
start. He designated seven natural lands that the University already held as the beginning nucleus of a reserve system. Then I asked my department for a spring's leave and
a jeep to lay out the details of a statewide plan. With my sleeping bag and fishing rod
and camping gear aboard, I visited every UC campus, asking the same questions of the
field scientists on the staff: "What are your favorite wild places to teach and do research?
Why?" And then we visited many of them.

A plan emerged that would encompass the ecological diversity of the state. We envisioned 44 reserves: some near each campus for local teaching; other big, multihabitat

NRS RESERVE ESTABLISHMENT TIMELINE

Year indicates when existing reserves joined the NRS.

1965
Box Springs Reserve
Dawson Los Monos Canyon Reserve
Frances Simes Hastings Natural History
    Reservation
Kendall-Frost Mission Bay Marsh Reserve
Philip L. Boyd Deep Canyon Desert
    Research Center
Scripps Coastal Reserve

1966
James San Jacinto Mountains Reserve

1968
Hans Jenny Pygmy Forest Reserve

1969
Año Nuevo Island Reserve
Elliott Chaparral Reserve

1970
Bodega Marine Reserve
Coal Oil Point Natural Reserve
San Joaquin Marsh Reserve

1972
Burns Piñon Ridge Reserve
Valentine Eastern Sierra Reserve:
    Valentine Camp

1973
Santa Cruz Island Reserve
Valentine Eastern Sierra Reserve:
    Nevada Aquatic Research Laboratory

1974
Chickering American River Reserve

1976
Motte Rimrock Reserve

1977
Carpinteria Salt Marsh Reserve

1978
Jack and Marilyn Sweeney Granite
    Mountains Desert Research Center
Landels-Hill Big Creek Reserve

1979
Stebbins Cold Canyon Reserve

1983
Jepson Prairie Reserve

1987
Younger Lagoon Reserve

1991
Emerson Oaks Reserve
Quail Ridge Reserve

1992
Donald and Sylvia McLaughlin Natural
    Reserve

1994
Heath and Marjorie Angelo Coast Range
    Reserve

1995
Stunt Ranch Santa Monica Mountains
    Reserve

1996
Fort Ord Natural Reserve
Sedgwick Reserve

2001
Kenneth S. Norris Rancho Marino
    Reserve

2004
Sagehen Creek Field Station

2007
Blue Oak Ranch Reserve

2009
Sierra Nevada Research Station:
    Yosemite Field Station

2011
Steele/Burnand Anza-Borrego Desert
    Research Center

2012
White Mountain Research Center

reserves to serve a given ecological zone of the state; still other smaller, single-habitat reserves designed to include the especially important habitat types. The NRS was the result. It now encompasses more than 100,000 acres in 33 reserves,[1] many with facilities and staff, and is by far the most complete, most magnificent such system dedicated to higher education and research in the world. It is certainly the most important thing I ever attempted to do. I gave the idea a push, and the will and very diverse skills of literally hundreds of other people have built and sustained it.

1. By 2012, the NRS encompassed more than 750,000 acres in 38 natural reserves.

EVOLUTION OF THE UC NATURAL RESERVES: AN INTRODUCTION

Peter S. Alagona

Peter S. Alagona is an assistant professor of history and environmental studies at UC Santa Barbara. He is interested in the history of land use, natural resource management, environmental politics, and ecological science in California and the West. His research projects include using the NRS as a case study to explore the role of biological field stations in modern American environmental history.

THE HISTORY OF THE UC NATURAL RESERVE SYSTEM

During the nineteenth and early twentieth centuries, scientists in California lacked the extensive libraries, museum collections, and laboratory facilities typical of older and wealthier academic institutions in Europe and the American Northeast. What they did have was a vast and sparsely populated hinterland with mountains, deserts, grasslands, oceans, shorelines, waterways, and forests. California attracted scientists who stressed observation of the environment over experimentation and who looked to the landscape instead of the laboratory for their subjects of study (Smith 1987). This tradition of natural science scholarship fostered the creation of the California Academy of Sciences, the Museum of Vertebrate Zoology (MVZ) at UC Berkeley, and the largest network of university-affiliated wildland research sites in the world: the NRS.

The idea of the NRS first began with a professor of zoology named Joseph Grinnell, who had a vision for how to transform California's ecological bounty into a resource for

Joseph Grinnell planted the seeds of a UC reserve system by encouraging the establishment of Hastings Natural History Reservation. (Courtesy of the Museum of Vertebrate Zoology, UC Berkeley)

scientists. As director of the MVZ since its establishment in 1908, Grinnell had done more than anyone else to promote research and education about wildlife in the West. Over three decades, he transformed the museum into the premier research center of its kind in western North America.

In 1937, near the end of his long career in science and conservation, Grinnell set out to create a new model institution for field research in the biological sciences. For this endeavor, Grinnell turned to the bucolic hardwood rangelands and chaparral-covered slopes of California's central Coast Ranges. There he hoped to create the University's first wildland site dedicated to teaching and research.

In founding a field station, Grinnell had a number of good examples to follow. The country's first biological field station, Woods Hole Marine Laboratory in Massachusetts, opened in 1888. By 1940, foundations and universities in the United States had established at least 48 field stations from New England to Arizona (Kohler 2002). Biological field stations proliferated during the Progressive Era (1885–1920) and then again during the New Deal (1933–38), both periods of scientific innovation and widespread public concern about natural resource degradation.

Grinnell's efforts to establish a UC field station were inspired, in part, by the increasing pace of development in California. From the beginning of his tenure at the MVZ, Grinnell had organized and led expeditions to survey the state's flora and fauna. He feared that many native species would disappear soon after the arrival of the ax and the plow (Star and Griesemer 1989). To find research sites protected from future development, Grinnell turned to the national parks. His work there inspired many important changes in National Park Service policies. But working in the parks required navigating political and bureaucratic obstacles at an agency with priorities that often superceded research and education. In the end, Grinnell felt that only a natural reserve owned by the University would provide the permanent protection necessary for long-term teaching, research, and monitoring of California's ecosystems.

These efforts to establish a UC field research station would be Grinnell's last work. In May 1939, the 62-year-old died suddenly of a heart attack at his home in Berkeley (Anonymous 1939). Just two weeks after his death, the UC Regents voted to accept Grinnell's proposal and established Hastings Natural History Reservation.

After World War II, the University's tremendous growth catapulted it into a position of international prominence in many areas of scientific research. The future of natural history, however, remained uncertain. By 1950, natural historians and other field biologists, who had experienced so much success in the previous decades, were being marginalized at research universities by laboratory-based physical and biomedical sciences. Traditional, field-based disciplines such as zoology and botany lost members, funding, and support. By all accounts, the 1950s and 1960s represented a low point for natural history throughout the United States.

The University of California was no exception to this trend. The MVZ and Hastings Natural History Reservation came under growing scrutiny from critics who viewed these institutions as antiquated. Suggestions were made to sell Hastings or convert it into an agricultural experiment station. But Grinnell had worked hard to gain the support of Robert Gordon Sproul, president of the University from 1930 to 1958. Sproul remained steadfast in his support for Hastings after Grinnell's death. "The University of California is engaged in an infinite variety of investigations aimed at the extension of human knowledge," Sproul wrote about Hastings in 1956, "but I don't know of any other which proceeds so steadily and surely with such quiet conviction and persistent effectiveness" (Sproul 1956).

When Clark Kerr succeeded Sproul as University president in 1958, Kerr continued the tradition of supporting campus reserves. It helped that Hastings generated its own operating budget through its endowment and external grants. The following year, Kerr increased the University's commitment to the idea of field stations when he endorsed the establishment of two more natural reserves: Boyd Deep Canyon Desert Research Center, near the town of Palm Desert in the Coachella Valley, and Box Springs Reserve, near the brand-new UC Riverside campus. These additions to UC lands marked a crucial departure from the standard model at other research universities, which had at most one terrestrial and one marine station. The acquisition of three total reserves suggested the possibility of a much larger endeavor at the University of California (Herring 2000).

It did not take long for the wisdom of these decisions to become apparent. The birth of the modern environmental movement in the early 1960s was a response to public anxiety over the nation's smoggy skies, polluted waterways, and use of chemicals such as DDT. Meanwhile, California was preparing to implement its historic Master Plan for Higher Education (1960), which aimed to make college accessible for millions of future students. To realize this goal, the state embarked on the most ambitious college and university development plan ever conceived. It was at this fortuitous moment that forces within the UC system emerged to argue for the preservation of natural lands by the University.

In 1963, Kenneth S. Norris, then an assistant professor at UCLA, suggested forming a UCLA Natural Study Area for University Teaching and Research. This relatively modest proposal was to be the precursor to a university-wide program of natural reserves.

On June 4, 1963, Norris wrote to President Kerr, requesting that he establish an all-university committee to develop and recommend policies concerning natural land holdings and acquisitions with the UC system:

> A large number of University of California staff members rely upon natural areas for teaching or research purposes, or both. Included are botanists, zoologists, geologists, meteorologists, archaeologists, geographers, and others. In fact, many staff members find the study of natural animal and plant populations essential to their research efforts. The explosive growth of California's human population is destroying natural terrain at an alarming rate, and once destroyed, it cannot be reconstituted. The University needs to plan carefully both for present staff use and for the future, with regard to these natural areas. California is completely unique in the diversity of natural terrain within its borders, and this diversity is now a strong asset for teaching, graduate, and staff research. We need to protect these advantages by careful planning.

Norris's correspondence indicates that this request was the result of a year and a half of discussion and correspondence with staff members from UC campuses at Berkeley, Davis, Santa Barbara, Riverside, and Los Angeles.

Norris enlisted several senior UC faculty members to campaign for a university-wide reserve system. This distinguished group included Norris's mentor, zoologist Raymond Cowles, and botanist Mildred Mathias, both of UCLA; botanist G. Ledyard Stebbins of UC Davis; and zoologist A. Starker Leopold of UC Berkeley. It also included several energetic young scholars, particularly Leopold's former student Wilbur Mayhew of UC Riverside. Their common goal was to consolidate the University's existing field stations into a single system and expand that system into a statewide network of natural reserves that would capture representative samples of California's extraordinary natural diversity.

Norris's careful strategizing soon bore fruit. On January 22, 1965, the UC Regents voted to establish the Natural Land and Water Reserves System, now known as the Natural Reserve System. Norris began traveling to every corner of California to evaluate sites for inclusion in the system. Along the way, he developed a method to rate potential reserves in terms of their resource

In addition to founding the NRS, Ken Norris was an expert on whale and dolphin behavior. He became the first to demonstrate echolocation in dolphins and described the fluid social patterns of Hawaiian spinner dolphins (*Stenella longirostris*). (Courtesy of the Norris Collection)

values, preexisting facilities, accessibility, and proximity to a UC campus. Norris's writings became a basis for later acquisition efforts and prioritization reports that would shape the future composition of the system (Norris 2010).

The system grew rapidly in the late 1960s and early 1970s and more gradually thereafter. Reserve lands were acquired in a variety of ways, through land purchases, leases, and donations. Early additions included Santa Cruz Island Reserve, James San Jacinto Mountains Reserve, Hans Jenny Pygmy Forest Reserve, Elliot Chaparral Reserve, and several others. By 1970, the UC reserve system was already the largest and most diverse network of university-based field stations in the world.

The UC natural reserves have contributed not only to basic field science but also to law and public policy. In the 1970s, scientists working at Hastings Natural History Reservation published research that demonstrated the ecological importance of California's native oak trees and hardwood rangelands (Alagona 2008). In the 1980s, scientists working at Sierra Nevada Aquatic Research Laboratory conducted key studies on the biological consequences of excessive water diversions from Mono Lake. Today, scientists at Sweeney Granite Mountains Desert Research Center are participating in planning processes to protect the eastern Mojave from overdevelopment for wind and solar energy.

Since its inception, the NRS has contributed immeasurably to the University of California's core missions of teaching, research, and public service. Many challenges lie ahead as public funding dwindles and climate change threatens to transform the state's most important and cherished landscapes. But the NRS will continue to flourish through the talents and dedication of its faculty, staff, and students. To use one of the metaphors that Grinnell popularized, the NRS has assumed a crucial niche as a leading institution for the study of ecological change on the Pacific Coast. Its task now will be to record the environmental history of the future.

PRINCIPLES GUIDING THE SELECTION, OPERATION, AND USE OF NRS SITES

The NRS's protected wildland sites encompass many of the state's major ecosystems, preserved in as undisturbed a condition as possible to support university-level research and teaching. From the inception of the system, a set of fundamental, guiding principles has governed the selection, operation, and use of NRS reserves. As the NRS has grown and matured, these principles have built a system that enables high-caliber scholarship and thoughtful stewardship to exist side by side.

Key to the system's success has been the quality of its lands. Reserve sites are chosen with care for their natural integrity, ecological variety, and inclusion of special characteristics not found elsewhere in the system. Of primary concern is the viability of each site's ecosystems. The *NRS Acquisition Guidelines* (NRS 2003) recognize that if a site is not "pristine," it may still qualify as an NRS reserve: "The natural relationships should be essentially intact . . . and the reserves should be of sufficient size so that the natural balance of the community may be maintained with the survival of the plant and animal elements assured."

MILDRED E. MATHIAS (1906–95)

UCLA Professor Mildred E. Mathias (NRS Collection)

If the NRS can be said to have a mother, that person would be Mildred Mathias. An internationally recognized botanist, conservationist, and UCLA professor, Mathias laid the foundations of a reserve system admired by field scientists around the world. "Expanding populations with accompanying urbanization have made the establishment of this system a matter of urgency if we are going to be able to continue the study of the natural environment," Mathias wrote in a 1970 article about the NRS for the journal *Biological Conservation*.

Mathias understood the forces of landscape change all too well. An expert on the taxonomy of the Apiaceae (carrot family), she had traveled throughout the Americas and East Africa for her research in ethnobotany and plant pharmacology. But field experiences in California made it clear to her that the state needed to protect lands for research and education.

In 1979, Mathias recalled collecting plant specimens with her botany classes in and around the Los Angeles campus. "Then, all of a sudden, freeways went through, dormitories went up, and we lost all the teaching sites that were nearby." Urban development across one of her research transects in the Mojave Desert east of Palmdale "ruined 25 years of records. . . . But of course we had no control over the land. And some of these long-term records are more and more valuable the longer they're kept, so it was sort of tragic to see this go" (Mathias 1982).

These firsthand experiences galvanized Mathias's work on behalf of the NRS. In 1968, she assumed the chair of the system's University-wide Faculty Advisory Committee and remained in the post for 22 years.

During that time, Mathias guided nearly two dozen properties into the reserve system. She listened to landowners who needed ways to pay inheritance taxes or mounting medical bills, yet wanted their lands to remain in a natural state for perpetuity. Mathias also conducted delicate negotiations with land trust organizations, investigated appraisal values of potential reserve lands, and soothed feuding heirs. Her dedication to the system is commemorated by the NRS graduate student research grants program, which is named in her honor.

Another major goal of the system is to include examples of California's most characteristic habitats. As the guidelines state, each site "should possess exceptional value in illustrating, interpreting, and protecting examples of the major habitat types of California" (NRS 2003). A reserve is considered to have "added value" if it also possesses special features. These may include important variations of common habitat types such as different successional stages or variations in soil; significant gene pools, such as isolated populations or populations at extreme limits of a species range or habitat type; "type localities"—species, soil, or geological types first described on site; transition zones (ecotones) and interfaces between adjacent habitat types; the presence of a rare or an endangered habitat type or species; and the presence of geological, archaeological, or paleontological features of importance.

From the start, a fundamental tenet of the NRS has been to conserve the natural resources in the system for future generations of University research and instruction. The Regents of the University of California first established this guiding principle in the NRS's original charter, calling for "the preservation of a natural environment in as undisturbed a condition as possible so that present and future faculty members and students may do research and make observations on a variety of natural environments" (UC 1965).

Early on, NRS founder Norris (1966) recognized the need to balance the goal of preserving these natural resources with the goal of performing scientific experimental manipulation on the reserves:

> Simple observation, untempered by the experimental check, often gives equivocal or misleading results. Hence, to be useful for our scientists, some degree of manipulation of either the biota or physical conditions can usually be expected to be necessary for studies done within the reserves.

To allow for some degree of manipulative research while protecting natural resources, a zoning system was developed. This system allows limited manipulations in portions of a reserve, leaving the remainder undisturbed.

Yet the long-term goal of preserving the NRS's natural resources has remained paramount. Experiments that might degrade the habitat, harm native biodiversity, or damage the ecosystem functions of a reserve for any appreciable period of time are not permitted. Minor specimen collecting is permitted when natural processes could rapidly restore ecological conditions to their original state (NRS 1999). The NRS has recently recommended guidelines for the removal of field equipment upon project completion.

The health of the ecosystem is always given prime consideration in the management of reserves. Prior to approval, proposed reserve uses are always weighed in terms of the potential impacts on natural systems. Neither introductions of new species or genes nor major habitat alterations are permitted. Features the reserve was created to protect receive particular consideration for long-term protection.

WILBUR (BILL) MAYHEW (1920–)

UC Riverside Professor Wilbur "Bill" Mayhew (NRS Collection)

"Teaching field science without natural areas is like playing baseball without a bat," according to Wilbur "Bill" Mayhew, one of the three cofounders of the NRS (Gomez-Pompa 1998). A founding faculty member of the Riverside campus, Mayhew spent much of his career securing well-preserved California landscapes for natural classrooms.

As a young zoology professor, Mayhew brought his students to one open space after another, only to see the land eventually succumb to bulldozers. While revisiting sites in Egypt he'd seen while serving in World War II, Mayhew became alarmed at how much land had been developed since. Determined to prevent this from happening in California, Mayhew began a program to acquire land for University teaching and research years prior to the formation of the NRS. For example, in the late 1950s, he suggested to then state assemblyman Philip Boyd that he personally donate 3,000 acres in the Coachella Valley to the University—land that today forms the nucleus of Boyd Deep Canyon Desert Research Center. In 1964, Mayhew secured the acreage for Box Springs Reserve just one day before the US Bureau of Land Management was to have sold it to a developer.

Once the NRS was founded in 1965, Mayhew accumulated properties across the state at the breakneck pace of five new reserves per year. Self-effacing and able to put anyone at ease, he often inspired skeptical property owners with the mission of the NRS: to contribute to the understanding and wise stewardship of California's landscapes for university-level research, teaching, and public service. Ultimately, Mayhew was an integral partner in acquiring 16 NRS sites. "We used to kid him that his ulterior plan was to walk across California, all on lands he had managed to save," wrote fellow NRS founder Norris (1997). Mayhew recalled the ribbing in a 1998 oral history this way: "They were accusing me of being the governor of the fifty-first state" (Mayhew 1998).

Friends marveled that the unassuming Mayhew became the de facto real-estate mogul of the NRS. Mayhew responded that it was for the right cause: "If I were out trying to make some money on land, I couldn't do it. But doing it for the University, I could talk to the devil himself to try to get the land" (Mayhew 1998).

Mayhew neglected his own academic career in his pursuit of land for the NRS to conserve. He stopped publishing entirely, reasoning that his science might help one or two people a year, but each reserve would benefit generations of students and scientists to come.

In practice, the faculty manager and management advisory committee for each reserve evaluate project proposals. Approval is based on criteria such as a project's dependence on the habitats and features of the reserve, the need for protection from vandalism or interference, and the availability of the resources and land required for the project. Pursuits such as photography and writing are considered as valid for reserve use as natural science research.

Collectively, the NRS sites form a living catalog of the state's diverse natural resources. As stated in the NRS's 1985 20-year review, "An essential component of the University of California, the reserves are as important to field scientists as chemistry

Long isolation from the mainland has made Santa Cruz Island Reserve an ideal site to study island biogeography and the conservation of rare species. (Lyndal Laughrin)

labs are to medical researchers. Though a laboratory can always be rebuilt, a natural ecosystem, once gone, can never be replaced. The habitats it supported are lost forever, the value of its species will never be realized. In this context, the NRS also serves as a library—an irreplaceable storehouse of living ecosystems, each millions of years in the making" (NRS 1985).

In the same report, Ken Norris echoed this theme as he addressed the future of the system:

> The specific educational value of the NRS will always be unpredictable. Experience teaches us that scholars of many kinds will use the reserves. There will be botanists, geologists, entomologists, naturalists, and scientists from many other disciplines as well; writers, photographers, and poets should also feel free to apply.
>
> These people are going to uncover new stories of the animals and plants and the geology and soils of natural systems. We can't know now what scientific questions might arise, but we can make sure that the resources to answer those questions are available. What we are doing is opening the doors and providing the opportunities for those who follow in our footsteps. (NRS 1985)

The future will continue to bring competing pressures on the operations and uses of NRS sites. Meanwhile, the system's guiding principles will ensure the long-term value of the NRS for years to come.

Philip L. Boyd Deep Canyon Desert Research Center, named after the former UC Regent and mayor of Palm Springs who donated the land to the university. (Christopher Woodcock)

To scan a list of NRS reserves is to gain a sense of the many donors who have helped transform the reserve system from a distant dream into solid reality. Sites such as James San Jacinto Mountains Reserve, Landels-Hill Big Creek Reserve, and Sweeney Granite Mountains Desert Research Center, to name a few, honor donors who appreciate nature conservation and the role of protected areas in advancing the mission of the University of California. The NRS has also benefited from a long list of philanthropists whose names are not commemorated by reserves, some of whom wish to remain anonymous. Named or not, their gifts of land, resources, infrastructure, and financial assistance have allowed the NRS to evolve into the large network of protected natural areas that it is today.

Similarly, the NRS has partnered with many organizations over the years to preserve California's biodiversity in the form of research reserves. Partners such as the California Department of Parks and Recreation, The Nature Conservancy (TNC), the National Park Service, the US Army, the USDA Forest Service, numerous land trusts, and many other groups have been instrumental in helping the NRS obtain and protect lands for reserve use. The NRS continues to work closely with conservation organizations and government entities. In some cases, the NRS shares land management responsibilities for reserves with other organizations. In other cases, the NRS shares oversight of a reserve because new techniques or approaches to the stewardship of natural resources are best shared and vetted by all responsible individuals and groups.

Donors and partners are essential to the NRS in a number of ways. First, donors and partners identify and provide access to parcels of land that have the potential to become NRS reserves. When a property joins the NRS, donors and partners may establish a secure financial footing for a fledgling reserve in the form of an endowment. Donors and partners also have played a significant role in drafting conservation easements and other forms of legal protection and continue to provide support through public outreach, education, and media support.

One example in the more recent history of the NRS comes from the David and Lucile Packard Foundation. In 1998, the foundation gave generously to establish the Kenneth S. Norris Endowment Fund for the California Environment on behalf of the NRS. This gift was provided to enable the NRS to realize its far-reaching potential in the areas of research, teaching, and public service. Specifically, the Packard Foundation gift enables the NRS to plan for the long-term investment in its diverse assemblage of wildland sites as well as its multidisciplinary faculty, students, and visiting scientists who come to the NRS, all sharing a common interest in and concern for the natural environment.

TNC has been perhaps the NRS's most dynamic partner to date. Santa Cruz Island Reserve is protected, owned, and managed by TNC, although the NRS owns and manages its own research facilities and infrastructure on the island. Angelo Coast Range, Blue Oak Ranch, Boyd Deep Canyon Desert Research Center, Emerson Oaks, Jenny Pygmy

J. ROGER SAMUELSEN, NRS DIRECTOR, 1974–91

SPECIAL THANKS TO NRS DONORS AND OTHER PARTNERS

Shortly before I stepped down as NRS director in 1991, Ken Norris invited me to join his students on field trips to the Big Creek and Granite Mountains reserves. Around the evening campfire at Big Creek, I shared a story about the generosity of the former landowners and others in bringing the property into the NRS in 1978. I also cited our collaboration with The Nature Conservancy and the Save the Redwoods League. TNC was the lead negotiator with the landowners and cultivated many of the individual gifts. SRL pledged $500,000 to cover acquisition costs. Afterward, student after student asked me to convey their deep appreciation to those who had made it possible for them to experience and learn from the splendor of Big Creek's diverse habitats.

At Granite Mountains, I reviewed for the students the long years of negotiations with the Southern Pacific Company, the Bureau of Land Management, and private landowners. Gifts from the David and Lucile Packard Foundation and the Max C. Fleischmann Foundation funded the purchase of key parcels of the reserve. I also mentioned a matching grant from the Ford Foundation in the early years of the NRS as well as the time and commitment of UC Regent William (Bill) A. Wilson and his committee, who raised more than $2 million from foundations, companies, and individuals to meet the terms of the grant. This was the money used to acquire sites for the NRS that were not available by outright gift.

On the way home from the Granite Mountains, I wrote a letter to Bill Wilson that said

The combined efforts of conservation partners have made wild places like Landels-Hill Big Creek Reserve part of the NRS. (Christopher Woodcock)

in part "the Granite Mountains Reserve would not have become a reality were it not for the long-term commitment and perseverance of good friends and supporters like you. Why have you helped us over the years? Not for financial gain and not for publicity or recognition but because you love the land as the students love the land and you value the laws of nature as the students value the laws of nature." Many other donors of land, money, and time come to mind as I recount the history of the NRS—Philip Boyd, Bruce and Jean Burns, Ida Dawson, Fanny Hastings, Charles and Ottie Motte, and Carol Valentine, to name a few. They shared Regent Wilson's passion for the natural world. We, along with current and future students, faculty, and researchers, are in their debt.

Forest, Jepson Prairie, and Landels-Hill Big Creek reserves are also protected by TNC, as is Oasis de los Osos, a satellite property of James San Jacinto Mountains Reserve.

The NRS recognizes the tremendous responsibility that comes with custody of some of earth's rarest ecosystems. However, through its careful stewardship, science-based management, and commitment to training and research, the NRS has established a sterling conservation reputation. The vision of donors and partners past and present will help the NRS continue to grow with new reserves, research centers, and field stations.

THE NRS MISSION: RESEARCH, TEACHING, AND PUBLIC SERVICE

A NATURAL LABORATORY FOR RESEARCH

Researchers use NRS reserves as "outdoor laboratories"—places where they can analyze natural systems, illustrate important ecological and evolutionary principles, and attain a better understanding of how humankind impacts the world and how the world supports humankind. NRS researchers address such immediate global problems as wildland conversion, the loss of native biodiversity, environmental deterioration, climate change, and water conservation. They also investigate the human histories of California, look for supernovae, and listen for earthquakes, among many other projects. In short, the research conducted at NRS reserves spans the breadth of intellectual endeavor.

At present, the NRS consists of 38 sites encompassing more than 750,000 acres. Yet the system has an even broader impact than a simple tally of its acres suggest. Many NRS reserves offer research and housing facilities in areas where accommodations are difficult to find. Such remote NRS sites are considered "gateway reserves" because they enable users to access vast tracts of protected public lands. In California alone, the US Bureau of Land Management and the USDA Forest Service manage approximately 15.2 million acres and 28 million acres, respectively, while the California Department of Parks and Recreation oversees roughly 1.4 million acres. NRS reserves are adjacent to as much as 1.5 million acres of protected public lands. At the same time, science research conducted at gateway reserves helps inform the management of public lands. In these ways, the influence of NRS reserves reverberates far beyond reserve borders.

NRS lands represent an astonishing array of California ecosystems. Some, such as vernal pools, are now rare; others, such as oak woodlands and coniferous forests, constitute a large percentage of state wildlands. The fact that these lands are protected for the long term adds immeasurably to their value for research.

One example of longstanding research within the NRS is the work of ornithologist Walter Koenig at Hastings Natural History Reservation. Formerly the resident zoologist at Hastings and now at the Cornell Lab of Ornithology, Koenig has studied the social behavior and population biology of the acorn woodpecker (*Melanerpes formicivorus*) for more than 25 years (Koenig 1981a, 1981b; Koenig and Knops 2002). By banding generations of woodpecker families and observing their behavior day in and day out, Koenig's work has revealed the complex social system of these woodpeckers and their intimate relationships with oak trees. His findings, amassed over the course of decades, are helping land managers protect declining woodpecker populations from California to Colombia.

Another long-term experiment conducted at the Angelo Coast Range Reserve seeks to document the impact of predicted climate change on California's grassland ecosystems. Blake Suttle of Imperial College, London, and Meredith Thomsen of the University of Wisconsin at LaCrosse, began their research at Angelo as UC Berkeley doctoral students; today they continue their studies at Angelo with their own graduate students.

In 2000, Suttle subjected large plots in a meadow on the reserve to irrigation regimes that simulated three different rainfall patterns predicted by climate models. Over the succeeding years, Suttle, Thomsen, and their students documented the responses of native vegetation, insects, and spiders in the experimental plots. In plots receiving more water in the spring, native perennial bunchgrasses persisted only through the first year. In plots receiving extra water later in the year, native, nitrogen-fixing forbs fueled profuse growth among non-native annual grasses (Suttle et al. 2007). The experiment revealed that species interactions can produce unexpected impacts powerful enough to alter the fate of ecosystems over time. This study epitomizes the kind of critical information that scientists could never glean from a greenhouse or laboratory, but only from work in a protected natural area where large-scale field manipulations can be maintained and followed over many years.

Some NRS reserves support unique physical or biological features, such as diminutive rodents that hop rather than walk, contenders for the world's tallest trees, and soils profoundly inhospitable to plant growth. Research on these specialized organisms and environments is possible elsewhere but rarely in sites protected from disturbance or destruction.

One example of an increasingly rare ecosystem available to scientific study in the NRS can be found at Jepson Prairie Reserve, a landscape rich in vernal ponds, pools, and swales. Wildflowers restricted to these wetland habitats bloom in concentric circles the colors of buttercream, cobalt, and canaries. The federally protected California tiger salamander (*Ambystoma californiense*) uses the vernal ponds at Jepson Prairie to breed, lay eggs, and metamorphose into adult form. Employing a novel trapping approach at the reserve, UCLA professor H. Bradley Shaffer not only discovered how far these secretive amphibians migrate from their natal pond but also determined which life history stages of the California tiger salamander are most vulnerable to upland habitat loss (Trenham and Shaffer 2005). The study's results have altered approaches to land-use planning and nature reserve design, with biologists now taking into account the salamander's requirement for extensive uplands as well as undisturbed wetlands to complete its life cycle.

Research at NRS reserves extends well beyond the traditional field sciences. Quail Ridge Reserve, nestled in the inner Coast Ranges northeast of San Francisco Bay, is the site of experiments that promise to transform both field ecology and wireless communications technologies. The Quail Ridge Reserve Wireless Mesh Network, or QuRiNet, consists of 20 permanent "nodes" and 40-foot towers strategically positioned along the reserve's mountainous terrain. Sensors placed across the reserve acquire information such as ambient temperature and relative humidity. The network relays these data in real time to users off site. Because this sensor network is located in a remote landscape where wireless interference and electromagnetic noise is absent, the researchers are able to study network design and improve message routing. The researchers also are applying this technology to track the movements of animals in real time (Wu et al. 2007; Wu and Mohapatra 2011).

NRS users are in no way limited to conducting research on land. A notable aspect of the reserve system is the array of marine reserves, which stretches from Bodega Marine Reserve in the north to Kendall-Frost Mission Bay Reserve near the Mexican border—a transect of more than 500 miles. State and federal marine sanctuaries adjacent to most

Reserves such as Sweeney Granite Mountains Desert Research Center enable researchers to study natural landscapes without fear of their plots or equipment being disturbed. (Jan Goerrissen)

NRS coastal reserves expand the protected natural resources further. Such a large-scale canvas enables researchers to compare species and conditions in one portion of the state with those of another, at a spatial magnitude relevant to marine species and their management. The ability to conduct such studies over the long term is particularly crucial at a time when environmental and human changes are occurring on a global scale.

One project using NRS marine reserves systemwide is the Partnership for Interdisciplinary Studies of Coastal Oceans (PISCO). Established in 1999 by marine biologists from UC Santa Barbara, UC Santa Cruz, Stanford University, and Oregon State University, PISCO is a research and monitoring program established to understand the dynamics of coastal ecosystems along the west coast of North America. PISCO researchers conduct regular biological surveys in the rocky intertidal and kelp forest ecosystems of Santa Cruz Island, Coal Oil Point Natural, Landels-Hill Big Creek, Bodega Marine, and Kenneth S. Norris Rancho Marino reserves. Among other findings, this large-scale experiment has demonstrated the value of marine protected areas such as fish nurseries, advanced efforts to conserve marine habitats, and tracked the impacts of climate change on ocean health.

Vital but unsung benefits of NRS reserves are the opportunities to connect with others working at the site. Reserve users make new friendships, obtain collegial advice, and become inspired by those they meet around the campfire, in a field truck, or preparing a meal in the communal reserve kitchen. In this way, the social environment at reserves can be as invigorating as the landscape. Chance encounters spark discussions that lead to interdisciplinary collaborations or seed lifelong career connections. At the same time, students have a firsthand opportunity to gain field experience, conduct their own studies, and interact with leading scientists in an informal setting.

A class in ecological field methods at Norris Rancho Marino Reserve. More than 150 University of California courses teach field skills at reserves each year. (Don Croll)

To further encourage research at reserve sites, the NRS sponsors the Mildred E. Mathias Graduate Student Research Grants program. This prestigious program, established more than two decades ago, honors Mildred Mathias, one of the founders of the NRS. The NRS awards Mathias Grants each year to promote UC graduate student research at NRS sites, giving young scientists crucial experience in the design and implementation of field research projects. Since 1988, faculty judges have awarded more than 300 grants and provided more than half a million dollars in award funds. In addition to this financial support, each grant recipient is invited to the biennial Mathias Symposium where students have the opportunity to meet colleagues and present the results of their research.

SUPPORTING UNIVERSITY-LEVEL LEARNING

How can anyone begin to understand the dynamics of an ecosystem without actually experiencing it? Chaparral is just a word until one has crawled through it, or watched the flush of new growth following fire, or listened to the hum of insects and the songs of chaparral birds. Chaparral even has a distinctive odor. It is not merely an assortment of uninteresting spiny shrubs or just another scrub vegetation. It is an intricately woven web of life to be seen, heard, and smelled, not just read about.

MILDRED E. MATHIAS (1973)

The NRS is often described as a "classroom without walls" or a "library of ecosystems." Instructional programs conducted outdoors emphasize education through direct observation. In the field, students learn by doing. They readily absorb concepts that can be difficult to teach in a traditional classroom, such as different ways to observe animal behavior, the interconnectedness of species, and the importance of evolutionary relationships. Not least of these lessons is gaining a sense of confidence about being in a natural environment.

The NRS supports instruction in a wide variety of disciplines at field sites. These range from botany to zoology, archaeology to environmental planning, and public health to the performing and visual arts. Virtually all topics of study are welcomed at NRS sites. Photography and outdoor writing—two areas involving landscape interpretation and inspiration—are considered as valid as natural science research at reserves.

Perhaps the course most closely associated with NRS reserves is UC Santa Cruz's Natural History Field Quarter. Begun by NRS cofounder Ken Norris in 1973, this course takes students on a natural history journey across the state. Since its commencement over a quarter century ago, when students climbed onto a belching bus with a built-in library, nearly a thousand UC Santa Cruz students have come to consider themselves Field Quarter alumni. Taught for the last 30 years by Professor

Coal Oil Point, 2003, oil on canvas (Copyright 2012 Hank Pitcher)

Steve Gliessman, a leader in agroecology, and Breck Tyler, a marine biologist at UC Santa Cruz's Long Marine Laboratory, the course provides students opportunities to learn field natural history skills and the practical application of those skills for the preservation and management of California's natural ecosystems.

Field visits to NRS reserves introduce Field Quarter students to bioregions across the state. Stops include Sweeney Granite Mountains Desert Research Center in the Mojave Desert, Santa Cruz Island Reserve in the Channel Islands, and Angelo Reserve in the temperate rainforests along California's North Coast. Far from the daily pressures of campus life, students slow down, learn to see nature's patterns, and observe principles of ecology, geology, conservation biology, evolutionary biology, and geomorphology. The NRS's suite of protected areas ensures that students acquire both essential field techniques and a deep appreciation for nature that they can apply in many avenues of life.

Another innovative field course taught at the NRS reserves is the product of a collaboration between Bruce Tiffney, a paleobotanist, and Hank Pitcher, a fine artist. More than two decades ago, the two UC Santa Barbara professors agreed that keen observation is essential for both natural sciences and art and that drawing is a way of learning how to see. Together, artist and botanist taught a series of courses that combined art with natural history. An early field course about observing the natural world from both scientific and artistic perspectives developed into a series teaching the techniques of scientific illustration alongside those of scientific description. This science-cum-art curriculum, a staple of the College of Creative Studies at UC Santa Barbara, includes *plein air* classes at Coal Oil Point and Sedgwick reserves and culminates in a three-weekend immersion course in landscape painting.

In sum, more than 150 undergraduate courses across the UC system are offered at one or more NRS reserves. These courses span an extraordinary breadth of disciplines and serve as a testament to the great environmental diversity of California. Students and faculty have left a long legacy of learning, mentoring, and appreciation for areas protected by the NRS and its partners. For educating minds young and old about California's sublime natural wealth, the NRS is unsurpassed here and around the globe.

SERVING THE PEOPLE OF CALIFORNIA

A middle school student from Richmond, California, examines a bee he captured while visiting Hastings Natural History Reservation. Thousands of schoolchildren from across the state take field trips to UC natural reserves each year. (Lobsang Wangdu)

University-level teaching and research are the principal activities on NRS reserves, and benefit the public indirectly. The NRS serves the public directly by making its reserves and facilities available to government agencies, conservation groups, and similar organizations—and by collaborating with these entities to protect California's natural resources.

The University of California is one of four trustee agencies recognized under the California Environmental Quality Act with regard to sites within the NRS. This designation gives it jurisdiction by law over the reserves' natural resources affected by a project, whose resources are held in trust for the people of the State of California (14 CCR 15386). As a trustee agency, the NRS is accountable to the public for all of its lands. NRS reserves thus serve the public good by helping to preserve biodiversity through the protection of natural ecosystems.

While reserve use is typically by permission only—and though all uses of reserves must be consistent with the University's teaching and research objectives—the NRS makes every reasonable effort to allow the general public to visit its reserves and to learn of the work conducted there. Public programs sponsored by or held at reserves include open houses, lecture series, botany walks, stargazing evenings, weeding weekends, and many other events.

Another way in which the NRS serves the public is by providing environmental education opportunities for elementary and secondary school youth. Resident reserve staff and their families often personally host groups of schoolchildren, design instructional projects, compile collections and databases, teach students, and coordinate teaching demonstrations by scientists.

The NRS has hosted an extraordinarily successful youth education program known as Adventure Risk Challenge (ARC) at Sagehen Creek Field Station, Sedgwick Reserve, and Yosemite Field Station. This six-week program, designed for underserved high school students with leadership potential, combines an intensive literacy and science focus with an outdoor, place-based, experiential curriculum. All activities are based on models of inclusive education, so that young people are encouraged to regard others collaboratively in a spirit of acceptance.

ARC's *Summer Literacy and Leadership Program* includes backpacking, kayaking, river rafting, and daily physical training. Program graduates not only finish high school but go on to attend colleges and universities across the country. In 2011, ARC was awarded the Human Diversity Award from the Organization of Biological Field Stations, which recognizes field station programs that increase the involvement of traditionally underrepresented groups in the field sciences.

Another award-winning public service program conducted at NRS reserves is run by the Cold Creek Docents, an environmental education affiliate of Mountains Restoration Trust. Docents conduct weekly field programs at Stunt Ranch Reserve and work with Stunt Ranch staff to educate local schoolchildren and others about the natural world. Most programs offer hands-on activities in such fields as geology, ethnobotany, and chaparral ecology. Over the past 35 years, the Cold Creek Docents have helped instill a conservation ethic and a sense of stewardship for Santa Monica Mountain's Cold Creek watershed in more than 100,000 students.

In addition, NRS personnel provide technical consultation on such important community concerns as watershed protection, fire suppression, regional resource management, and potential land-use impacts. These and other services connect reserves to their communities, forging stronger links between the people of California and their environment.

A SENSE OF PLACE

The UC natural reserves were conceived as tangible entities: wildlands that could be protected and studied in perpetuity. But years of research, management, and human attention have imbued each reserve with more abstract qualities. Stewardship—caring for the land to preserve its natural integrity—is part of the mission of the NRS and an ongoing pursuit at each reserve. For those who remove invasive weeds, improve habitat for wildlife, and guard against trespass and damage, the act of stewardship enhances the value of reserves. In the words of Wallace Stegner, "No place is a place until things that happened in it are remembered in history, ballads, yarns, legends, or monuments" (Stegner 1992). By experiencing the land and its changes across weeks, seasons, and years, people infuse each reserve with a sense of place. This sense of place enhances the human value of the reserve much the way a handsome frame heightens the beauty of a painting.

NRS reserves are remembered by discoveries rather than physical monuments. Discovery at NRS reserves can take myriad forms: an undergraduate who changes her career path after a memorable field course; a professor who uncovers a new plant-pollinator relationship; an urban child who finds wonder in the natural world for the first time. Discoveries at NRS reserves can lead to fine artwork, sound poems, and sketches of plants and animals in their natural habitats. Other discoveries are remembered in the ballads, yarns, and miscellaneous doggerel jotted down and retold over the campfires of field quarter classes. Only a handful of those findings can be described here. Instead, we invite readers to use the following pages as a starting point for discovering what makes each UC natural reserve a truly singular place.

HEATH AND MARJORIE ANGELO
COAST RANGE RESERVE

The undisturbed waters of the South Fork Eel River have made Angelo Coast Range Reserve a center for stream research. (Christopher Woodcock)

Rugged and steep, the Heath and Marjorie Angelo Coast Range Reserve lies within the vast conifer forest that once extended across much of the northwestern United States. Buffered by large tracts of federally owned land, the reserve protects approximately three miles of the South Fork Eel River and the watersheds of three of its tributaries. Angelo's boundaries embrace a mosaic of habitats once found throughout the region, including one of the largest tracts of old-growth Douglas-fir (*Pseudotsuga menziesii* var. *menziesii*) remaining in California. Terraces adjacent to the stream channels form the only level ground in a landscape of narrow valleys and sharp ridges. Meadows cover nine of these large terraces, providing islands of native and European grasses and forbs within the coniferous forest. Mature stands of Douglas-fir and coast redwood (*Sequoia sempervirens*) cloak the valley, with forest openings revealing stands of chaparral and oak woodland. Together, these natural features have made the Angelo Reserve a magnet for research in aquatic ecology and how water moves through the environment.

This drainage has supported many types of people. In the late prehistoric era, the Cahto people hunted game, collected acorns, and dug bulbs, corms, and roots for food throughout the Eel River watershed. The first European settlers arrived in the 1880s,

HEATH AND MARJORIE ANGELO COAST RANGE RESERVE

Administering Campus: UC Berkeley

Established: 1994

Location: Mendocino County, on South Fork of Eel River; 20 miles west of Laytonville; 150 miles north of San Francisco

Size: Approximately 4,300 acres, plus access to 3,500 acres of US Bureau of Land Management property

Elevation: 1,240 to 4,231 feet

Average Precipitation: 80 inches per year

Average Temperatures:

    August average 85°F, August maximum 100°F

    Winter average 32°F, winter minimum 18°F

Facilities: Laboratory-dormitory complex provides two three-bedroom houses, one group facility for 35, a science center with two lab rooms, a classroom, a computer room, and office space

Databases: Aerial photos, maps, climate and hydrology records, extensive species inventories, herbarium, insect collection, stand-age data, bibliography, and small library

logging trees and planting orchards that can still be seen today. In 1930, seeking a quieter life, Heath and Marjorie Angelo sold their San Francisco manufacturing business and bought an old homestead along Elder Creek. Over the next two decades, the couple purchased surrounding parcels to protect the adjacent forests from logging. In 1959, the Angelos donated a substantial portion of their land and sold the rest to The Nature Conservancy (TNC), forming this conservation organization's first nature reserve west of the Mississippi River. TNC donated the land to the University of California for inclusion in the NRS in 1994 and continues to protect the site through a conservation easement.

Three undisturbed watersheds—rare in the north Coast Range—are completely contained within reserve boundaries. Elder, Fox, and Skunk creeks all flow into the South Fork Eel River. Since 1967, the US Geological

The striking purple flowers of Douglas iris (*Iris douglasiana*), a native species widespread across central and northern California, are found throughout the grassy meadows and forest openings at Angelo Coast Range Reserve. (Peggy L. Fiedler)

Exclosure devices are installed in the streams at Angelo Coast Range Reserve
by UC Berkeley Professor Mary E. Power and her team to study the ecology
of California's North Coast river ecosystems. (NRS Collection)

Survey has monitored Elder Creek, the largest of these tributaries, as a purity benchmark
for natural waters. Elder Creek's seasonal flow regime offers a glimpse of how river flows
wax and wane in a watershed free of dams, logging, and pavement. The mixed boulder-
gravel beds of the South Fork and its larger tributaries provide a spawning habitat for
runs of steelhead (*Oncorhynchus mykiss*) and habitat for the coastal giant salamander
(*Dicamptodon tenebrosus*).

Healthy waterways at the Angelo Coast Range Reserve have provided a pristine setting
for freshwater ecology research. UC Berkeley professor Mary E. Power has conducted mul-
tifaceted research into the structure of food webs within Angelo's streams. Over a 20-year
period, Power and her students and colleagues studied changes in the food webs connecting algae, the main energy source for river life, to grazing and predatory invertebrates, to
fish, including juvenile steelhead (Power 1990; Wootton et al. 1996; Power et al. 2008).
By using large, flow-through cages in the Eel River to enclose or exclude fish, Power has
demonstrated that in summers following scouring winter floods, fish exerted "top-down"
control on algal proliferations by eating invertebrates that either grazed algae or fed on these
grazers. This long-term field study documented the importance of scouring winter floods
for rejuvenating food webs. After a flood, a creek can better support the growth of top predators like steelhead and maintain ecosystem services that protecting river health. The loss of
fish may be followed by infestations of mosquitoes and other disease-carrying insects, while
streams that once ran healthy and clear can become clogged with algae (Estes et al. 2011).

Water is the inspiration behind yet another major research project conducted at Angelo
by the W. M. Keck HydroWatch Center. This research unit was created at UC Berkeley to
study how water travels through a steep, forested landscape. Climate researcher Inez Fung
and her team of interdisciplinary scientists have installed an array of wireless sensors at

PROFESSOR MARY E. POWER,
DEPARTMENT OF INTEGRATIVE BIOLOGY, UC BERKELEY

UC Berkeley Professor Mary E. Power (Lobsang Wangdu)

When I first came to Berkeley, I traveled four hours away from the Bay Area in an effort to find natural areas where I could set up experiments that would not be disturbed by others. However, even when I went as far into the Mendocino forests as I could go, four-wheelers would find my inconspicuous experimental chambers and crush them.

A natural area protected by a public agency or land trust wouldn't work for my research because such groups usually don't allow obvious experimental manipulations. Also, even when agreements are made with some of the managing agencies, misunderstandings and inconsistencies in the way these sites are managed can disrupt field research after considerable effort has been invested. So I am incredibly grateful that the visionary founders of the NRS set up this system of large natural ecosystems, protected for university level teaching and research.

Angelo Coast Range Reserve encompasses sunny, main stem rivers; dark headwaters; and wonderful mixed forests, meadows, and small wetlands, offering a field site where we can watch nature unfold without multiple disruptions from human beings. To me, Angelo is an incredible treasure—a place where you can really invest your heart and spend decades learning about how an ecosystem works.

Field ecologists live within their systems for a while and study them deeply. Many of my students have focused primarily on field sites at the Angelo Reserve. Some former students are now young faculty all over the country and the world, and they bring their students—my "grandstudents"—back to Angelo. Together we build on what each of us knows.

There are very few other sites in the world protected for long-term levels of research and none in a reserve system that spans seven degrees of latitude and 14,000 feet of elevation in a state as rich in natural history as California. The NRS is truly unique and, in my opinion, one of the most important gifts and ongoing legacies that the University of California will leave to the world.

Angelo Coast Range Reserve streams contain a full complement of aquatic species, including the cardinal meadowhawk dragonfly (*Sympetrum illotum*). (Jeffery T. Wilcox)

Angelo to track the movement of moisture within the Elder Creek watershed. Sensors monitor not only total rainfall and streamflows but also the movement of sap through trees, microclimate conditions in the canopy, and water table levels via deep, rock-penetrating wells. Fung and her colleagues seek to predict how climate change and forest cover will affect rainfall, ecosystem health, and the availability of California's fresh water supply.

Angelo's jagged topography has attracted the interest of yet another landscape-scale science program: The dense tree canopy that obscures the contours of the reserve makes its hills and valleys nearly impossible to map. But a mapping technique called LIDAR (light detection and ranging) can create a vegetation-free digital version of the landscape. UC Berkeley professor William Dietrich and his colleague Collin Bode have used LIDAR data from Angelo to develop methods of landscape analysis for interpreting and predicting environmental conditions from LIDAR maps. Digitally stripped of surface structures, the maps can reveal ancient landslides, earthquake faults, and shifts in river topography that indicate how the landscape formed.

Trees that once thwarted mapmakers are a boon for scientists exploring life in Angelo's forest canopy. Scientists can study the complex world within coast redwoods via a forest canopy access system—the first of its kind in California. Platforms in the canopies of six redwood trees are linked to each other by a system of five wire cable bridges designed to be harmless to the trees themselves.

Among those who study Angelo trees in depth is UC Berkeley biology professor Todd Dawson. Dawson investigates how water moves up to and through the tree canopies of Angelo's mature forest. Dawson and his colleagues have discovered that large trees like old Douglas-fir use their roots to draw moisture from deep underground during the day, depositing it in shallower soils at night. This phenomenon, known as hydraulic lift, makes more water available to other forest plants throughout California's long, hot summers. Redwoods are shallow-rooted but supplement their water intake in other ways. Dawson and his students also collected water samples from both fog and redwood tissues and compared their isotopic ratios. Their findings have demonstrated that the redwood trees supplement their water intake with the mists that shroud these forests in summer.

The protected watersheds of Angelo Coast Range Reserve have supported research into natural processes that touch all Californians: water, forests, the evolution of landscapes, and food webs that support fish and wildlife. As competition for environmental resources intensifies over the twenty-first century, research at Angelo will be instrumental in helping scientists keep earth's vital systems healthy.

BODEGA MARINE RESERVE

The marine layer lifts over Bodega Marine Reserve, revealing diverse coastal ecosystems and the facilities of Bodega Marine Laboratory. (Christopher Woodcock)

Perched at the western edge of the North American continent, along the rugged north-central coast of California, Bodega Marine Reserve is a dramatic meeting place of land and sea. Its boundaries extend from the mudflats of Bodega Harbor inland through salt marsh, over sand dunes, through coastal prairie and coastal scrub, and down rocky cliffs to the waves of the Pacific Ocean. One of the richest marine upwelling regions along the Pacific Coast lies directly offshore, while the San Andreas Fault Zone runs through the reserve itself. These natural features, plus the facilities of Bodega Marine Laboratory, make the reserve a prime site for research and education.

The history of the Bodega Bay region is as rich as its environment. Coast Miwok were the first known residents, as evidenced by the remnants of villages around the harbor and by shell middens on Bodega Head. In the early 1800s, Russian trappers established an outpost on Bodega Head. By 1841, they had hunted the area's southern sea otters nearly to extinction

BODEGA MARINE RESERVE

Administering Campus: UC Davis

Established: 1970

Location: Bodega Head in Sonoma County, 70 miles north of San Francisco

Size: Approximately 500 acres; UC owns more than 300 acres but manages almost 6,400 acres, including the newly expanded Bodega Head State Marine Reserve

Elevation: Terrestrial elevation is 0 to 190 feet. Subtidal elevation is 266 feet deep in Bodega Head State Marine Reserve

Average Precipitation: 34 inches per year, ranging from 13 to 73 inches over 32 years

Average Temperatures:

September maximum 64°F

January minimum 43°F

Facilities: Laboratories, library, classrooms, office space, research vessels and equipment, 40-bed dormitory, 14-bed bunkhouse, 3 cottages/apartments for visiting scientists, lodge with three single- and three double-occupancy rooms plus shared kitchen

Databases: Climate data from 1967; intense meteorological, oceanographic, biological, and photographic monitoring began in 1987; Bodega Marine Laboratory staffed library includes hundreds of publications on reserve-based research

and abandoned their settlements. American ranchers and potato farmers arrived in their wake and stayed for the next century. In the early 1960s, the University of California purchased the reserve lands as the future site of Bodega Marine Laboratory. At about the same time, Pacific Gas and Electric Company (PG&E) acquired the southern portion of Bodega Head to build a nuclear power plant. In 1964, plans for the power plant were scuttled after heated public debate and the discovery that the San Andreas Fault runs directly underfoot. This land was later sold by PG&E to the California Department of Parks and Recreation. In 1961–62, Alfred Hitchcock filmed *The Birds* in the Bodega Bay area; a number of scenes were filmed on reserve lands.

The nudibranch *Limacia cockerelli* feeds exclusively on the orange-brown colonial bryozoan *Hinksina velata*. This sea slug breathes through the orange-tipped gill plumes on its back. (Jackie Sones)

The ocean's influence extends across every inch of the reserve. Cool ocean waters insulate this coastline from pervasive inland heat and chilling winter frost. Upwelling of cold, nutrient-rich water due to prevailing northwesterly winds in spring and summer supports a remarkable diversity and abundance of marine life near shore. These waters are protected as Bodega Head State Marine Reserve, which extends three nautical miles beyond the shoreline of the reserve. Here the intertidal zone grades into subtidal habitats. Beyond the beach and rocky edges, the marine floor is granitic, interspersed with sand and dissected by surge channels. Kelp grows in profusion along the shallow bottom, with sponges and nudibranchs common in deeper water. Rockfish (*Sebastes* spp.) and lingcod (*Ophiodon elongatus*) use this nearshore habitat to breed.

Rocks of Bodega Head Marine Reserve are encrusted with gooseneck barnacles (*Pollicipes polymerus*). Barnacles flutter their feathery legs, or cirri, through seawater to capture particles of plankton and detritus. (Jackie Sones)

The San Andreas Fault Zone separates Bodega Head peninsula from the mainland American Plate and passes through the northeastern corner of the reserve, the adjacent dunes, and the harbor. The fault zone consists of a mélange of crushed rock and marine sediments overlain with windblown dune deposits. Fault movements carried the rocks of Bodega Head north from southern California over roughly 20 million years.

Reserve lands straddle the peninsula of Bodega Head, which are bordered to the north and south by state park lands, and to the east by Bodega Harbor. At the north end of the reserve, partially stabilized coastal dunes rise 16 stories above sea level. European beachgrass (*Ammophila arenaria*), an introduced species planted in the twentieth century to prevent dune erosion, is now the most abundant plant throughout the dunes. Reserve staff and the California Department of Parks and Recreation are working together to restore this degraded ecosystem. A few areas, however, still support a mostly native dune plant community with indigenous shrubs and shifting sands.

Directly west of the dunes stretches the long, narrow strand of Salmon Creek Beach, which is fully exposed to the pounding surf. A more protected pocket beach lies in Horseshoe Cove immediately south of the laboratory buildings. This cove marks an area where waves have eroded marine terrace sediments. A line of coastal bluffs rises from the southern tip of Salmon Creek Beach. Wave action has carved the base of these granitic cliffs into broad rocky benches riddled with tidepools. Diverse intertidal communities, bathed in frothing surf, flourish on this rocky shore. Hundreds of species of marine algae produce a colorful, undulating landscape that serves as food and shelter for mollusks, crabs, fish, and sea urchins.

Grasslands lie along the edges of the coastal bluffs. Generations ago, Bodega Head grasslands were dominated by native perennials such as California brome (*Bromus carinatus*) and blue wild rye (*Elymus glaucus* subsp. *glaucus*). Grazing livestock reduced the native cover of these perennials and provided openings for non-native, invasive species to establish. Today one-third of the plant species in this habitat are non-native. However, a rich mixture of native

Shorebirds probe the mudflats of Bodega Head for clams, worms, and other invertebrates. (Galen Rowell, Mountain Light Photography)

plants near the coastal bluffs still produces a brilliant floral display each spring. The protected leeward slopes of the bluffs host coastal scrub dominated by bush lupine (*Lupinus arboreus*).

Freshwater wetlands are scattered throughout the reserve in depressions and low, freshwater seeps. Marsh plant communities vary according to distance from standing water, with bur-reed (*Sparganium eurycarpum*), spikerush (*Eleocharis macrostachya, E. rostellata*), and panicled bulrush (*Scirpus microcarpus*) at water's edge giving way to horsetails (*Equisetum arvense, E. hyemale* subsp. *affine, E. telmateia* subsp. *braunii*), umbrella sedge (*Cyperus eragrostis*), and monkeyflowers (*Mimulus guttatus*) on higher ground. Rushes (*Juncus* spp.) and non-native velvet grass (*Holcus lanatus*) fringe the drier edges. Many animals depend on these wetlands as sources of drinking water.

The reserve adjoins Bodega Harbor, where sand and mud substrates support meadows of eelgrass (*Zostera marina*). These marine flowering plants provide habitat and nursery areas for small fish and invertebrates. Leopard sharks (*Triakis semifasciata*), bat rays (*Myliobatis californica*), juvenile rockfish, and Pacific sanddabs (*Citharichthys sordidus*) patrol the mudflat and eelgrass beds during high tide. At low tide, western sandpipers (*Calidris mauri*), dunlin (*C. alpina*), sanderlings (*C. alba*), and other shorebirds probe the mud with their beaks in search of crustaceans and worms. Local tidal flats and eelgrass beds are crucial foraging habitats for shorebirds on winter migration: as many as 10,000 shorebirds have been tallied in Bodega Harbor each winter.

Ocean waters west of the reserve attract large numbers of coastal and pelagic birds. A

Powerful Pacific waves shape the organisms and shorelines of Bodega Marine Reserve. (Jackie Sones)

few, such as pelagic and Brandt's cormorants (*Phalacrocorax pelagicus* and *P. penicillatus*) and pigeon guillemots (*Cepphus columba*), nest on the rocks and cliffs of Bodega Head. California sea lions (*Zalophus californianus*) and harbor seals (*Phoca vitulina*) frequent coastal waters, as do their predators, great white sharks (*Carcharodon carcharias*). Gray whales (*Eschrichtius robustus*), particularly females with calves, are commonly sighted swimming north on spring migration. Southern sea otters (*Enhydra lutris nereis*) once abundant enough to support a pelt industry, now are seen infrequently along Bodega Head.

Bodega Marine Reserve operates in close partnership with Bodega Marine Laboratory. The laboratory is located within the reserve and offers a flow-through seawater system, wet labs, classrooms, a library, and housing. Together, the reserve and lab constitute one of the world's most active research and educational field sites in marine and coastal environments. Over the years, scientists have focused numerous studies on the interplay between ocean conditions and marine populations in this region of California. The shifting ranges of tidepool species, coastal current monitoring, and the timing and locations of plankton blooms are just a few of the long-term studies being conducted at the reserve. The extensive meteorological and oceanographic data collected by the laboratory and reserve provide researchers with additional insights into global ecological patterns.

Bodega Reserve hosts dozens of university courses on subjects ranging from the atmospheric sciences to oceanography, and geology to research diving. At the reserve, students can clamber across an active earthquake fault, collect limpets and anemones, and analyze ocean water samples collected on site. At the end of the day, they can rest and share experiences in well-appointed reserve dorms and kitchens. For all these reasons, the outdoor learning experiences at Bodega Marine Reserve are unparalleled by any campus classroom.

CHICKERING AMERICAN RIVER RESERVE

Chickering American River Reserve features pristine meadows and coniferous forests intermixed with alpine lakes and soda springs. (Christopher Woodcock)

Located in the headwaters of the North Fork of the American River, Chickering American River Reserve is the only NRS site on the windward western slopes of the Sierra Nevada. The thin soils of this remote, high-elevation region support an impressive variety of mountain habitats. Coniferous forests, aspen groves, subalpine meadows, montane chaparral, alpine lake wetland margins, and rock-strewn fell-fields can all be found within its borders. Several springs with waters enriched in calcium bicarbonate and other minerals bubble up across the property.

Rich in flora and fauna, Chickering Reserve harbors at least 1,000 plant species. It also lies within the habitat ranges of high-elevation mammals such as the American pika (*Ochotona princeps*), yellow-bellied marmot (*Marmota flaviventris*), American marten (*Martes americana*), and fisher (*Martes pennanti*). The 100 documented bird species include northern goshawks (*Accipiter gentilis*) and California spotted owls (*Strix occidentalis occidentalis*), and the 15 reptile and amphibian species include the foothill yellow-legged frog (*Rana boylii*), a declining species that has persisted primarily in California's least-polluted streams.

In addition to great natural diversity, the Chickering Reserve preserves reminders of an earlier era in California history. These include petroglyphs carved into granite and

CHICKERING AMERICAN RIVER RESERVE

Administering Campus: UC Berkeley

Established: 1975

Location: Placer County, 5 miles southeast of Donner Pass on the North Fork of the American River. Access is 11 miles past the town of Soda Springs on a dirt track

Size: Approximately 16,800 acres

Elevation: Reserve elevation is 6,000 to 8,000 feet. North Fork of the American River land is 4,800 to 8,800 feet

Average Precipitation: 49 inches per year; average snowfall is 332 inches per year

Average Temperatures:

    January minimum 7°F

    July maximum 86°F

Facilities: None; the site is best suited for day use

Databases: Inventory of vertebrates, plant list

basalt that probably date to 5,000 years before the present. These petroglyphs are attributed to the Martis people who summered in the area. In more recent times, the area attracted visitors to Soda Springs Hotel, an early "destination resort" and an important stopping point for Sierra Nevada travelers from the 1870s to the 1890s. The resort hotel burned down in 1892, was rebuilt, and then burned once again in 1925. This unusual mountain parcel ultimately was made available to the NRS by the Chickerings, a family of conservation-minded pioneers.

The Chickerings first arrived in North America in the seventeenth century, when the intrepid Mary Chickering, a widow, and her five sons set sail from England for New England's shores in the early 1600s. The family settled in Massachusetts and over the next few generations produced a Lexington minuteman, Harvard clergymen, and more than a few New England lawyers. Many decades later, with the ink still fresh on his law degree, William Henry Chickering left the East Coast for the new state of California. In 1873, he established a law firm in San Francisco that continues to this day as Chickering & Gregory, P.C. In 1927, William's son Allen L. Chickering

The American pika (*Ochotona princeps*) lives within rocky outcroppings atop high mountains such as those at Chickering American River Reserve. Pikas cut grasses and other herbaceous species in summer, piling their harvest into stacks to dry for winter food. (Max Eissler)

purchased a Sierra Nevada getaway from railroad magnate Leland Stanford. This property, formerly known as Soda Springs, is now the Chickering American River Reserve.

Allen L. Chickering was an early member of the Sierra Club, joining in 1896. He also served as chairman of the board of Rancho Santa Ana Botanic Garden and was director of the San Francisco Botanical Garden at Strybing Arboretum. As a member of the Save-the-Redwoods League council for 28 years, he donated significant sums to protect redwood forests within the state park system. A California wildflower enthusiast, he published a horticultural treatise on the mariposa lilies (*Calochortus* spp.).

Allen's son Sherman matched his father's accomplishments in nature conservation. Also a lawyer at Chickering & Gregory, Sherman Chickering was a life member of many wildlife and wilderness organizations. He served for three terms as president of the

Twin Lodgepole Pines, 2010, woodcut print (Tom Killion)

California Fish and Game Commission and on the California Academy of Sciences Board of Trustees from 1972 until his death in 1993.

Sherman Chickering was a talented California botanist and made contributions to the *Jepson Manual*, the bible of California flora. He wrote in one of his journals, "I think I ammost proud of the herbarium and botany of wildflowers I have collected in the area of the North Fork of the American River. My eight volumes of photographs and pressed flowers have been pored over by some of the foremost botanists of the state."

In 1975, Sherman Chickering and his family established one of the first conservation easements in California on their Soda Springs property. Such easements restrict development in perpetuity. Most landowners stop there. But the Chickerings wished to put their land to additional beneficial use and granted limited access to their Sierra Nevada property to researchers and students affiliated with the NRS. The fact that many rare and declining species still thrive on reserve land is a testament to the light touch of NRS scientists and the farsighted conservation commitments of the Chickering family.

The white globe lily (*Calochortus albus*) and its relatives the mariposa lilies are among the most picturesque and widespread wildflowers in California. (Baotran Ellner)

The conifers at Hans Jenny Pygmy Forest Reserve may appear at first glance to be saplings, but often are centuries old. Nutrient-poor soils and inhospitable conditions stunt their growth. (Christopher Woodcock)

Immense ocean waves, sculpted sandstone, and fog-shrouded forests imbue the Mendocino coast with a wild and timeless feel. Yet it is the presence of a less obvious feature—a series of five wave-cut marine terraces rising from the water's edge—that makes this landscape a natural curiosity. These sequentially exposed coastal terraces can be described as a veritable museum of rare soil types. The Hans Jenny Pygmy Forest Reserve supports a forest of Lilliputian trees atop the oldest and highest of these coastal terraces.

The earliest human inhabitants of the Mendocino area were the Northern Pomo. These Native Americans are believed to have used reserve lands as a place to pick huckleberries (*Vaccinium ovatum*) but little else. Centuries later, the gold rush of 1849 brought both a skyrocketing Western population and a sudden market for lumber from the North Coast region. In the 1960s, Mendocino sawmills gave way to artists and tourists, leaving the pygmy forests vulnerable to resort development. To preserve a portion of this rare ecosystem, in 1963 the University of California bought terrace land south of the town of Mendocino with funds from the Kearney Foundation of Soil Science. This property became part of the NRS two years later, and it remains protected by The Nature Conservancy (TNC), which owns land adjacent to the reserve.

HANS JENNY PYGMY FOREST RESERVE

Administering Campus: UC Berkeley

Established: 1970

Location: Mendocino County, 2 miles southeast of Mendocino; 150 miles north of San Francisco; a 3.5-hour drive from Berkeley campus

Size: Approximately 70 acres

Elevation: 591 feet

Average Precipitation: 39 inches per year

Average Temperatures:

    September maximum 59°F

    January minimum 47°F

    Annual mean 53°F

Facilities: Limited trail system, walk-in soil pit, no on-site structures or campgrounds

Databases: Results from soil surveys

The marine terraces of the Mendocino Coast have risen rapidly to an elevation of approximately 650 feet above sea level over the last 500,000 years—a breakneck pace in geological terms. During periods of sea level rise, when a warming climate melted the glaciers, waves cut the shoreline into a gently sloping underwater terrace. The terrace ended in a narrow beach at the base of a low cliff. When sea level fell again during the next period of glaciation, retreating waves deposited up to 30 feet of gravel, sand, and clay over the new terrace. Coastal winds blew sand atop the bluffs, building dunes. Meanwhile, the floor of the Pacific Ocean continued to slide beneath the North American Plate, uplifting the entire coastline. Over time, each terrace was raised above sea level, exposing the next layer of sediments to interglacial sea level rise.

Each of the five terraces is approximately 100 feet higher and 100,000 years older than the one below. Each step in this ecological staircase supports a distinct association of soils, microbes, plants, and animals. While giant coast redwood (*Sequoia sempervirens*) and century-old Douglas-fir (*Pseudotsuga menziesii* var. *menziesii*) loom over the lower slopes and alluvial stream bottoms, they may be only finger-thick and waist-high on the highest and oldest terrace. Such pygmy forests, which grow on extremely impoverished soils, showcase the startling effect soil can have on vegetation (Westman and Whittaker 1975; Westman 1975, 1978).

Conditions for this diminutive forest were made possible by three factors: a moist, cool climate; poorly drained soils; and flat topography. The heavy rains of a North Coast fall and winter, which range from 17 to 61 inches annually, cannot percolate through the

The highly acidic, saturated soils of the Hans Jenny Pygmy Forest Reserve terrace provide ideal growing conditions for western Labrador tea (*Rhododendron columbianum*). (James André)

Fetid adder's tongue (*Scoliopus bigelovii*) prefers the moist shade of redwood forests and north coast plant communities. It emits an unpleasant odor to attract gnat pollinators. (Peggy L. Fiedler)

terrace soil's deep iron hardpan. Water pools atop each terrace's sandstone bedrock. The trapped rainwater soaks tree roots and surface soils for months at a time. Tannin-rich needles dropped by the conifers turn the water into an acidic tea. As winter progresses, however, the water flows along the gently sloped bedrock toward the next lower terrace, progressively leaching the soil of nutrients as it travels. Springtime brings drier skies and draws down the local water table by as much as six feet.

At least a half-million years of this process, known as podzolization, has left the pygmy forest with extremely nutrient-impoverished soils, particularly on the fifth and highest terrace occupied by the Jenny Reserve. The ash-gray soils of the reserve are so acidic that they are even shunned by worms. Trees that take root in this podzol are stunted and spindly. Because each terrace has been exposed for a different amount of time, the soils, microbes, plants, and animals associated with each one is distinct. The first (and youngest) terrace contains fertile grasslands that can survive constant salt spray and a high water table. The second terrace contains conifers that are massive in size. Only on the third and higher terraces has enough time passed to produce podzolized soils and a pygmy forest.

The reserve's pygmy forest hosts several endemic co-nifer species, including Bolander's pine (*Pinus contorta* subsp. *bolanderi*) and pygmy cypress (*Hesperocyparis pygmaea*), which is found only on podzolized soils. The harsh soil environment produces trees that grow to a maximum height of less than three feet with stems less than one inch in diameter. Bolander's pine is closely related to shore pine (*P. c.* subsp. *contorta*), a species common on the first terrace, and likely evolved in response to the region's highly weathered soils. Both pine species are capable of growing into large trees under more favorable conditions. Wildlife in the reserve is notable for its scarcity, as the dwarfed vegetation offers little shelter or food for larger animals. However, one insect, Helfer's blind weevil (*Raymondionymus helferi*), is endemic to the forest.

The list of researchers who have studied Mendocino's pygmy forest over the last century includes some of the most eminent names in California plant ecology and soil science. Perhaps the most august is UC Berkeley professor Hans Jenny, for whom the Pygmy Forest Reserve is named. A Swiss-born and trained chemist, Jenny's landmark *Factors of Soil Formation* (Jenny 1941) offers a simple mathematical expression of factors from the physical environment that contribute to the formation of soil. In a eulogy to Jenny, his UC Berkeley colleagues wrote, "The Pygmy Forest became an ecological Rosetta Stone for Hans, and he dedicated much of his postretirement life to deciphering its relationship to his five factors of soil formation . . . His intellectual obsession with the Pygmy Forest also led Hans to a renewed perception of the uniqueness and fragility of soil ecosystems . . . he waged a series of successful campaigns to preserve a number of such unique areas in California" (Amundson et al. 1992).

It is fitting that a textbook example of Jenny's greatest body of work is protected within the NRS. Within this site, Jenny's Rosetta Stone continues to offer insights to students fascinated by one of California's rarest ecosystems.

After retiring from the faculty of UC Berkeley, Hans Jenny spent much of his time studying Mendocino's pygmy forests. Along with his wife, Jean, he campaigned to preserve the distinctive California landscapes now protected at Jughandle State Park and Jepson Prairie Reserve. (Dennis Galloway, UC Berkeley)

JEPSON PRAIRIE RESERVE

In early spring the vernal wetlands of Jepson Prairie Reserve transform into kaleidoscopic landscapes adorned with flowers of many hues. (John W. Wall)

In the baking heat of a Central Valley summer, the expansive fields of Jepson Prairie Reserve resemble ordinary meadows. But in spring, this bunchgrass prairie bursts into rainbow carpets of wildflowers. Pools of rainwater dot the landscape, concealing rare salamanders and tiny fairy shrimp. Once widespread throughout the region, few such vernal wetlands and their assemblages of native species remain.

The most prominent natural features of the reserve are its vernal pools and ponds, seasonal bodies of water that form in the rainy season atop an impermeable subsurface layer of clay. When it rains, the clay swells and prevents water from draining. Water ponds on the surface of the soil for weeks or months. Specialized vernal pool plants and animals have adapted to these ephemeral wetlands. Jepson Prairie Reserve shelters an outstanding example of a vernal wetland amid the agricultural development that has overtaken much of California's Great Valley.

JEPSON PRAIRIE RESERVE

Administering Campus: UC Davis

Established: 1983

Location: Solano County, 70 miles from San Francisco, 25 miles from Davis campus

Size: Approximately 1,560 acres

Elevation: 5 to 25 feet

Average Precipitation: 17 to 20 inches per year

Average Temperatures:

    January average 46°F

    July average 87°F

Facilities: None; site is best suited for day use

Databases: Flora and fauna lists in Jepson Prairie Handbook, geographic information system (GIS), and meteorological

Native Americans considered the area too wet for year-round habitation. However, the Southern Patwin and other indigenous peoples gathered plant materials, hunted elk and waterfowl, and fished for tadpole shrimp in the area. After European settlement, the hardened soils at Jepson Prairie also protected the site from being plowed. Instead, domestic sheep and cattle replaced wild herds of pronghorn (*Antilocarpa americana*) and tule elk (*Cervus canadensis nannodes*).

Over the last 50 years, agriculture and urbanization have decimated the natural habitats of the Central Valley. By the mid-1970s, the pace of destruction so disturbed Jean Jenny—wife of UC Berkeley soil scientist Hans Jenny, for whom the NRS's Jenny Pygmy Forest Reserve is named—that she founded an organization to protect the Jepson Prairie region. In 1980, the group helped convince The Nature Conservancy (TNC) to buy Olcott Lake, a seasonally inundated playa at Jepson Prairie Reserve, as well as the surrounding bunchgrass prairie. Two years later, TNC dedicated this landscape as the Willis Linn Jepson Prairie Preserve, to be protected in perpetuity. In 1983, the University of California signed an agreement with TNC to promote research and teaching at the site; soon afterward, Jepson Prairie Reserve was brought into the NRS. TNC transferred ownership and management of the property to the nonprofit Solano Land Trust in 1997 but reserved a conservation easement to continue protecting the land. Today, the NRS and Solano Land Trust jointly manage Jepson Prairie Reserve.

An undescribed species of native bee in the genus *Panurginus* forages on *Downingia pulchella*, a widespread vernal pool wildflower. Solitary native bees live in burrows within Jepson Prairie Reserve's uplands. Their emergence in spring coincides with the flowering of preferred vernal pool species. Females prepare a ball of pollen and nectar that they seal into a new burrow with their eggs. Offspring feed on the pollen until they emerge at roughly the same time as next year's spring bloom. (Leslie Saul-Gershenz)

After breeding in Jepson Prairie Reserve vernal wetlands, California tiger salamanders travel upland to wait out the hot, dry summer in the burrows of the California ground squirrel (*Spermophilus beecheyi*). (Vide Ohlin)

In addition to a vast mosaic of small vernal pools and swales, Jepson Prairie supports two large playa lakes also underlain by a continuous layer of clay. The largest of these is Olcott Lake. Each spring, the lake and other vernal pools dry down over the course of a few weeks. Millions of native wildflowers bloom in spectacular succession as the water recedes, forming concentric rings of color. The higher, drier outer rings are typically dominated by yellow goldfields (*Lasthenia* spp.) and yellow carpet (*Blennosperma nanum* var. *nanum*). Drying of the middle pool elevations reveals white meadowfoam (*Limnanthes douglasii* subsp. *rosea*), navarretia (*Navarretia* spp.), and popcornflower (*Plagiobothrys* spp.). Finally, the pool bottoms become a carpet of blue downingias (*Downingia* spp.). The deeper playa lake bottoms host species with even greater tolerance for long-term inundation, extreme salinity, and severe alkalinity. The rare tiny annuals Solano grass (*Tuctoria mucronata*) and Colusa grass (*Neostapfia colusana*), found only in this soil type and habitat, are listed as federal endangered species.

Many other threatened or endangered species are found at Jepson Prairie as well. Among these are vernal pool fairy shrimp (*Branchinecta lynchi*), conservancy fairy shrimp (*Branchinecta conservatio*), and vernal pool tadpole shrimp (*Lepidurus packardi*), which hatch in the pools within hours of rainfall. More vivid is the lentil-sized Delta green ground beetle (*Elaphrus viridis*), known only from the 10-square-mile area surrounding the reserve. In spring, this metallic-green beetle hunts along the edges of playa pools for tiny invertebrate prey.

Also at Jepson Prairie, the California tiger salamander (*Ambystoma californiense*)

Researchers seine Olcott Lake at Jepson Prairie Reserve for immature
California tiger salamanders. (Jerry Booth)

spends most of its life cycle in deep burrows across Jepson Prairie's grasslands.
Adult salamanders emerge on rainy winter nights and migrate to larger vernal pools
and playa lakes to mate and deposit eggs. After metamorphosing in the pools, juvenile salamanders migrate to upland ground squirrel burrows to spend the dry
months of the year. Researchers at Jepson Prairie have tracked California tiger
salamanders traveling more than a half mile between the pools and their upland
habitat burrows (Shaffer and Trenham 2005; Trenham and Shaffer 2005). Scientists now recognize that upland habitats are critical for this salamander and similar
amphibians.

Jepson Prairie also boasts vigorous populations of native perennial grasses in the
drier uplands. Purple needlegrass (*Stipa pulchra*), California melic (*Melica californica*),
and California semaphore grass (*Pleuropogon californicus*) are particularly abundant. Tidally influenced sloughs, which bracket the northern and southern boundaries of the
reserve, support marsh and riparian species such as willows (*Salix* spp.) and saltgrass
(*Distichlis spicata*).

When wildflowers are not in bloom, the most striking landscape features at Jepson
Prairie are the mima mounds. From 1 to 6 feet high and 10 to 100 feet across, these
humps occur in regularly spaced patterns. Mima mounds have mysterious origins.
Ice-age freeze-and-thaw dynamics, prehistoric gopher mounds, and seismic activity are
among the possible causes.

Willis Linn Jepson, namesake of Jepson Prairie Reserve, is synonymous with botany
in California. Born and raised in the town of Little Oak not far from the reserve, Jepson understood the uniqueness of Solano County's landscape. He was both a founding
member of the Sierra Club and the first to document and describe the unique vernal

pools of the western Sacramento Valley. As a product of modern conservation agreements and a resource for field scientists in the Central Valley, Jepson Prairie Reserve is a living tribute to one of California's greatest botanists.

Born near Vacaville, Willis Linn Jepson first visited Jepson Prairie in the 1890s. Through his dedication to field exploration and an encyclopedic knowledge of California flora, Jepson become the preeminent expert on California botany in the first half of the twentieth century. (Archives, University and Jepson Herbaria, University of California, Berkeley)

DONALD AND SYLVIA
MCLAUGHLIN NATURAL RESERVE

Gray pines (*Pinus sabiniana*) and serpentine outcroppings characterize the former gold mine lands of McLaughlin Natural Reserve. (Deborah L. Elliot-Fisk)

Gold holds a central place in the identity of California. The gold rush of 1849 propelled a formerly sleepy backwater into a mecca for global commerce. And each spring, poppies (*Eschscholzia caespitosa, E. californica*) cover hills with molten-gold blooms. Powerful geologic forces brought both gold and poppies to the open grasslands and oak-studded hills east of Clear Lake. The site's precious metals have been mined away, but its exotic geology and endemic plant communities remain, attracting botanists, earth scientists, and other researchers to Donald and Sylvia McLaughlin Natural Reserve.

In 1978, the Homestake Mining Company discovered gold at what is now McLaughlin Reserve. The find proved to be the largest gold deposit found in California in the twentieth century, totaling more than four million ounces. McLaughlin gold was the result of tectonic plate movements that brought hydrothermal intrusions to the region roughly

DONALD AND SYLVIA MCLAUGHLIN NATURAL RESERVE

Administering Campus: UC Davis

Established: 1993

Location: Napa, Lake, and Yolo Counties, northwest of Davis; 2 hours from Davis campus

Size: Approximately 7,000 acres

Elevation: 1,245 to 2914 feet

Average Precipitation: 29.8 inches per year

Average Temperatures:

  July average 76.2°F

  January average 45.2°F

Facilities: 6,000-square-foot field station with 23 beds, classroom, laboratory, greenhouse, Wi-Fi, computer, kitchen, showers, laundry, gym, storage space, and shop space

Databases: Natural history handbook with species lists; meteorological, air quality, water quality, and aquatic ecology databases in various formats

California poppies brighten McLaughlin Reserve's grasslands with gold each spring. (Catherine M. Watters)

two million years ago. Magma bodies heated groundwater, boiling it to the surface through fractures in the earth's crust. The resulting hot springs carried dissolved gold and other metals to the surface, where they precipitated into veins of opal, chalcedony, and quartz flecked with microscopic crystals of gold. Typical of most hot-spring gold deposits, the McLaughlin deposit contained very low concentrations of this precious metal—roughly 0.10 ounces per ton of ore in the case of the Homestake Mine—making open pit mining the most efficient method of extraction.

After an extensive environmental review process that included requisite environmental protection such as postmining revegetation of disturbed soils and monitoring for and preventing mine waste pollution, Homestake Mining Company was granted permits to operate an open pit mine at the site. As part of its permit application,

The serpentine soils of McLaughlin Reserve host a large variety of native wildflowers, including larkspur (*Delphinium hesperium* subsp. *hesperium*) and tidy tips (*Layia platyglossa*). (Cathy Koehler)

Homestake proposed to establish an environmental field station on the land after mining ceased.

In 1985, the company approached the University of California to operate the field station. A UC faculty assessment found the site's extensive serpentine plant communities valuable for scientific research. Initially, in 1993, the UC Regents and mining company agreed to establish a temporary agreement for a reserve on an approximately 280-acre site with exceptional native serpentine plant habitats. Once the mine closed in 2003, an agreement was signed for a nearly 7,000-acre reserve, while the Land Trust of Napa County established a conservation easement to prevent commercial use and development of the property. The reserve was named for Homestake's former chairman, Donald McLaughlin, who also served as a UC Regent, and for his wife, Sylvia, a conservationist instrumental in preserving nearby San Francisco Bay from development and pollution. Several years later, Homestake Mining Company, which was eventually acquired by Barrick Gold of North America, donated more than 1,000 acres of land within the reserve to the University and established a generous reserve endowment.

The unique serpentine plant communities on the reserve are a product of the same geologic processes that joined California to the western edge of North America. Remarkably different geologic formations lie next to each other, resulting in soils of benign chemistry lying adjacent to others rich in heavy metals such as nickel, chromium, and cobalt. At the same time, these deposits also contain too much magnesium and too little calcium to support most plants.

McLaughlin Reserve's Hunting Creek in winter (Cathy Koehler)

McLaughlin harbors a wide array of native plants that have evolved to tolerate in-hospitable serpentine soils. Unusual plant communities on the reserve include mixed serpentine chaparral, which is dominated by the serpentine-endemic McNab cypress (*Cupressus macnabiana*), and serpentine grasslands. These unusual species assemblages have made McLaughlin Reserve a center for native serpentine plant studies. For example, UC Davis plant ecologist Kate Scow and her colleagues have investigated the combined effects of grazing, fire, and soil chemistry on native and exotic plant species diversity and the effects of exotic species on serpentine flora (Batten et al. 2006). Other botanical research has included studies of how soil microbes facilitate non-native plant invasions and how plant species that can tolerate normal and serpentine soils adapt to local conditions.

The reserve is equally valuable for wildlife research. The broad expanses of open space in the region support large predators and many species of small mammals.

Vegetation mosaics across the reserve provide diverse habitats for bird species, and year-round water in man-made ponds and in spring-fed creeks supports amphibians, fish, and aquatic invertebrates. Wildlife studies at McLaughlin have included research on how aquatic predators affect the rate of tadpole development in Pacific chorus frogs (*Pseudacris regilla*) and long-term population trends in stream invertebrates (Mazor et al. 2009).

Reserve lands disturbed by mining excavations are in the process of being reclaimed, providing opportunities for research into the reclamation of contaminated landscapes. One study at McLaughlin investigated whether soil microbes can ameliorate the effects of heavy metals in revegetation of mine tailings (Holloway et al. 2009). Such research can inform the restoration of other lands impacted by mining, turning the legacy of extraction at McLaughlin Reserve into a different form of California gold.

Rufous hummingbirds (*Selasphorus rufus*) are among the five hummingbird species netted and banded at McLaughlin Reserve as part of an international effort to monitor the population dynamics and health of these tiny birds. (Dave Menke)

QUAIL RIDGE RESERVE

Quail Ridge Reserve occupies a peninsula formed by the dam construction; reservoir waters now buffer the reserve from invasive species. (Lobsang Wangdu)

East of the vineyards of Napa Valley, tucked within the folds of the Inner Coast ranges, stretch the waters of one of California's largest reservoirs, Lake Berryessa. The lake bustles with boats of all sizes during the long summer months. But a quieter remnant of this area's original charms can be found along the waterway's southern shore. Located on a small, rugged peninsula, the slopes of Quail Ridge Reserve are clad in native oak woodland, chaparral, and outstanding examples of native perennial grasslands.

Quail Ridge's geological history begins beneath the sea. Roughly 140 million years ago, the young Sierra Nevada and Klamath Mountains began to rise beneath the Pacific Ocean. Their uplift triggered landslides that occurred for over 75 million years under a mile or more of water. Further uplifting, folding, and faulting produced the Coast Range.

The Inner Coast Range region was eventually inhabited by the Southern Patwin.

QUAIL RIDGE RESERVE

Administering Campus: UC Davis

Established: 1991

Location: Napa County, on a southern peninsula of Lake Berryessa; 27 miles from Davis campus

Size: Approximately 2,500 acres

Elevation: 440 to 1,516 feet

Average Precipitation: 24 inches per year

Average Temperatures:

> January average 46°F

> July average 82°F

Facilities: Several overnight options are available for small groups or solo researchers. The field station includes a laboratory/workspace. Camping areas are available for class use.

Databases: Natural history handbook with species lists, meteorological, GIS layers, and herpetological arrays

Though no evidence of native settlements has been found on the reserve, over 150 village sites were identified in the area now flooded by the lake. The Southern Patwins likely visited Quail Ridge to harvest acorns, pine nuts, berries, and game. In 1843, the area became part of a Mexican land grant bestowed to two brothers, Sisto and José de Jesus Berelleza. The Berellezas, for whom the reservoir is named, ranched livestock from Vacaville in Solano County to Capay Valley in Yolo County until the early 1850s. After the United States annexed Alta California, the valley where the brothers had built their houses was divided into family farms. The town of Monticello grew up in its center, prospering amid fields growing pears, walnuts, grapes, and alfalfa.

Damming of the area's largest stream, Putah Creek, put an end to these halcyon times. In 1957, the US Bureau of Reclamation completed 270-foot high Monticello Dam at Devil's Gate, a steep and narrow canyon of Putah Creek. Six years later, the community of Monticello was inundated under 1.6 million acre-feet of dam water. Monticello Dam created the second-largest body of water in California after Shasta Reservoir and formed a peninsula out of Quail Ridge.

The "Chi-ca-go" call of the California quail (*Callipepla californica*) is often heard in the chaparral habitats of Quail Ridge Reserve. (Mike Hamilton)

A variable checkerspot (*Euphydryas chalcedonia*) butterfly rests on the common wildflower bluedicks (*Dichelostemma capitatum*). (Baotran Ellner)

Researchers at Quail Ridge Reserve are developing ways to use pattern recognition algorithms to automatically identify California newts (*Taricha torosa*) entering and exiting reserve ponds. (David Gubernick)

In 1984, local community members began purchasing land on the peninsula with an eye to preserving its natural ecosystems. Some formed the nonprofit Quail Ridge Wilderness Conservancy in 1989, which was instrumental in bringing the ridge into the NRS in 1991 and continues to facilitate land acquisition for the NRS. Today the reserve consists of a patchwork of parcels owned by the Conservancy, the California Department of Fish and Game, the US Bureau of Land Management, the US Bureau of Reclamation, and the University of California. Together with the Napa County Land Trust and Wildlife Conservation Board, these entities have formed a unique partnership to cooperatively manage the reserve lands, to conserve the natural features and wildlife on the reserve, and to foster research and education. The reserve also includes some private lands.

Positioned on the inland edge of the North Coast Ranges, Quail Ridge Reserve experiences a pronounced rain shadow. Its extremely dry Mediterranean climate favors drought-resistant species. Exposed, south-facing slopes feature stands of chaparral dominated by chamise (*Adenostoma fasciculatum*), Parry manzanita (*Acrtostaphylos parryana*), and buckbrush (*Ceanothus cuneatus*). As with most chaparral species, the small, leathery leaves of these shrubs help minimize water loss.

An unusually diverse mix of oaks is found at Quail Ridge. These include valley (*Quercus lobata*), interior live (*Q. wislizenii*), blue (*Q. douglasii*), black (*Q. kelloggii*), and scrub (*Q. berberidifolia*), plus hybrids of black and interior live oak. The grey-blue boughs of foothill pines (*Pinus sabiniana*) stand out amid the darker olive foliage of the live oaks. The dense canopy of north-facing woodlands shelters an understory of colorful spring wildflowers, including baby blue-eyes (*Nemophila menziesii*), hound's tongue (*Cynoglossum grande*), and shooting stars (*Dodecatheon hendersonii*).

An unusual abundance of native grasses grows in areas where the oaks thin into savannah. California's state grass, purple needlegrass (*Stipa pulchra*), and its sister species,

The Quail Ridge Reserve Network provides not only a test bed for wireless network research but also a place to collect climate and other data about the environment from distant portions of the reserve. (Christopher Woodcock)

foothill needlegrass (*S. lepida*), are abundant across the reserve, as are june grass (*Koeleria macrantha*), California fescue (*Festuca californica*), and California melic (*Melica californica*). Yet even on the reserve, invasive European annual grasses are not uncommon.

The reserve's location at the eastern edge of the Coast Ranges puts it at the nexus of two major biogeographic regions. Salamanders are plentiful in the moist and cool Pacific Border region of the coast, while the warm, dry Sierra Madrean region typical of central Mexico features more snakes and lizards. Quail Ridge supports robust populations of reptile and amphibian species common to both regions. Of the 106 reptile and amphibian species found in California, 20 percent have been documented on the reserve (UC Davis 2004).

Research at Quail Ridge has focused primarily on the reserve's flora and fauna. Studies conducted include investigations into the factors that influence the distribution of native perennial grasses (Harrison et al. 2002; Bakker et al. 2009), habitat choice in the brush mouse (*Peromyscus boylii*; Mabry 2008; Mabry and Stamps 2008), and the evolutionary relationship between the deer tick (Ixodidae) and the bacterium *Anaplasma phagocytophilum*, which causes the tick-borne illness anaplasmosis in humans and domestic animals (Nieto et al. 2010; Wright et al. 2011).

In recent years, the reserve has become a popular site for testing wireless network technologies. The sharp folds of the Coast Range isolate Quail Ridge Reserve from the electromagnetic interference that pervades cities and their environs. Precipitous topography makes relaying messages from one network node to the next challenging. UC Davis professor of computer science Prasant Mohapatra and colleagues have developed a wireless communication network on the reserve to support two very different types of research. Computer scientists use the system to test network performance and design as well as wireless equipment. Field researchers use the network to gather and transmit a wide range of environmental data. Network tasks include relaying measurements of soil temperatures to determine microclimate characteristics, tracking animal movements with radio telemetry, and recording the arrival of salamanders at the reserve's breeding ponds. The rising importance of wireless communications in field research promises to make Quail Ridge a state-of-the-art center for computing innovations for years to come.

Dense coniferous forests are interspersed among scree slopes and wet meadows at Sagehen Creek
Field Station, a landscape characteristic of the Sierra Nevada crest. (Christopher Woodcock)

Immediately east of the Sierra Nevada crest, within a glacier-carved basin, snow melts
and collects to form the clear headwaters of Sagehen Creek. For eight miles, the stream
winds past thick conifer forests, soggy fens, and open meadows, through a landscape
teeming with trout, aquatic insects, and boreal forest mammals. Researchers have
flocked here for over half a century to study the environment of the northern Sierra
Nevada, encouraged by the warm cabins and convivial conversation at Sagehen Creek
Field Station.

Deep snows and long winters make the Sierra crest a challenging place to live.
Though no permanent Native American habitation sites have been found in the Sagehen Basin, both the Washoe of the eastern Sierra Nevada and the Martis of the western
Sierra trekked here to hunt and gather food in summer. The discovery of gold and sil-
ver in the Sierra Nevada in the mid-nineteenth century also attracted immigrants from

SAGEHEN CREEK FIELD STATION

Administering Campus: UC Berkeley

Established: 1951 (joined NRS in 2004)

Location: Nevada County, 8.4 miles north of Truckee on Highway 89

Size: Approximately 9,000 acres by agreement with the USDA Forest Service

Elevation: 5,900 to 8,700 feet; station facilities located at 6,390 feet

Average Precipitation: At 6,390 feet, the annual precipitation for water is 34.67 inches; the annual precipitation for snow is 202.8 inches.

Average Temperatures:

January 13°F to 40°F

July 37°F to 79°F

Facilities: Housing in 22 buildings for up to 59 people year-round. Library/computer lab; two classrooms; communal kitchen, eating area, and deck; office space; fish observation house. Electricity with backup generator, wireless network with satellite Internet service, VCR, slide and LCD projectors. Flush toilets, showers, sinks, and washing machines. Heat is available in all buildings.

Databases: Extensive climate, species, precipitation, stream condition, and photo databases

around the world. Sheep and cattle were run in nearby meadows to feed the miners, and a logging industry sprang up to house the new arrivals. The Sagehen area was effectively logged out by the early 1900s, though the remains of narrow gauge logging railroads, flumes, a sawmill, and logging skid trails still can be found in the basin.

A desire to conserve the region's natural resources led the federal government to establish the Tahoe National Forest in the first years of the twentieth century. Similar concerns led UC Berkeley biology professor A. Starker Leopold to launch a California wildlife and fisheries studies program in 1949. Seeking a base for the program's fisheries arm, Leopold and fellow professor Paul Needham camped and fished their way across the Sierra Nevada until they found Sagehen Creek. The stream was everything they sought: small enough to manipulate with experiments, subject to severe winter weather, and so healthy it supported nine species of native fish. Wasting no time, the researchers opened Sagehen Creek Field Station in 1951 under a special-use permit from the USDA Forest Service. The field station put the conservation ideas proposed by Starker's famous father, Aldo Leopold, into action.

More than half a century of wildlife studies followed, with students and researchers often doubling as a construction crew to expand the facilities. In 2004, the field station joined the NRS. Two years later, the entire 9,000-acre basin was designated the Sagehen Experimental Forest by the Forest Service. Sagehen is now a center for cooperative

Sagehen Creek Field Station includes a fen featuring mineral-rich waters and carnivorous plants such as the round-leaved sundew (*Drosera rotundifolia*). (Christopher Woodcock)

research to guide the sustainable management of Sierra Nevada forests, conducted by university and government scientists.

Rock and snow are central players in the environment of the Sagehen Basin. Ancient volcanic eruptions covered the area in layers of ash, andesite, and mudflows. Subsequent faulting uplifted and steepened the Sierra Nevada range. During this process, glaciers carved deep valleys throughout much of the Sierra, leaving glacial moraines scattered across the basin and a small cirque hollowed into the headwaters of Sagehen Creek.

Yet glaciers failed to remove the volcanic cap that overlies Sagehen's granite foundation. These volcanic rocks can store water underground for decades. Fed by a deep winter snowpack, the extensive groundwater system in the Sagehen Basin bubbles up to the surface as springs and fens. The mineral-rich fen waters support a number of unusual plants, including two species of carnivorous sundews (*Drosera angelica, D. rotundifolia*). Located at the edge of the rain shadow of the Sierra Nevada, the Sagehen Basin spans a significant precipitation gradient. In early spring, the snow cover may be 15 feet deep at the basin's highest point yet absent at its lower edge.

The creek that first drew UC researchers to the Sagehen Basin has been a focus of reserve science since the founding of the field station. Sagehen Creek is one of few streams in the eastern Sierra with a diverse fish assemblage, which is supported by a rich complement of caddisflies, stoneflies, mayflies, and other aquatic insects.

Among the earliest structures built on the site was an underground chamber to observe trout behavior in Sagehen Creek. Known today as the fish observatory, the building replaces a reach of the stream bank with a long wall of glass, permitting fish watchers to record fish behavior in relative comfort year round. Using the

Efforts are under way to restore the endangered Lahontan cutthroat trout to the protected waters of Sagehen Creek. (Tim Torell, courtesy of the Nevada Department of Wildlife)

observation chamber and other methods, researchers have conducted pioneering studies into the life history of native Lahontan cutthroat (*Onchorhyncus clarki henshawi*) and rainbow (*O. mykiss*) trout, as well as non-native brook (*Salvelinus fontinalis*) and brown (*Salmo trutta*) trout living within Sagehen Creek and nearby waterways. Efforts to restore the threatened Lahontan cutthroat trout to Sagehen Creek are now under way.

An orphaned black bear (*Ursus americanus*) cub is tucked into a winter den at Sagehen Creek Field Station to ease its return to the wild. (Lobsang Wangdu)

The Sagehen Basin hosts an impressive 600 species or so of vascular plants. Vegetation typical of the Great Basin to the east, such as Wyoming big sagebrush (*Artemisia tridentata* subsp. *wyomingensis*) and antelope bitterbrush (*Purshia tridentata*), is found in dry, lower elevations. These native shrubs merge into open Jeffrey pine forest (*Pinus jeffreyi*), red fir (*Abies magnifica*), and western white pine (*Pinus monticola*) stands, especially along dry ridgelines. Along Sagehen Creek, a dense riparian zone grades into fens at lower elevations. Fed by mineral-rich waters, the fens are dominated by mosses (e.g., *Drepanocladus aduncas*), sedges (*Carex* spp.), bog blueberry (*Vaccinium uliginosum* subsp. *occidentale*), and other plants that can survive in saturated soil conditions.

The Adventure Risk Challenge program hosted at Sagehen Creek Field Station combines intensive English literacy courses with rock climbing, backpacking, and other outdoor skills. (UC Berkeley Adventure Risk Challenge Program)

Mammal species in the Sagehen Basin range in size from shrews (*Sorex* spp.) to black bears. Many of the mammals found in the basin have been the subjects of long-term studies, including beavers (*Castor canadensis*), martens, chipmunks (*Tamias* spp.), and weasels (*Mustela erminea, M. frenata*). During the winter of 2008, a motion detection camera employed to track American martens (*Martes americana*) in the Sagehen Basin captured instead a photograph of a wolverine (*Gulo gulo*). The first wild wolverine documented in California since the 1920s, it was still living in the Sagehen area as of 2010.

The Sagehen Experimental Forest, which surrounds the reserve, serves as a research site to test forest management techniques such as thinning and undergrowth removal for the Sierra Nevada. For example, a century of fire suppression has allowed a huge fuel load of dead branches, undergrowth, and other fuels to accumulate, putting regional forests at risk of catastrophic wildfire. Scientists are applying various methods to reduce fuel loads while improving wildlife habitat in experimental Sagehen forest plots. By mapping resulting changes in vegetation and modeling how fire would behave in each area, scientists are developing ways to keep the forests of the West resilient and healthy. over the long term.

STEBBINS COLD CANYON RESERVE

One of few NRS sites open to the public, Stebbins Cold Canyon Reserve offers challenging hiking along its steep and forested slopes. (Christopher Woodcock)

Stebbins Cold Canyon Reserve is nestled in the Coast Ranges near the southeastern corner of Lake Berryessa. Formed around a tributary of Putah Creek, the rugged slopes and dense vegetation of this north-facing canyon evoke a wilder California from long ago. One of few sites in the NRS open to both academic research and public use, this corner of the Vaca Mountains is an attractive site for day hikes and a prime location to study natural history.

Native Americans have lived in this region for thousands of years. As far back as 2,000 years before the present, the Southern Patwin hunted brush rabbits (*Sylvilagus bachmani*), grizzly bears (*Ursus arctos horribilis*), tule elk (*Cervus canadensis nannodes*), and other game in the region and used bedrock mortars along Cold Creek to grind acorns. As recently as 1838, the Patwin still lived along Putah Creek in large numbers but were displaced by Spanish and Mexican settlers soon afterward. After California joined the United States, the canyon was opened for livestock grazing. In the 1930s, homesteader John Vlahos grazed goats and cattle here. Vlahos built several structures in the canyon and used one as cold storage for goat cheese, giving the canyon its name. The University of California acquired the property and its healthy native plant and wildlife communities to establish Stebbins Cold Canyon Reserve in 1984.

STEBBINS COLD CANYON RESERVE

Administering Campus: UC Davis

Established: 1979

Location: Solano and Napa Counties, 20 miles west of Davis campus; 6 miles west of Winters; 0.5 miles east of Monticello Dam

Size: Approximately 600 acres

Elevation: 300 to 2,500 feet

Average Precipitation: 20 inches per year

Average Temperatures:

　　January average 46°F

　　July average 82°F

Facilities: None; site is best suited for day use

Databases: Natural history handbook with species lists; GIS layers

The canyon itself began as a river delta on the California coast millions of years ago. Eons of deposition compressed the particles into sandstones, mudstones, and shales. The rise of the Coast Ranges tilted these sediments into near-vertical planes and stranded them more than 40 miles from the sea. Cold Creek cut down through the softest mudstone layers, while the walls of the canyon are made of more resistant sandstones.

Cold Creek flows directly into Putah Creek, one of only three perennial streams that empty into the Central Valley from the Coast Range. Aquatic and terrestrial animals once traveled freely between both watersheds. However, the construction of a major dam on Putah Creek just upstream from Cold Canyon and a highway that crosses Cold Creek at the mouth of the canyon have likely limited the dispersal of many species into or out of the reserve.

Like much of California, the reserve experiences wet winters and dry summers, but summers at the reserve are particularly harsh due to the canyon's location and topography. Relatively little rainfall and coastal fog filter past the Coast Ranges

Yellow-rumped warblers (*Setophaga coronata*) are versatile foragers. These songbirds skim insects off the surface of rivers, snatch them from midair, and pluck them from spider webs. Yellow-rumped warblers also supplement their diet with berries in fall. (Dave Menke)

Jumping spider
1999

Stebbins Cold Canyon Reserve is home to the jumping spider *Habronattus americanus*, which stalks its prey with exceptionally acute eyesight. Males of this species are among the most colorful spiders in North America. This stamp was part of an insects and spiders stamp sheet issued in 1999 by the US Postal Service. (US Postal Service)

Stebbins Cold Canyon Reserve is a popular destination for school field trips. (Lyndsay Dawkins, Jeff Falyn)

and into the reserve. The canyon's steep walls trap heat, while the southern and western ridges shield the drainage from cooling delta breezes.

Almost devoid of flat surfaces, the reserve is a patchwork of different microclimates and plant communities. Chaparral stands cover the northern slopes and are dominated by chamise (*Adenostoma fasciculatum*), scrub oak (*Quercus berberidifolia*), toyon (*Heteromeles arbutifolia*), and poison oak (*Toxicodendron diversilobum*). Adjacent southern slopes are populated by non-native grasslands, which can tolerate drier, hotter conditions. Moister grasslands grade into blue oak (*Q. douglasii*) savannas. Interior live oak (*Q. wislizenii*) woodlands shade cooler hillsides with more available water. The narrow channel of Cold Creek is lined by riparian forest brightened by the magenta blooms of western redbud (*Cercis occidentalis*) in early spring.

Wildlife abounds in this protected canyon. As is true in nearly every ecosystem, most of these organisms lack a backbone. The rare and protected valley elderberry longhorn beetle (*Desmocercus californicus dimorphus*) spends most of its existence inside the branches of elderberry (*Sambucus nigra* subsp. *caerulea*) shrubs growing along Cold Creek, while Pacific banana slugs (*Ariolimax columbianus*) slide across the mossy trail banks and fallen leaves.

Public access is controlled at most NRS reserves, but Stebbins Cold Canyon Reserve is open to the public. Located a short drive from Sacramento and the San Francisco Bay Area, the reserve has become a favorite destination for school groups, hikers, amateur naturalists, and others seeking a natural antidote to urban life. Its close proximity to the

UC Davis campus attracts a number of university-level courses and researchers as well. More than 20,000 people visit each year.

The reserve is named for G. Ledyard Stebbins, among the most influential botanists of the twentieth century and a giant in the field of evolutionary biology. A professor at UC Berkeley, then UC Davis, Stebbins was one of the architects of the modern synthesis: the view that evolution is the result of interactions among genetics, prehistoric events, natural selection, and morphological evolution. A devoted conservation biologist, Stebbins was one of the founding members of the California Native Plant Society. Formed in 1965, the society is a statewide, nonprofit organization of lay botanists and professional scientists dedicated to the conservation of California's native plants. The group has blossomed into a widely influential conservation organization with 33 regional chapters.

At the dedication of the reserve, Professor Stebbins said he found it far more satisfying to have a natural reserve named for him than a campus building. When he died in 2000, at the age of 94, his ashes were scattered across the canyon that honors his memory.

The reserve is named for G. Ledyard Stebbins, a much-beloved UC Davis genetics professor, California botanist, and one of the architects of the modern synthesis of evolution. (Debbie Aldridge/UC Davis)

AÑO NUEVO ISLAND RESERVE

Now abandoned to animals and the elements, the former lightkeeper's residence looms over Año Nuevo Island Reserve. (Kathleen M. Wong)

Few places on this earth today belong solely to the animals. Yet the most populous state in the nation still harbors a throwback to those wilder times. Año Nuevo Island is located just an hour's drive south of bustling San Francisco. This wave-tossed scrap of dry land is prime real estate for seals, sea lions, and seabirds of many kinds. A half mile from shore, these marine species can rest and raise their young safe from mainland predators and human development. And thanks to a partnership between the University of California and the California Department of Parks and Recreation, the island has become a locus of trailblazing research into the mysterious lives of marine animals.

Año Nuevo Island lies at the western tip of a marine terrace midway between San Francisco and Santa Cruz. Since its formation 105,000 years ago, incremental movements of the San Andreas Fault System have raised this terrace above the waves. When first sighted by Spanish explorer Sebastian Vizcaino around New Year's Day

AÑO NUEVO ISLAND RESERVE

Administering Campus: UC Santa Cruz

Established: 1969

Location: San Mateo County, near the Santa Cruz County line; 0.62 miles offshore of Point Año Nuevo. The island is part of Año Nuevo State Reserve, owned by the California Department of Parks and Recreation.

Size: Approximately 25 acres, including the area of small rocky islets and coves immediately adjacent to the main island

Elevation: 0 to 40 feet

Average Precipitation: 20 inches per year

Average Temperatures:

  September maximum 76°F

  January minimum 39°F, annual mean 56°F

Facilities: Historic buildings provide limited dormitory, kitchen, and field lab space; electricity provided by diesel generator; no running water; observation blinds serve major pinniped areas.

Databases: Pinniped records continuous since 1967. Census data for all pinniped species present on the island (northern elephant seals, Steller sea lions, California sea lions, and harbor seals). Resighting and breeding records for individually tagged northern elephant seals. Shorter term records for breeding seabirds (especially rhinoceros auklets) are maintained by PRBO Conservation Science and Oikonos. The National Marine Mammal Laboratory maintains resighting records for individually marked California sea lions present during the summer since 1996; extensive bibliography of published research.

1605, it was a narrow peninsula. Soon afterward, the ocean scoured a channel separating the point from the mainland. This gap continued to widen until the 1940s, when the channel eroded to bedrock in the 1940s. Much of the rock on the seaward side of the island has also eroded into tiny islets frequented by Steller sea lions (*Eumetopias jubatus*). Two sandy beaches flank the southeastern portion of the island, where elephant seals congregate.

The federal government built a light station in 1870 to help ships avoid the low-slung island in thick coastal fog. In 1872 a steam fog whistle was added to aid navigation around the rocky point, to be replaced several decades later by a lighthouse. The original light-keeper's dwelling was replaced in 1904 with a two-story, 15-room structure to house the keepers and their families. The station was closed in 1948 and replaced by an automated sea buoy. The lightkeeper's house has been abandoned to nesting birds and the explorations of curious sea lions. The fog signal building still shelters visiting researchers.

Rock platforms to the north and west of the island are favored by breeding Steller sea lions. The largest colony of pinnipeds gathers on Main Beach, the triangular promontory at the island's southeastern edge. (Daniel P. Costa)

Infancy is brief for northern elephant seal pups (*Mirounga angustirostris*). Pups bulk up fast on fat-rich milk because their mothers depart for the ocean within one month of giving birth. The young seals learn to swim and hunt on their own. (Kathleen M. Wong)

PROFESSOR DANIEL P. COSTA, DEPARTMENT OF ECOLOGY AND
EVOLUTIONARY BIOLOGY, INSTITUTE OF MARINE SCIENCES, UC SANTA CRUZ

UC Santa Cruz Professor Daniel P. Costa (Courtesy of Daniel P. Costa)

Año Nuevo Island Reserve has been the backbone of my research program for my entire career. The opportunity to have access to a pinniped colony half an hour from campus and to be able to have facilities there has been essential to my work. Anywhere else in California, if you wanted to go to a research site such as this, you'd have to go to the Channel Islands, which requires a plane flight or boat trip and takes the better part of a day to get there and organize logistics.

At Año Nuevo, we can test ideas and equipment in our backyard and then apply what we find on expeditions elsewhere, to the Galápagos, Alaska, and the Antarctic. In a real sense, Año Nuevo Island Reserve is an extension of our lab, allowing undergraduates to work with large animals in the field. It would be impossible for them to get this experience anywhere else.

The unique nature of the Año Nuevo Island Reserve and our research there has made us attractive to collaborators worldwide. The island attracts not only graduate students from all over the world—Australia, Japan, Germany, the United Kingdom—but also colleagues who want to work with us because of the natural laboratory we have available. We benefit and they benefit.

The story of the reserve begins in 1967, when the state closed the island to the public to protect the growing population of seals and sea lions and established the area as a reserve devoted solely to research. A year later, the California Department of Parks and Recreation granted permission to UC Santa Cruz to use the island as a research facility. In 1969, the University obtained a use agreement for the island, beginning a long collaboration with the California Department of Parks and Recreation. Año Nuevo Island Reserve joined the UC Natural Reserve System (NRS).

Today, Año Nuevo Island supports magnificent populations of pinnipeds. Five different species are periodically resident at the reserve, including California sea lions (*Zalophus californianus*), Steller sea lions (*Eumetopias jubatus*), and harbor seals (*Phoca vitulina*). Most numerous by far are northern elephant seals (*Mirounga angustirostris*). Hunted for the oil that could be rendered from their blubber, only a few dozen were

A rookery of Brandt's cormorants (*Phalacrocorax penicillatus*) surrounds the abandoned lightkeeper's house in summer. The vivid blue throat patch is part of the cormorant's breeding plumage. (Pat Morris)

thought to exist by the early twentieth century. The first recorded pups were born on the island in 1961. The island and associated mainland colonies of this species are more accessible to researchers than any other pinniped breeding colony in the world. Each winter, the two-ton males engage in bloody battles for mating rights with females who come ashore to give birth. Females and juveniles return to molt in spring; males follow in summer. Juveniles haul out on its beaches to rest in fall. southern sea otters (*Enhydra lutris nereis*), gray whales (*Eschrichtius robustus*), and great white sharks (*Carcharodon carcharias*) are also sighted around the island during winter.

In summer, seven species of seabirds congregate to breed on Año Nuevo.. The birds nest on offshore islands for protection from mainland predators such as rats and foxes. Of special note is the rhinoceros auklet (*Cerorhinca monocerata*), named for the vertical bump on its beak. This relative of the puffin digs nest burrows into the island's soft soils. Año Nuevo Island constitutes the auklet's southernmost breeding. However, sea lions wandering across the crown of the island have eroded the native vegetation and collapsed auklet burrows. To protect the auklet colony, a portion of the island has been fenced with a log palisade and replanted with grasses. Ceramic nest burrows designed and made by UC Santa Cruz art students were buried beneath the soil to provide trample-resistant nests.

Año Nuevo Island Natural Reserve has been the center of a decades-long research program on the northern elephant seal initiated by UC Santa Cruz professor Burney Le Boeuf and colleagues in the 1970s. Le Boeuf's research on northern elephant seal breeding behavior and male competition at Año Nuevo remains a classic study on animal behavior (Le Boeuf et al. 2000). Professor Dan Costa, his colleagues, and students have continued studying many other aspects of this colony. For example, by attaching time-depth and satellite GPS tags to the heads of elephant seals and other pinnipeds (Boehlert et al. 2010; Block et al. 2011), Costa and associates have mapped where the seals go on their annual ocean journeys and how they spend their travel time. Onboard instruments such as thermometers allow researchers to assemble temperature profiles of ocean currents; chlorophyll sensors observe the productivity of local waters; and accelerometers glued to seals' jaws indicate when and where animals are grabbing and swallowing fish. The research techniques first developed with northern elephant seals at Año Nuevo have been applied many other marine species, including southern elephant seals (*Mirounga leonina*). Data from these marine mammals have been used to map the bathymetry of the ocean floor and to explain accelerated rates of glacial melt in Antarctica (Padman et al. 2010).

A network of marine scientists from around the world has applied similar tags to ocean species ranging from albatross to great white sharks and sea turtles to sunfish. To date, the Tagging of Pacific Predators (TOPP) project has tracked more than 2,000 animals from 23 species. TOPP has yielded a remarkable portrait of previously unknown migration pathways and critical habitats. For example, TOPP discovered that marine predators congregate to hunt in areas with steep temperature and salinity gradients. These and other remarkable insights into the lives of marine animals are a testament to the global reach of Año Nuevo science research.

BLUE OAK RANCH RESERVE

The wooded hills of Blue Oak Ranch Reserve have a timeless feel, yet are just a few miles from Silicon Valley. (Christopher Woodcock)

Next door to metropolitan San Jose, midway up the western face of Mount Hamilton, stretches an iconic California landscape. Groves of majestic valley and blue oaks spread their branches over grasslands brightened by spring wildflowers and split by rocky arroyos. Spectacular views of southern San Francisco Bay and the Santa Cruz Mountains can be seen across the Santa Clara Valley. Further up the mountain cluster the white domes of the University of California's Lick Observatory, which offer breathtaking views of the night sky. These lands are part of Blue Oak Ranch Reserve, one of the newest reserves within the NRS. Habitat protected by Blue Oak Ranch is the culmination of more than two decades of conservation planning and ecological restoration. In its short history as an NRS reserve, hundreds of university students and faculty have come to learn, teach classes, and conduct field research, while interest in exploring the reserve's natural landscape continues to grow.

BLUE OAK RANCH RESERVE

Administering Campus: UC Berkeley

Established: 2007

Location: Santa Clara County, 11.2 miles east of downtown San Jose

Size: Approximately 3,200 acres

Elevation: 1,489 to 2,855 feet. Mount Hamilton summit is 4,200 feet.

Average Precipitation: 23.7 inches per year

Average Temperatures:

July 62.2°F to 78°F

January 36.5°F to 48.3°F

(Both temperature and rainfall statistics were taken from the National Weather Service station atop Mount Hamilton, 5 miles from the reserve.)

Facilities: Reserve is for day use or overnight camping at this time. A network of roads gives access to most areas within the property. New facilities are being planned.

Databases: ArcGIS data library, airborne and satellite imagery for Mt. Hamilton Range, Google Earth KML for boundary and local features, species lists (vertebrates and plants), bibliography, and climate records for Mt. Hamilton and City of San Jose. On-site weather station in operation since August 2008; two microclimate sensor networks will be in place by March 2009.

Long before Europeans landed in North America, Werwersen Ohlone people lived in the vicinity of Mount Hamilton. In 1839, the area became part of Rancho Cañada de Pala, a Mexican land grant made to José de Jesus Bernal. Bernal built a homestead and raised cattle and horses on the rancho. Between 1850 and 1880, as many as six different families ranched and subsistence farmed the area. At the turn of the century, Joseph D. Grant, son of a wealthy San Francisco merchant, bought most of the land in the area. In addition to ranching the site, Grant hunted large game with guests such as Leland Stanford and Herbert Hoover.

The land remained in livestock ranching and farming until the 1960s, when the property was consolidated into Blue Oak Ranch. In 1972, investors bought the ranch intending to establish a vineyard. But the plan never came to fruition, and in 1990 the land was sold. A perpetual conservation easement was recorded against the property in 2000. The owner of the conservation easement interest is The Nature Conservancy (TNC); the conservation easement remains in effect and continues to protect the property today. The land was transferred to the UC Regents in 2007, when it joined the NRS.

Reserve boundaries enclose four watersheds, enabling research to be conducted at

Wisps of fog obscure a valley oak at Blue Oak Ranch Reserve. (Christopher Woodcock)

Wildlife no longer common in the metropolis of San Jose abounds at Blue Oak Ranch Reserve. A camera equipped with a motion sensor at the reserve captured this view of a mountain lion (*Puma concolor*) on the move. (Jeffery T. Wilcox)

the watershed scale. Roughly two-thirds of the reserve is drained by three tributaries of Arroyo Aguague, which then joins Upper Penitencia Creek, which in turn joins Coyote Creek before flowing into San Francisco Bay. The remainder of the reserve belongs to the Smith Creek watershed in the Arroyo Hondo drainage. Livestock ponds across the reserve are fed by springs, seeps, or runoff from winter rains. The deepest of these hold water year round. Isolated water sources in a dry landscape, these ponds support several reptiles and amphibians of special concern—the California tiger salamander (*Amybstoma californiense*), the foothill yellow-legged frog (*Rana boylii*), the California red-legged frog (*Rana draytonii*), and the western pond turtle (*Clemmys marmorata*)—making Blue Oak Ranch Reserve a refuge for rare species in a populous region of the state.

Blue oak (*Quercus douglasii*) and valley oak (*Q. lobata*) woodlands dominate the reserve, interspersed with coast live (*Q. agrifolia*) and black oak (*Q. kellogii*). These woodlands grade into riparian forest, Diablan sage scrub, wildflower fields, and native perennial grasslands. Both blue and valley oak woodlands are in decline throughout California due to livestock grazing, urban development, new diseases such as sudden oak death, and a low survival rate for seedlings. Prescribed fires, such as those set on the reserve in an experimental program, may aid oak regeneration by opening grassland canopies and reducing competition from non-native grasses.

The precipitous slopes of Arroyo Hondo canyon offer a wide range of microclimates, with vegetation adapted to cool and moist environments growing on north- and east-facing slopes and plants adapted to hot, dry conditions growing on west- and south-facing slopes. Such habitat diversity attracts birds from the Pacific Flyway needing to refuel during their annual migrations and provides dispersal corridors for numerous aquatic and terrestrial animal species.

Despite past agricultural uses of the area, there are still native California grasslands in many locations across the reserve. Native grasses are most abundant in the understory of the mixed evergreen woodland, under individual oak trees in oak woodlands, and along open ridge tops and adjacent slopes. Dominant species include purple needlegrass (*Stipa pulchra*), perennial species of barley (*Hordeum brachyantherum* subsp. *brachyantherum*), melic grasses (*Melica californica, M. imperfecta, M. torreyana*), and wildryes (*Elymus glaucus* subsp. *glaucus, E. triticoides*). Of the 462 plant species documented on the reserve, almost 80 percent are native.

The most conspicuous rodent on the reserve is the California ground squirrel (*Spermophilus beecheyi*). Its presence has attracted an abundance of northern Pacific rattlesnakes (*Crotalus oreganus oreganus*). Ground squirrels and rattlesnakes are entwined in an ancient relationship that offers a prime example of coevolution in action. Biology professor Rulon Clark of San Diego State University is currently studying the elaborate predator-prey interactions between the two species at the reserve. Adult squirrels are immune to rattlesnake venom and will mob and bite snakes to ward the predators away from their pups. To warn snakes that they've been spotted, mother squirrels lash their

Northern Pacific rattlesnakes and California ground
squirrels have been locked in an evolutionary arms race
for thousands of years. Adult squirrels typically are
immune to snake venom and warn away snakes with
a combination of sand kicking, tail lashing, and other
harassment. Scientists at Blue Oak Ranch Reserve are
studying interactions between the two species.
(Squirrel: Jeffery T. Wilcox. Snake: Michael Hamilton)

tails back and forth. This seemingly visual signal is detected as infrared heat by the snakes'
temperature-sensitive pit organs. Other squirrels in the colony may provoke the snake to
rattle—a tip-off about the reptile's size and potential striking distance. Clark attaches radio
transmitters to the snakes and records video
of ground squirrel-rattlesnake encounters in
the wild. His team is also using robotic squirrels to home in on rattlesnake responses to
squirrel antipredator behaviors.

Clark's research at the reserve is facilitated
by a long-range, high-speed wireless mesh network developed by reserve director Michael P.
Hamilton and UC Berkeley biology professor
Todd Dawson. The wireless network relays live
video images and animal-tracking data to the
reserve headquarters and provides solar power
for additional field equipment. A second sensor network called the *Very Large Ecological
Array* gathers minute-by-minute variations in
environmental parameters such as soil moisture, temperature, humidity, wind speed, and
solar radiation. Data from more than 50 nodes
can be viewed online in real time and are also
stored for later analysis. The wireless sensor
network can detect minute variations in conditions in tree canopies, on the ground, and
within the soil. Understanding how these
microsites differ can help scientists learn the
environmental tolerance ranges of plants, how
native versus introduced grasses alter the be-
lowground ecosystem, and how climate affects
the annual abundance of acorns. Wireless network research at Blue Oak promises to deliver
a new level of detail to studies of the natural
environment.

CARPINTERIA SALT MARSH RESERVE

Expanses of pickleweed (*Salicornia pacifica*) dominate the middle marsh zone of Carpinteria Salt Marsh Reserve. (Christopher Woodcock)

To a bird winging over the southern California coast, Carpinteria Salt Marsh is an oasis encircled by roads, greenhouses, warehouses, and homes. Its maze of tidal channels, located some 12 miles east of Santa Barbara, wind through a gray-green expanse of low-slung pickleweed. In a region of California where 93 percent of the estuarine wetlands have been degraded or filled, the reserve and surrounding protected lands provide valuable habitat to shorebirds, rare plants, and an unusual mix of northern and southern coastal species.

Carpinteria Salt Marsh was once part of the much larger El Estero wetland that is now largely occupied by the city of Carpinteria. The surviving estuary serves as the outlet of two perennial creeks and several smaller streams that drain the Santa Ynez Mountains and Carpinteria Valley. The mountain range, which extends west to Point Conception, marks the boundary between the northern and southern California biogeographic regions. Relatively cool and moist conditions prevail to the north, while warmer, drier

CARPINTERIA SALT MARSH RESERVE

Administering Campus: UC Santa Barbara

Established: 1977

Location: Santa Barbara County, due west of the city of Carpinteria; 20 miles east of Santa Barbara campus

Size: Approximately 120 acres owned by the University; approximately 230 acres total habitat area

Elevation: 3 feet below mean sea level to 10 feet above mean sea level

Average Precipitation: 15 inches per year

Average Temperatures:

 August maximum 75°F

 January minimum 42°F

Facilities: Interpretative area, teaching amphitheater, and nature trail at Carpinteria Salt Marsh Nature Park on Ash Avenue; some facilities available at UC Santa Barbara; no on-site research or housing facilities.

Databases: Bibliography of marsh-based inventories/research, historic/current aerial photos, species lists, synoptic collections, geographic information system (GIS), marsh management plan with extensive site information, and selected databases at website

conditions are more typical of the south. Together with nearby Goleta Slough, the marsh represents the northern range limit of several species characteristic of southern California estuaries, including shoregrass (*Monanthochloe littoralis*) and the light-footed clapper rail (*Rallus longirostris levipes*).

The Carpinteria coastline is rich in tar seeps. Lower sediment layers of the marsh are veined with asphalt—remnants of former tar pits. Between 25,000 and 40,000 years ago, Pleistocene megafauna such as the dire wolf (*Canis dirus*), mammoth (*Mammuthus* spp.), and giant bison (*Bison latifrons*) became trapped in the natural asphalt and died. Their fossilized bones were excavated from the area in the late 1920s. Plant material deposits featuring coast redwood (*Sequoia sempervirens*), Monterey pine (*Pinus radiata*), and manzanita (*Arctostaphylus* spp.) preserved in the asphalt indicate that the climate during this time was similar to temperate Big Sur. Spanish explorers called the area *carpinteria*, or carpenter's shop, after the Chumash Indians they observed building and waterproofing oceangoing canoes onshore with local tar.

After more than 7,000 years in the Carpinteria Valley, native Californians lost their domain to European settlers. The newcomers farmed the alluvial plains. In 1896, the first offshore oil field in the United States was built to tap petroleum deposits near the Carpinteria coast. Residential development starting in the late 1920s channelized streambeds and hardened the modern edges of the marsh with freeways and roads.

As much as half of the Carpinteria Valley and its extensive salt marsh ecosystem has been diked and filled—a common scenario that has made California coastal wetlands rare. (Bruce Perry)

A snowy egret (*Egretta thula*) flushes fish, crustaceans, and insects by shuffling its feet in shallow marsh water. (Will Sooter)

In 1966, UCLA professor Kenneth S. Norris, along with professor Carl Hubbs of Scripps Institution of Oceanography, identified Carpinteria Salt Marsh as an acquisition priority for the nascent NRS. Through a combination of gifts and purchases, the University of California acquired 120 acres in the central portion of the marsh and added the site to the NRS in 1977. Adjacent properties are conserved by private groups and the land trust for Santa Barbara County. The salt marsh ecosystem protected by this collective is now one of the most studied coastal wetland ecosystems in the world.

California's smallest butterfly is the pygmy blue (*Brephidium exile*). Frequenting salt marshes, this species lays its eggs on salt-tolerant plants such as pickleweed (*Salicornia pacifica*), pigweed (*Amaranthus* spp.), and sea-blite (*Suaeda* spp.), which serve as food for its larvae. (Cristina Sandoval)

Carpinteria Salt Marsh Reserve safeguards an unusually complete cross-section of estuarine habitats. Its tidal wetlands are punctuated by salt flats and willow (*Salix exigua, S. lasiolepis*) thickets. Higher marsh habitats, sandy beach, remnants of coastal dunes, and a rocky reef are found here too. This exceptional variety of habitats attracted the attention of early botanists, whose plant collections have helped reconstruct the area's original floristic diversity. Roughly 45 percent of the plant species found within the historical limits of the estuary and its sand dunes are native. Of the 11 rare plant species present, 2—an experimental population of Ventura marsh milk-vetch (*Astragalus pycnostachyus* var. *lanosissimus*), once presumed extinct, and salt marsh bird's beak (*Chloropyron maritimum* subsp. *maritimum*)—are listed as endangered by the US Fish and Wildlife Service. Salt marsh bird's beak is also protected by the state.

The Carpinteria estuary supports many resident bird species. These include shorebirds such as marbled godwits (*Limosa fedoa*), wading birds such as great blue herons (*Ardea herodias*), and even passerines such as Belding's savannah sparrows (*Passerculus sandwichensis beldingi*). Arrow gobies (*Clevelandia ios*) swim through the meandering channels, while ghost shrimp (Thalassinidee) excavate burrows in the wetland muck. The estuary also provides habitat for migratory long-billed curlews (*Numenius americanus*) and species of special interest such as western snowy plovers (*Charadrius nivosus nivosus*). And like many estuarine habitats, Carpinteria Salt Marsh functions as a nursery for marine flatfish such as diamond turbot (*Hypsopsetta guttulata*), starry flounder (*Platichthys stellatus*), and California halibut (*Paralichthys californicus*).

Carpinteria Salt Marsh Reserve was the site of research that has fundamentally changed the way scientists view ecosystem relationships. In fieldwork conducted at the reserve, UC Santa Barbara professor Armand Kuris and his former student, Kevin Lafferty, now with the US Geological Survey, came to realize that parasites—tiny, plentiful, and ubiquitous throughout most food webs—likely exert important controls on all manner of ecosystems around the world (Kuris and Lafferty 1994; Lafferty et al. 2006).

The trematode fluke *Euhaplorchis californiensis* requires a series of hosts to complete its life cycle (Lafferty et al. 1994). Fluke eggs are excreted in bird droppings across the mudflats, where they are consumed by native California horn snails (*Cerithidea californica*). Once inside a snail, the parasite hatches and gradually castrates its host, altering the snail's behavior. Castrated snails do not expend energy seeking mates and reproducing—instead, they continue to graze on algae while leading a celibate lifestyle. The parasite siphons off the host's energy for its own use, growing from a thousand times smaller than its host snail to up to 40 percent of the host's body weight. Size means everything to the fluke at this life stage; the larger one is, the more eggs it can produce.

In the next stage of its life cycle, the fluke becomes a free-swimming larva that abandons its snail to seek out a third host, the California killifish (*Fundulus parvipinnis*). Rather than being ingested by the killifish, larval flukes attach themselves to the fish's gills and, from there, work their way into its brain. A fish with flukes in its brain will flail on or near the surface of the water, drawing the attention of predatory birds. Once the fish is ingested by a shorebird, the trematodes it carries can begin their life cycle anew in an avian host (Lafferty and Morris 1996).

Schoolchildren visit Carpinteria Salt Marsh Reserve on field trips throughout the year. (Wayne R. Ferren Jr.)

In work conducted at UC Santa Barbara with fish collected from the reserve, Lafferty determined that killifish parasitized by the fluke were 30 times more likely to be eaten by birds than uninfected killifish. In this way, the fluke helps control killifish population numbers in the marsh. Lafferty also calculated that horn snails infected by the trematodes grow more slowly than uninfected snails, so that without the parasite, the snail population would roughly double. A doubled snail population would decimate the estuary's algal beds, leaving other grazers in the ecosystem short of food. Over time, this effect would cascade through the entire marsh food web. A healthy estuarine ecosystem, the scientists realized, includes snails, killifish, and shorebirds but also the fluke parasite that these three species share. Because a degraded system typically will not support one or more of the fluke's hosts in sufficient numbers to allow the trematode to complete its life cycle, scientists are now using the presence of this parasite as an indicator of estuary health (Lafferty et al. 2006).

COAL OIL POINT NATURAL RESERVE

At Coal Oil Point Reserve, a colony of endangered birds coexists with surfers, sunbathing students, and residents who enjoy strolling the beach. (Christopher Woodcock)

Coal Oil Point Natural Reserve is one of the best and last examples of a southern California coastal strand ecosystem where sand dunes, wave-tossed beaches, and muddy wetlands all converge. Devereux Slough is the dynamic center of the reserve. Winter rains flood this estuarine wetland, which dries by late summer into salt flats and hypersaline ponds. These seasonal habitat changes attract thousands of migratory birds throughout the year, inspiring the National Audubon Society to designate it an Important Bird Area. An innovative public outreach program developed at the reserve enables surfers and sunbathers to share the beach with a colony of threatened shorebirds.

Named for the petroleum seeps in the Santa Barbara Channel, the beach at Coal Oil Point is often flecked with black tar balls. Several drilling platforms collect the up to 900 barrels of oil and approximately 50 barrels each day less than a mile from shore. Despite the industrial cast of the seascape, the reserve itself has largely been spared

COAL OIL POINT NATURAL RESERVE

Administering Campus: UC Santa Barbara

Established: 1970

Location: Santa Barbara County, on UC Santa Barbara's West Campus, overlooking the Santa Barbara Channel

Size: Approximately 170 acres

Elevation: 0 to 40 feet

Average Precipitation: 14 to 21 inches per year

Average Temperatures:

    August maximum 75°F

    January minimum 42°F

Facilities: Small lab on site; housing, laboratories, and research support available on adjacent Santa Barbara campus

Databases: Extensive monthly climate records; some records of lagoon temperature, salinity, and dissolved oxygen; plant and animal lists; historic/current aerial photos; published management plans for plants, animals, and hydrology; natural-resource GIS; and comprehensive catalog of research on UC Santa Barbara wetlands under development

from development. In 1919, Englishman Colin Campbell and his Chicago heiress wife Nancy Leiter bought the slough and adjacent land to develop an estate. In 1945, after the Campbells' deaths, the lands surrounding their mansion were bought by UC Santa Barbara. Recognizing the integrity of the site's coastal vegetation, the UC Regents made Coal Oil Point Reserve part of the NRS in 1970.

The reserve sees heavy use by scientists and students. Proximity to the Santa Barbara campus makes it a popular teaching site for university courses ranging from botany and invertebrate zoology to plein air painting. Scientists use the reserve to monitor habitat use by migratory birds, research dune and estuary plant restoration, and conduct range surveys of marine invertebrates. Natural offshore oil seeps make the reserve an ideal place to study the effects of petroleum on the environment. Research topics have included the metabolism of toxic hydrocarbons by marine

In the 10 years since the western snowy plover protection program began, more than 500 nests have been recorded at Coal Oil Point Reserve. (Larry Wan)

CRISTINA SANDOVAL, DIRECTOR, COAL OIL POINT RESERVE

Coal Oil Point Reserve Director Cristina Sandoval (Courtesy of Cristina Sandoval)

I like the everyday challenge of being faced with a problem and having to create a solution. This position allows for a large amount of creativity. The success of the snowy plover program wasn't just a coincidence or my hard work but was possible because of an organization like the NRS. I was able to think about the best thing to do for the plovers and then do it quickly.

When I first came to Coal Oil Point Reserve there were no signs or fences, so visitors didn't know it was an NRS reserve. Instead, there were parties and cars on the beach. We slowly established our reserve boundary and stationed docents on the beach to inform people that the land was protected. Now people know that Coal Oil Point is a reserve of the University; that once you're there, you have to tread lightly; and that there are things you can and cannot do. As a result, we've seen a big increase in wildlife species and abundance.

The plovers are an example of that. We didn't want to close the entire beach to the public to protect the plovers. This would have created a big crisis with the local community. We needed to instead balance recreational use of the beach with the well-being of the plovers.

Backed by data on how plovers use the beach, we developed a plan to fence only a part of the beach off from the public to protect the birds. We received a great deal of support from state agencies that oversee protection efforts of the snowy plover because we took a scientific approach to management. It was critical to have data to demonstrate why our management approach would be a good solution to the problem of public access versus endangered species protection.

When I started at Coal Oil Point Reserve, I was a scientist who had mostly dealt with insects and spiders. You're alone much of the time in your research, so having highly developed social skills is not essential. It turns out my job as an NRS reserve manager is mostly managing people. I've learned how to talk to people in a way that gets a friendly smile back when telling them to do something they don't want to do. The reserve job rocked me out of my comfortable scientist's chair; it made me a better, more thoughtful person.

invertebrates, bacterial mats that decompose oil, and how petroleum carbon contributes to the local food web.

The beachgoing public is the most conspicuous presence on the reserve. Surfers flock to the offshore break, sunbathers bask on the strand, and residents take their dogs for walks. Unrestricted access to the reserve's Sands Beach was permitted for many years after the reserve was first established. But in the summer of 2001, scientists noticed that a pair of federally protected western snowy plovers that had succeeded in hatching two marshmallow-sized chicks in a recently revegetated section of beach dunes. Those tiny balls of fluff marked the first recorded snowy plover chicks on the reserve in over 30 years. The bird's presence prompted reserve director Cristina Sandoval to restrict access to the plover habitat in the dunes and upper beach.

Sandoval understood that this sparrow-sized shorebird needed protecting from human disturbances. The US Pacific population of snowy plovers was listed as federally threatened in 1993, when the entire population consisted of about 1,300 individuals and an estimated 80 percent of its preferred nesting habitat had been greatly altered. Today approximately 2,000 breeding pairs live along the US Pacific coast, 90 percent of them in California. One of the plover's biggest success stories has unfolded at Coal Oil Point Reserve.

Shortly before the first plover chick appeared, US Geological Survey biologist Kevin Lafferty studied plover behavior at the reserve. He determined that human beachgoers and their dogs were constantly disturbing the birds while they ate, rested, and incubated their eggs. Lafferty's research prompted a more comprehensive level of protection for reserve plovers (Lafferty 2001a, 2001b). Using Lafferty's data, reserve director Sandoval designed a management plan to protect plovers at Coal Oil Point. The easy solution would have been to prohibit all public access to the beach. Instead, Sandoval sought to change visitor behavior. Trails were rerouted around potential nesting areas; signs featuring maps, explanations, and reminders to keep dogs on leash were posted; and rope

Docents give beach visitors a glimpse of Coal Oil Point's resident plovers. (Kevin Lafferty)

fences to keep people and animals out of the sensitive upper beach were installed. Key to the program has been a cadre of docents recruited and trained by the Santa Barbara Audubon Society to educate beachgoers about the plovers.

Begun in August 2001, the Snowy Plover Docent Program at Coal Oil Point Natural Reserve continues to play a crucial role in plover protection to this day. The 70 volunteer docents patrol the beach daily, from dawn to dusk. Docents watch over the plovers, educate visitors about the birds, and request that people respect the boundaries of their nesting area. The program has succeeded beyond anyone's expectations. Although only one chick was hatched the first year of the program, nesting on the reserve has increased dramatically over the years, with an average of 30 pairs nesting each year at Coal Oil Point. The program is now considered a model for balancing human and environmental needs in protected areas.

Efforts to aid the snowy plover have benefited the reserve in many ways. For example, areas of beach open to the public have been trampled bare of vegetation, while the area sectioned off for plovers includes untrammeled dunes featuring plants that include native beach primrose (*Camissonia cheiranthifolia*) and sand verbena (*Abronia maritima*). In the presence of healthy plover populations, researchers have noted higher numbers of shorebirds such as whimbrels (*Numenium phaeopsis*) and western gulls (*Larus occidentalis*). In turn, beach visitors are gaining a better understanding of the local ecosystem. A program designed to protect one bird has made a visit to Coal Oil Point Reserve an infinitely richer experience.

FORT ORD NATURAL RESERVE

The dense, Lilliputian vegetation at Fort Ord Natural Reserve by morning light (Christopher Woodcock)

Fort Ord Natural Reserve is tucked behind coastal sand dunes at the southeastern edge of Monterey Bay, merely a mile from the Pacific shore. Its sandy soils support stands of live oak woodlands and maritime chaparral, a unique vegetation type restricted to the foggy landscapes along California's coast. A history of military ownership has largely preserved this unique coastal ecosystem from development. With the closure of the military base and the creation of a UC Natural Reserve on the site, scientists have been able to study a nearly intact community of rare plants found almost nowhere else in the world.

Fort Ord was established by the US military in 1917, during preparations for World War I. For the next 77 years, lands that now belong to the reserve served primarily as a training ground for army infantry maneuvers. Following the closure of the 15,000-acre base in 1994, ownership was transferred to various federal, state, and local jurisdictions.

FORT ORD NATURAL RESERVE

Administering Campus: UC Santa Cruz

Established: 1996

Location: Monterey County, 4 miles north of downtown Monterey, 40 miles south of Santa Cruz

Size: Approximately 600 acres

Elevation: 70 to 190 feet

Average Temperature: 59°F

Average Precipitation: 18 inches per year

Facilities: Primitive campground available for research and class use. The site is suited for day use and primitive camping. Hotels and other overnight accommodations are nearby.

Databases: Baseline-survey data collected for the Fort Ord Base Closure Habitat Management Plan (HMP); excellent sets of aerial maps; plant and vertebrate species lists are available; and an invertebrate species list is under development. Databases of rare annual plant distributions, perennial shrubs composition, rough occurrence patterns of some vertebrates, and selected material on invertebrate distribution are available.

Approximately 1,000 acres were given to the University of California, 400 of which were set aside for development. The remaining 600 acres were incorporated into the NRS in 1996 as the Fort Ord Natural Reserve. Three hundred sixty-seven acres nearby were set aside in the form of the Salinas River National Wildlife Refuge for the federally protected Smith's blue butterfly (*Euphilotes enoptes smithi*)—the first nature reserve established for a single insect in the United States.

From the reserve's inception, researchers from UC Santa Cruz have been studying the unique ecology of this environment. These efforts have provided important information on the natural history and conservation of the rare flora restricted to Monterey Bay maritime chaparral, a scrub community that varies regionally throughout California and the Pacific coast. All maritime chaparral types support one or more species of manzanita (*Arctostaphylos* spp.). Of the 95 species and subspecies of manzanita found in California, more than half occur only locally along the immediate coast. Like inland chaparral, maritime chaparral is punctuated with drought-resistant species such as coast live oak (*Quercus agrifolia*), California lilac (*Ceonothus cuneatus, C. dentatus*), sage (e.g., *Salvia mellifera*), and poison oak (*Toxicodendron diversilobum*).

Ground-hugging sandmat manzanita (*Arctostaphylos pumila*) and head-high wooly leaf manzanita (*A. tomentosa*) dominate maritime chaparral on Fort Ord Natural

Lace lichen (*Ramalina menziesii*) drips from a stand of stunted coast live oaks at Fort Ord Natural Reserve. (Peggy L. Fiedler)

Reserve. Open, sandy areas between manzanita shrubs support a variety of rare, threatened, or endangered herbaceous species such as sand gilia (*Gilia tenuiflora* subsp. *arenaria*) and Monterey spineflower (*Chorizanthe pungens* var. *pungens*). These two species are found only in California's central coast maritime chaparral and rely on disturbances to create open spaces to colonize. Shrubs such as chamise (*Adenostema fasciculatum*) and Monterey ceanothus (*Ceanothus rigidus*) add to the dense stands of vegetation, while the flowers of black sage, bush monkey flower (*Mimulus aurantiacus*), and California sagebrush (*Artemisia californica*) form a colorful, interlaced canopy. In spring, annual wildflowers sprout in abundance, filling open sandy areas relatively free of perennial species. Stunted coast live oaks, their branches dripping with lichen, grow in relatively small patches on higher sand ridges and north-facing slopes. Sandy, low-nutrient soils stunt plant growth.

Recent research at Fort Ord has illuminated how community interactions shape the ecology of the reserve. Exclusion plots installed and monitored by professor Laurel Fox of UC Santa Cruz and her students have demonstrated how foraging mule deer (*Odocoileus hemionus*), dusky-footed woodrats (*Neotoma fuscipes*), and brush rabbits (*Sylvilagus bachmani*) trim native shrubs and herbaceous

Bud burst of the wooly leaf manzanita. Diversity in manzanita species is a hallmark of California central coast maritime chaparral. (Peggy L. Fiedler)

The California legless lizard is abundant at Fort Ord Natural Reserve, where it forages for insects and spiders by burrowing into the sandy soil. It can be distinguished from a snake when it blinks—snakes have no eyelids—and by the fact that it detaches its tail to distract potential predators. (Michael Benard)

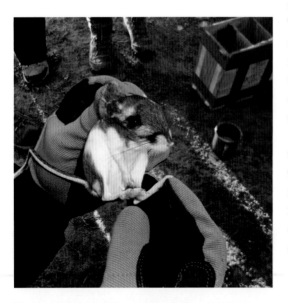

The Fort Ord Natural Reserve's proximity to UC Santa Cruz makes it a popular location for course field trips. This Heermann's kangaroo rat (*Dipodomys heermanni*) was trapped to give students an opportunity to examine a native herbivore up close and was released soon afterward. (Gage Dayton)

plants into shapes reminiscent of topiary (Deveny and Fox 2006). Research by San Francisco State University professor V. Thomas Parker suggests that small mammals such as dusky-footed woodrat and deer mice (*Peromyscus maniculatus*) may influence how maritime chaparral recovers after fire. These small mammals spend their nights foraging for seeds. Most are eaten immediately, while the rest are buried in underground caches to be eaten during leaner times of the year. But some animals inevitably die or forget where they stashed the seeds. Such forgotten seed caches likely serve as important seed banks for recruitment after fire.

The California legless lizard (*Anniella pulchra*) and Blaineville's horned lizard (*Phrynosoma blainvillii*) are two reptiles of special concern abundant throughout the reserve. The legless lizard is seldom seen, as it spends most of its life foraging for invertebrates beneath the surface of the soil. In contrast, Blaineville's horned lizard is commonly found in open sandy areas feeding on native harvester ants (*Pogonomyrmex* spp.).

Fort Ord is one of just a handful of areas that protect the unique flora and fauna of central California maritime chaparral. Ongoing research and educational opportunities at the reserve continue to provide insights into the ecology and conservation of this distinctive ecosystem.

FRANCES SIMES HASTINGS
NATURAL HISTORY RESERVATION

Hastings Natural History Reservation was the first field station within the University of California system and one of the inaugural seven reserves of the NRS. (Christopher Woodcock)

Hastings Natural History Reservation unfolds across the foothills of central California's Santa Lucia Mountains. It is located midway between the coast and the San Joaquin Valley, on the south-facing slopes of Carmel Valley. The reserve encompasses three narrow valleys, each containing oak-studded slopes, perennial grassland meadows, and dense stands of chaparral.

In many ways, Hastings embodies the platonic ideal of an NRS reserve. It is far enough from urban asphalt and pollution to have a healthy ecosystem, yet near enough to major cities for easy visitor access. A laboratory, overnight accommodations, extensive acreage, and an endowment to support ongoing research round out its amenities. In 1965, when the UC Regents approved the formation of the NRS, Hastings became one of the system's seven founding reserves. The Hastings story illustrates how a farsighted California family, supported by thoughtful stewardship and public service, sparked a legacy of world-renowned research.

Human history at Hastings extends back thousands of years. First Esselen, then Ohlone-Costanoan peoples walked a trail that passed through Hastings to travel between interior villages and the Pacific shoreline. Each year, they collected acorns within Carmel Valley's expansive oak groves and stored their harvests in granaries of willow stems woven

FRANCES SIMES HASTINGS NATURAL HISTORY RESERVATION

Administering Campus: UC Berkeley

Established: 1937; joined NRS 1970

Location: Monterey County (upper Carmel Valley); 26 miles southwest of Carmel; 142 miles from Berkeley campus

Size: Approximately 2,300 acres, plus access to approximately 28,600 acres from cooperating landowners

Elevation: 1,530 to 3,125 feet

Average Precipitation: 21 inches per year

Average Temperatures:

    July maximum 87°F

    January minimum 34°F

    Annual mean 63°F

Facilities: Fully functional field station with scattered houses, workshop, offices, group meeting room/kitchen, lab with bench/office for up to six investigators, housing for 38, kitchen facilities in each house, modest library and herbarium, and secure storage space in large barn. Wireless Internet at all buildings and much of the reserve; some cell phone coverage.

Databases: Extensive synoptic collections/field notes, complete herbarium, long-term weather data from on-site weather stations, photographic archive, aerial photos/ large-scale maps, extensive bibliography, GIS, and flora and plant lists

around large wooden posts set into the ground. In the late 1700s, the Spanish incorporated this route into the Mission Trail connecting their religious and military outposts. Later still, this trail became Carmel Valley Road.

In the 1860s, homesteader John Scott built the cabins and barn that form the heart of Hastings Natural History Reservation. The barn is among the oldest remaining structures on the Monterey Peninsula; its walls are made of boards blasted from logs using black powder. Until 1936, a series of owners cleared the oaks at Hastings and farmed almost all level ground. They used mule-drawn disc harrows to till the fields for oats and barley. Over time, these fields were abandoned as their productivity declined. But the legacy of farming at Hastings has been far reaching, converting large areas of former grassland savanna to monocultures of exotic, annual weeds.

In 1929, Russell and Frances Hastings of San Francisco bought the property as a hobby ranch. At Rancho del Pato Alegre, or Happy Duck Ranch, they raised a family for nearly two decades. In the late 1930s, Frances Hastings approached her close friend, Ida Sproul, about possible University of California uses for the ranch. Ida's husband was Robert Sproul, then president of the University of California. Joseph Grinnell, director

The Scott barn is among the oldest structures in the Monterey Area, dating from the 1860s. It is still used to store historic ranch items and field equipment. (David Gubernick)

of the UC Berkeley Museum of Vertebrate Zoology (MVZ), encouraged the arrangement, as indicated in a letter to Russell Hastings (1938): "My imagination pictures, in due course, the Hastings Reservation as a recognized 'mecca' to which will come, for periods of undistracted research, advanced students of ornithology, mammology, botany, entomology, ecology, etc., using the local fauna and flora as source of the living materials to be studied, with aid from the station records and the authentically identified reference collections. A pleasant picture, truly." Sproul and the Hastings concluded an informal agreement in 1937, allowing the University of California to use the ranch as a biological research station. When Frances Hastings died in 1963, she bequeathed the land to the University. Above and beyond their donation of the land, the Hastings also provided funds to support a resident research zoologist at the reserve. Decades later, their generous gifts continue to pay research and teaching dividends.

The first resident scientist at Hastings, Jean M. Linsdale, laid a sturdy research foundation for others to follow. Starting in the 1930s, he amassed an extensive museum collection of plants and animals at the reserve. Today, these collections represent long-term datasets virtually unrivaled in California. Their snapshots of central California in the early twentieth century are being reexamined to help predict shifts in California's environment during an era of accelerated climate change.

In the late 1950s, the focus of research at Hastings shifted to behavioral studies of birds and reptiles. In 1982, zoologist-in-residence Walter Koenig began investigating the social behavior and ecology of the acorn woodpecker (*Melanerpes formicivorus*). By banding nearly every bird on reserve grounds, he was able to follow the interactions and movements of many generations. Koenig established that these woodpeckers live in extended cooperative family groups that consist of several breeding males and females, the males often brothers and the females often sisters, plus a number of adult

Acorn woodpeckers live in communal family groups. Family groups collect acorns and store them in shared granaries, defending the cache against acorn poachers. (Bruce Lyon)

Researchers at Hastings Natural History Reservation mark acorns placed in granaries to track the collection, storage, and use of this key food resource by acorn woodpecker families. (Kathleen M. Wong)

and juvenile offspring. All help gather, store, and protect a cache of acorns that will see the family through the lean months of winter and spring. Koenig's landmark 30-year study of acorn woodpecker natural history is internationally celebrated (Mumme et al. 1989; Koenig and Dickinson 2004; Koenig et al. 2009). At the same time, biologist Janis Dickinson and colleagues developed a similar long-term study of social behavior of western bluebirds (*Sialia mexicana*) at Hastings (Dickinson et al. 1996; Dickinson and Weathers 1999).

Plant studies at Hastings are equally distinguished. Keith White's work on blue oak (*Quercus douglasii*) woodlands (White 1966), Monterey pine (*Pinus radiata*) forests, and relict native grasslands has provided the baseline for comparative studies across a 40-year time span. Throughout the 1970s and 1980s, Jim Griffin made meticulous maps of forest trees of California and studied the failure of valley and blue oak forests to regenerate. In 1988, Griffin and reserve director Mark Stromberg, with others, continued White's long-term study of native grasslands. They demonstrated that despite decades of rest from grazing and tilling, the old farm field at Hastings had not "returned to nature." Instead, the land had attained a new equilibrium of non-native annual species, primarily European grasses (Stromberg and Griffin 1996; Stromberg et al. 2001). This result strongly implies that the non-native golden hills of California are here to stay; only the most vigorous restoration and management efforts will allow native wildflowers and bunchgrasses to dominate the state's grasslands again.

The bones of a wild boar (*Sus scrofa*) lie in the meadow above the old ranch house at Hastings Natural History Reservation. By roiling large swaths of soil in their search for roots, small animals, and other foods, feral pigs disrupt ecosystems at many reserves across California. (David Gubernick)

Other well-known studies at Hastings have focused on the physiology of lace lichen (*Ramalina menziesii*; Matthes-Sears and Nash 1986, Boucher and Nash 1990), nutrient balance of oak woodlands, geology of plate tectonics, and mating strategies of black-widow spiders (*Latrodectus hesperus*). Over 600 publications from Hastings cover almost every aspect of oak woodland natural history alone.

Today, Hastings continues its transition from being a reserve studied by a small staff to being a field station accessible to researchers from around the world. In recent decades, visiting students and the general public have far outnumbered working scientists. Hastings's growing popularity demonstrates the value of protected areas to a populace eager for knowledge about California's natural heritage.

LANDELS-HILL BIG CREEK RESERVE

The shady slopes of Landels-Hill Big Creek Reserve provide a cool environment for redwoods and other conifers at the edge of the Ventana Wilderness. (Christopher Woodcock)

California's steepest coastal range, the Santa Lucia Mountains, plunges directly into the ocean at Big Sur. Along this spectacular coast, Landels-Hill Big Creek Reserve across steep canyons and forested ridgelines an hour's drive south of Monterey. Composed of largely undisturbed wilderness, this landscape experiences extreme climatic differences between ridgetop and shoreline. Kelp forests and rocky reefs hug the coast, while submarine canyons drop one-third of a mile deep directly offshore. The result is a dramatically compressed series of habitats bordered by massive redwoods above and tidepools below.

The natural abundance at Big Creek attracted native Esselen and Salinan people to the area for more than 6,000 years. Archeological surveys indicate the earliest inhabitants visited the area to collect marine fish and shellfish. Over time, their use of the land expanded to include acorn gathering and other terrestrial activities and eventually included the settlement of large inland villages near oak woodlands and grasslands. Through the late nineteenth and early twentieth centuries, homesteaders drove cattle over the mountains, encouraged tourism, and logged coastal forests. In the 1940s, many Big Sur buildings, including the renowned Nepenthe restaurant, were built with redwood timber extracted from the Big Creek watershed. In 1961, the seven families that owned what are now reserve lands combined their properties into Big Creek Ranch. In

LANDELS-HILL BIG CREEK RESERVE

Administering Campus: UC Santa Cruz

Established: 1977

Location: Big Sur Coast, Monterey County, 50 miles south of Monterey; two-hour drive from Santa Cruz campus

Size: Approximately 4,300 acres; an additional 5,500 acres is accessible by use agreement

Elevation: Reserve is 0 to 3,500 feet. Top of watershed at Cone Peak is 5,155 feet

Average Precipitation: 25 inches per year at coast; 40 inches per year along ridges; higher on upper peaks

Average Temperatures:

> For lower elevations (0 to 100 feet), August range is 52°F to 70°F and January range is 42°F to 60°F; for higher elevations (2,000+ feet), July range is 65°F to 85°F and January range is 43°F to 57°F

Facilities: Three campgrounds, visitor cabin/lab for 10 at Whale Point, small lab/library, 13 miles of trails, 10 miles of dirt roads, limited parking, and beach access for small boats onto marine reserve

Databases: On-site GIS; teaching collections; published surveys; computer text files for plants, animals, cultural/archaeological surveys; weather data; stream monitoring and marine fish monitoring; regional bibliographies

1978, the UC Regents acquired Big Creek Ranch with assistance from TNC, Save-the-Redwoods League, the former owners, and several other private donors. The reserve is named in honor of attorney Edward Landels, a ranch shareholder, and petroleum industry expert Kenneth Hill and his wife Dorothy, whose donations helped enable the University to acquire the property. Landels-Hill Big Creek Reserve remains protected by deed restrictions implemented by TNC.

Reserve hills rise in a tapestry of mixed hardwood and evergreen trees interspersed with grasslands and dense stands of chaparral. Cutting through the hillsides are cool, moist canyons carved by rushing streams and shaded by groves of coast redwoods (*Sequoia sempervirens*) and sycamores (*Platanus racemosa*). Higher slopes, clothed in Coulter pine (*Pinus coulteri*), descend through mixed oak and manzanita to coastal bluff scrub. Steelhead (*Oncorhyncus mykiss*) ply the clean, clear waters of Big Creek to spawn in gravel riffles. Because of its remoteness, Big Creek offers excellent habitat for sensitive species such as the California condor (*Gymnogyps californianus*) and California spotted owl (*Stryx occidentalis occidentalis*).

In addition to the reserve itself, the expansive and privately held Gamboa Point Property to the south is also available for research by agreement. The reserve and Gamboa

Esselen and Salinan peoples hunted, collected marine shellfish, and eventually settled in villages near the oak savannas of Landels-Hill Big Creek Reserve. (Galen Rowell, Mountain Light Photography)

Point properties include portions of three major watersheds, as well as several smaller streams that meander on their own to the ocean. All three watersheds drain the western flanks of Cone Peak, located 1.5 miles east of the reserve in the Ventana Wilderness. The peak rises 5,155 feet from the ocean in just 3.3 miles, forming one of the steepest coastal gradients in the contiguous United States.

Big Creek hosts an unusual mixture of plant and animal species, many near their geographic range limit or found nowhere else. This diversity reflects the reserve's location at the border of two biogeographic provinces, the cool Oregonian and warm Californian. Here, plants characteristic of the cool, foggy coast mingle with plants typical of drier southern climes, as well as with species common to montane forests. For example, ponderosa pines (*Pinus ponderosa* var. *pacfica*) characteristic of the Sierra Nevada grow near southern California's Quixote yucca (*Hesperoyucca whipplei*). Here the yucca approaches its northern range limit while the coast redwood approaches its southern limit. The effects of this ecotone apply to animals as well. Many intertidal invertebrates, but also amphibians and reptiles, exhibit high levels of hybridization and rapid shifts in species composition from north to south in the Big Sur region.

Recent periods of uplifting and faulting, interspersed with periods of partial submergence by an inland seaway, have contributed to the region's biogeographic flux. The rare Santa Lucia fir (*Abies bracteata*), found only along the central coastal California, is one example of this phenomenon. The disappearance of summer rains beginning approximately 11,000 years ago eliminated conifer forests once widespread in central and southern California. However, the uplift of the Santa Lucia Mountains enabled these relict conifers to persist on cool, bare rock slopes at high elevations. Other endemic species include the large, treelike Hoover's manzanita (*Arctostaphylus hooveri*) and Hutchinson's delphinium (*Delphinium hutchinsonae*).

The intertidal zone consists mainly of jumbled boulder fields separated by coarse sand and cobble beaches. Sharp rock pinnacles rise above the breakers from the seafloor. Giant kelp stands anchor close to shore, forming dense mats along the ocean's surface. This

Vicente Canyon, Big Sur, 2001, woodcut (Tom Killion)

The waters of Big Creek support a spawning run of
steelhead. (Christopher Woodcock)

REMARKS AT THE DEDICATION OF BIG CREEK RESERVE

ANSEL ADAMS, APRIL 29, 1978

Ansel Adams (Norden H. "Dan" Cheatham)

This ceremony celebrates the realization of a dream. It symbolizes the forward thrust of collective imagination, effort and conscience. It is a large step on the path of environmental realism—both tangible and intangible.

I have been involved in environmentalism (of many forms) for 60 years; first with the National Park concepts, then with the State Parks and Reserves, then with the various challenges of historic preservation and the protection of small but potentially significant works of nature and of man. My work has been more in the areas of photography and writing; I am definitely not a political "mover and shaker." I am one with those who believe that environment, in both physical and spiritual integrity, must in the end command our lives and the lives of those who will be upon the Earth in the millennia to come.

We are gathered to dedicate an important concept as well as an important reality. One of the most beautiful areas of our coast is now secure for purposes which relate to the mind and spirit of mankind. Credit for this achievement is due to many individuals and organizations (notably the Nature Conservancy, the University of California and the Save-The-Redwoods League). We must not overlook the great groundwork of William E. Colby and his colleagues which formulated and structured the concept of the California State Parks. It is hard to believe that in a little more than a century the idea of preservation was born and has grown steadily (and against much opposition!) into a basic pattern of our society. Since 1864 when President Abraham Lincoln signed the transfer of Yosemite Valley to the State of California, many important land-control actions have been effected, culminating in the establishment of the National Park Service in 1916.

Archibald MacLeish wrote so eloquently of the image of the earth floating in the void of Space; it is the lonely home of mankind and of all life. Man, presumably the highest form of life the earth has fostered, can now destroy the fragile miracle of the world. We well know what predatory man can accomplish in his greed for development, his ruthless exploitations under a misinterpretation of Free Enterprise, and his fouling of air, water and the beauty of life itself. We shudder at the prospect of unthinkable war, while we tolerate with confused submission the destruction of resources, obliteration of natural beauty and wonder, and invite the inroads of crime and terror. Does this represent the fate of the blue sphere turning in majesty for aeons around the sun?

Here on the Coast of California we are still in a relative paradise. There remains in this area land that has not been developed (but may be), shores that are clean (as yet), vistas that are pure and awe-inspiring. At this time, standing here in this magnificent and protected environment, all seems forever secure.

Nothing could be further from the truth! Just as it required a vast concerted effort by individuals and organizations to achieve the status of a Reserve for this immediate area (as it did for all the great conservation achievements of the past), so will it demand constant watching, working and persuading to secure what we now have and to acquire all that we may have of protected natural beauty in the years to come.

Hence, I am doubly grateful when I think of this extraordinary Reserve: for the fact of its existence and for the promise of further protection of one of the most rewarding sections of our priceless environment.

We must give our heartfelt thanks to all who have helped make this Big Creek Reserve a reality. And we all have our duty to carry on the interpretation, comprehension, and protection of the qualities of this unique and glorious region for all foreseeable time to come.

I thank you.

Ansel Adams

undersea forest harbors a diverse group of temperate reef fish, invertebrates, and marine algae. Rafts of southern sea otters (*Enhydra lutris nereis*) fasten themselves to kelp fronds, and up to 200 adult harbor seals (*Phoca vitulina*) and their pups can be seen resting on the beach north of the creek mouth. Indeed, the reserve shoreline is located at the center of California's Sea Otter Refuge.

Gray, blue, and humpback whales (*Eschrictius robustus, Blaenoptera musculus, Megaptera novangeliae*) spout near shore during their migrations, as do several species of dolphins. Seabirds frequent the ocean cliffs and ridge tops. Black oystercatchers (*Haematocarpus bachmani*) with bright red beaks nest on rocks along the shoreline, and a colony of Brandt's cormorants (*Phalacrocorax penicillatus*) nests on Square Black Rock alongside the iconic Big Creek Bridge of coastal State Route 1.

From the ocean's edge, the reserve extends approximately three miles offshore into Big Creek State Marine Reserve, which adjoins Big Creek State Marine Conservation Area.

The protected waters off Landels-Hill Big Creek Reserve shelter a wide variety of marine and intertidal species, including painted greenling (*Oxylebius pictus*), which eat crustaceans, mollusks, and marine worms. (Steve Lonhart)

The combined area of these two marine protected areas is nearly 22.5 square miles. Since 1994, fishing for any living marine resource from the state marine reserve has been prohibited; fishing is limited to a handful of species within the conservation area. Reserve personnel help keep an eye on offshore activities in both of these marine protected areas, which are administered by the California Department of Fish and Game. These protected areas offshore make the reserve equally prized for its marine as well as terrestrial features. For example, the Partnership for Interdisciplinary Studies of Coastal Oceans (PISCO), which tracks changes in the coastal ocean, rocky intertidal, and kelp forest ecosystems of the US Pacific coast, commenced its research at Landels-Hill Big Creek Reserve a dozen years ago. PISCO researchers still return annually to monitor species shifts.

Cliffs leave much of the reserve's 5.5-mile-long coast inaccessible by sea. A narrow cove at the mouth of Big Creek provides one of only a few landing points along this stretch of coast—a valuable asset for researchers studying the ocean environment. Easy access to both land and sea, combined with a spectacular array of protected habitats and species, ensures Landels-Hill Big Creek Reserve will continue to make major contributions to knowledge of wild coastal ecosystems.

KENNETH S. NORRIS RANCHO MARINO RESERVE

Kenneth S. Norris Rancho Marino Reserve protects two miles of rocky shoreline. (Christopher Woodcock)

Immediately south of the seaside community of Cambria, the Kenneth S. Norris Rancho Marino Reserve straddles the biogeographic boundary between northern and southern California. The reserve protects two miles of rocky shoreline, 500 acres of coastal prairie, and native forests of Monterey pine (*Pinus radiata*) and coast live oak (*Quercus agrifolia*). Privately owned and funded, this reserve offers a taste of California at its best: breathtaking vistas of the windswept coast, abundant and diverse marine life, and rocky shorelines.

Rancho Marino lies within the San Andreas Fault Zone, wedged between the inland Cambria and the offshore San Gregorio-Hosgri faults. The coastline of the reserve consists of an uplifted marine terrace bordered by a sea cliff to the west and the abrupt rise of the Santa Lucia Range to the east. Nine brief stream systems dissect the western slope of the coastal mountains on reserve property. These waterways rapidly concentrate heavy

KENNETH S. NORRIS RANCHO MARINO RESERVE

Administering Campus: UC Santa Barbara; operated under a use agreement with the landowner, who also funds the reserve's management and operation

Established: 2001

Location: San Luis Obispo County, bordering the south end of the town of Cambria

Size: Approximately 500 acres, including 2 miles of coastline, Monterey pine forest, and coastal prairie

Elevation: 0 to 702 feet

Average Precipitation: 18 inches per year; in flood years, 35 inches

Average Temperatures:

    July maximum 98°F

    January minimum 36°F

Facilities: A kitchen/meeting area, outhouses, and outdoor showers, accommodating up to 40 campers for short stays. Smaller groups have stayed up to 3 months. Two travel trailers provide 10 beds. UC manager's office and library are nearby. All other structures on reserve lands are excluded from NRS use, as per agreement with the owner.

Databases: Species lists of intertidal and terrestrial plants and animals, including beetles, birds and small mammals. Monitoring projects include Monterey pine demographic study, grazing plots, black abalone and limpet plots, photo monitoring of landscape, and California red-legged frog surveys.

Coastal terraces of Kenneth S. Norris Rancho Marino Reserve were once grazed by dairy cattle. Grazing is still used to encourage the growth of native species. Coastal sage scrub (foreground) and a native stand of Monterey pine (upper right) are also found on the reserve. (Don Canestro)

rainfall, dropping sediment on alluvial fans that cover the level marine terrace. Two of the nine drainages are dammed to provide stock ponds for cattle as well as breeding and foraging habitats for fish and frogs.

Plentiful coastal resources and a mild climate may have supported populations of Native Americans along the central California coast as far back as 10,000 years. These early inhabitants collected red abalone (*Haliotis rufescens*) and other invertebrates, fished the intertidal and near shore habitats, and gathered local plants such as acorns for food. Middens filled with shells, fish and mammal bones, tools, and various artifacts are scattered throughout the region. When Spanish explorer Juan Cabrillo first landed on the California coast in 1542, the Cambria region was a boundary zone between the lands of the Northern Chumash, or Obispeño, to the south, and Salinan ethnographic groups to the north.

In 1841, reserve lands were a small part of the 13,184-acre land grant of Rancho Santa Rosa, given to Julian Estrada by the Mexican governor. Less than 30 years later, mining magnate George Hearst bought Rancho Santa Rosa in addition to two nearby land grants, Rancho Piedra Blanca and Rancho San Simeon.

Over the next century, the Cambria region saw the establishment of cattle ranches, fruit orchards, a lumber industry for local Monterey pine, and mines for cinnabar, an ore of mercury. Most successful were Swiss dairymen who, by the turn of the twentieth century, were producing more than one ton of butter and one-half ton of cheese daily, primarily for San Francisco markets. Cattle still roam Rancho Marino as part of a program to enhance native vegetation and study the effects of grazing on California's coastal terrace prairies (Stromberg et al. 2002). Chinese seaweed farmers resided on the reserve lands from around 1900 to 1960, burning intertidal rocks in winter to encourage the growth of sea lettuce (*Ulva* spp.) to harvest the following spring.

Southern sea otters rest and forage for sea urchins, clams, and crabs in offshore kelp forests. (Mike Baird)

Colorful Loki's chiton (*Tonicella lokii*), a species of marine snail, is part of the diverse community of invertebrates residing in the tidepools and coastal rocks of Kenneth S. Norris Rancho Marino Reserve. (Jackie Sones)

Most impressive at Rancho Marino is the exceptionally rich marine life along the shoreline. With the goal of enhancing research and educational opportunities, in 2007 the waters adjacent to the reserve were included in the state's White Rock State Marine Conservation Area. The taking of any marine life is prohibited within the conservation area, with the exception of limited commercial harvest of giant (*Macrocystis pyrifera*) and bull (*Nereocystis luetkeana*) kelp. Cold upwelling waters nearby support one of the largest kelp beds in California. The reserve also supports research on the population dynamics and diseases of the southern sea otters (*Enhydra lutris nereis*) that forage for invertebrates within the kelp forest (Johnson et al. 2009).

Rancho Marino is a key site in a long-term ecosystem research and monitoring program called the Partnership for Interdisciplinary Studies of Coastal Oceans (PISCO). PISCO focuses on the kelp forests, rocky shoreline habitats, and coastal currents found across the more than 1,200 miles adjacent to the California Current. Research results are translated into policy recommendations, particularly regarding the sustainability of coastal ecosystems vulnerable to climate change and sea level rise (Oftedal et al. 2007). PISCO scientists are also monitoring California's innovative statewide

Dramatic surf is daily fare off Kenneth S. Norris Rancho Marino Reserve.
(Don Canestro)

network of marine protected areas, which includes White Rock State Marine Conservation Area.

Native Monterey pine forests are limited to five stands on the Pacific Coast, yet this conifer species is one of the most cultivated trees worldwide. Researchers at the reserve are working to understand forest dynamics by studying the demography of the pines (*Pinus* spp.) and their symbiotic relationships with fungi (Henry 2005).

Rancho Marino is named for biologist and professor of natural history Ken Norris. Professor Norris was not only a gifted educator beloved by his students but also a world-renowned marine biologist. As a coastal reserve featuring spectacular native habitats, the Kenneth L. Norris Rancho Marino Reserve honors this founding father of the NRS.

SANTA CRUZ ISLAND RESERVE

Prisoner's Harbor at Santa Cruz Island Reserve (Christopher Woodcock)

California's eight Channel Islands lie in a sweeping arc along the state's south coast between San Diego and Point Conception. Considered the Galápagos Islands of the north, these islands are evolutionary and ecological laboratories varying in size, complexity, and degree of isolation. The largest of these is Santa Cruz Island. Located 26 miles south of the city of Santa Barbara across the Santa Barbara Channel, Santa Cruz is separated from neighboring Santa Rosa and Anacapa islands by five to seven miles of open water.

The Channel Islands are the result of 30 million years of compression, faulting, and uplift interactions between the Pacific and North American lithospheric plates. During warm interglacial periods, most of the Channel Islands have been submerged. Glaciation in the Late Pleistocene led to lower sea levels and united the northern islands into a single large landmass known as Santarosae. Warmer conditions and rising sea levels

SANTA CRUZ ISLAND RESERVE

Administering Campus: UC Santa Barbara

Established: 1966; joined NRS 1973

Location: Santa Barbara County, in the Santa Barbara Channel; 24 miles long by 6 miles wide; 19 miles southwest of Ventura, CA

Size: Approximately 46,000 acres, the portion of the island owned by TNC

Elevation: 0 to 2,434 feet; reserve field station located at 201 feet

Average Precipitation: 20 inches per year at the island's central valley station

Average Temperatures:

Mean monthly maximum 71°F

Mean monthly minimum 50°F

Facilities: Field station with dormitory for 30+, private rooms that sleep 6 to 12, kitchen, dining hall, laundry, electricity, propane, library/conference room, and Internet; wet and dry lab; four-wheel-drive vehicles; 17-foot Boston whaler; five-person inflatable boat

Databases: Santa Cruz Island GIS (part of Channel Islands GIS) on site and at UC Santa Barbara; electronic Channel Islands bibliography; herbarium/invertebrate collections; flora of the island (Santa Barbara Botanic Garden 1995), plant, and bird species checklists (Channel Islands National Park)

over the past 10,000 years separated Santarosae into the four northern Channel Islands of today.

Santa Cruz is the most rugged and topographically diverse of the California Channel Islands. It is split east to west by a large central valley that marks the path of the Santa Cruz Island Fault. Volcanic, sedimentary, and metamorphic rock spanning 160 million years in age can be found on the island. Tectonic forces dragged the island to the confluence of two major ocean current systems. The cold California Current flowing south along the mainland coast brings colder water and air temperatures to the island's western and northern shorelines. The land and marine life here is typical of northern California. Along the eastern and southern shorelines of Santa Cruz Island, the California Counter Current brings warmer waters north from Baja California, attracting flora and fauna from more southerly regions.

These diverse geological substrates, topographical features, and ocean conditions have combined to produce a multitude of microclimates on the island. Coupled with the island's large size, these characteristics make Santa Cruz Island the most biodiverse of the California Channel Islands. Approximately 70 miles of coastline fringe the island and include sand and cobble beaches, giant kelp forests, protected coves, and exposed cliffs. The intertidal and nearshore subtidal communities have rich assemblages of algae, invertebrates, fish, and marine mammals.

Ocean currents originating from both north and south, combined with diverse shorelines ranging from sandy beaches to exposed cliffs, help make Santa Cruz Island the most biologically diverse of the northern Channel Islands. (Lyndal Laughrin)

Rare plants on Santa Cruz Island include the giant coreopsis (*Leptosyne gigantea*), a relative of the sunflower, which has a trunk for a stem and sheds its leaves to cope with summer drought. (Christopher Woodcock)

The Channel Islands fox (*Urocyon littoralis*) is one-third smaller than its mainland ancestor, the gray fox (*U. cinereoargenteus*). Different subspecies of this diminutive carnivore have evolved on six Channel Islands. (Lyndal Laughrin)

Divers often describe the underwater habitat as a cold-water version of tropical reef ecosystems.

Santa Cruz Island supports the greatest number of vascular plants of any California island with a total of 627 species, including 37 Channel Island endemics and 8 Santa Cruz Island endemics. As with most isolated archipelagoes, few nonflying vertebrates can be found on the Channel Islands. Native species include four mammals, seven reptiles, and three amphibians; almost all are endemic. The Channel Islands separated from the mainland relatively recently and remain quite close by, which may provide for modest gene flow from continental species. For these reasons, most island endemics differ from their continental relatives at a relatively subtle subspecies level, the Santa Cruz Island scrub jay (*Aphelocoma insularis*) being the one exception to this rule.

The history of humans on the Channel Island extends back thousands of years. The oldest dated human remains from North America were found on adjacent Santa Rosa Island. Dated 13,800 years before the present, this individual lived at a time when woolly mammoths and saber-toothed cats roamed California. The Chumash people of central California trace their ancestry to this earlier time. During the European contact period, approximately 2,000 Native Americans lived on Santa Cruz Island. The numerous cultural deposits left during this long human occupation have attracted substantial archaeological and anthropological research.

The Mexican Era inaugurated 150 years of cattle and sheep ranching on the island. University of California researchers began studying island archaeology, geology, and biology in the 1920s; a formal UC educational program on Santa Cruz Island originated in 1964 with UC Santa Barbara's Summer Field School in Geology. Two years later, the

LYNDAL LAUGHRIN, DIRECTOR,
SANTA CRUZ ISLAND RESERVE

Santa Cruz Island Reserve Director Lyndal Laughrin (Holli Harmon)

As a graduate student, I decided to study the Santa Cruz island fox. When I started, the island fox had only just been described as a new subspecies (*Urocyon littoralis santa-cruzae*). Part of my work was basic natural history, determining which plants, fruits, or insects the fox ate at different times of the year.

In 1970, the former manager of the field station left abruptly. Because I knew the ropes of the UC Santa Barbara Channel Islands Field Station, they gave me the job. And I'm still here.

On the island, you have to be pretty self-sufficient. You don't have easy access to other people to come and do jobs for you. At first, I had to do the basic plumbing, fix the tires, and change the oil in the field vehicles.

In the early days, the only communication we had was an old marine radio, and we'd call the marine operator to patch us into the phone system. Other people could listen in and hear what was happening on the island. Nowadays, with electronic banking and the Internet, you can live on a remote island and still have a lot of normal life conveniences.

I like the extreme diversity on this island. We have a pine forest where you can feel like you're up in the Sierra Nevada. You can hop over to the south side and feel like you're in Baja California. In the valley, you don't even know you're on an island; it gets very cold (freezing temperatures) in the wintertime and very hot in the summer, whereas around the coast, the ocean moderates temperatures.

I've always felt privileged and fortunate to be able to live and work here and be involved and stimulated by the programs we've had over the years. I can learn about archeology by following the archeologists around one day and the same with geologists the next day.

Santa Cruz Island is a wonderful natural laboratory and natural library. All you have to do is go out and sit on a hillside and you can immerse yourself in it.

geology camp facilities were designated the UC Santa Barbara Channel Islands Field Station through a long-term commitment between UC and Dr. Carey Stanton, owner of the cattle ranch on the western 90 percent of the island. Within a decade, the field station joined the NRS as Santa Cruz Island Reserve.

In 1978, TNC purchased the portion of the island owned by Dr. Stanton. TNC still owns, protects, and manages the island as Santa Cruz Island Preserve and generously allows the University to use it for research and educational purposes. Two years later, the federal government established Channel Islands National Park. The National Park Service acquired the portion of Santa Cruz Island not owned by Dr. Stanton and TNC in the late 1990s. Together, the Park Service and TNC initiated intensive programs to restore and conserve the island's natural and cultural resources. Their success stories include the complete removal of feral sheep and pigs, cessation of cattle ranching, removal of

Prisoners' Harbor, S.C.I., 1958, watercolor on paper (© the Estate of Richard Diebenkorn, courtesy Santa Cruz Island Foundation)

feral European honeybees (*Apis mellifera*), reintroduction of bald eagles (*Haliaeetus leucocephalus*), and recovery of the island fox (*Urocyon littoralis santacruzae*) (Roemer et al. 2001; Roemer et al. 2002). Current eradication efforts focus on problems with invasive Argentine ants (*Linepithema humile*) and a diverse list of non-native plant species, including fennel (*Foeniculum vulgare*) (Ogden and Rejmánek 2005) and yellow star thistle (*Centaurea solstitialis*). Many of the University's outreach programs with schoolchildren and adult visitors involve hands-on exotic plant removal and native habitat restoration projects.

Researchers, graduate students, and university-level classes from around the world come to Santa Cruz Island Reserve to study island biology. The information they gather and synthesize informs management decisions for Santa Cruz and other island ecosystems. In this way, the reserve contributes to the continued health and maintenance of this unique portion of California.

SEDGWICK RESERVE

The rolling hills of Sedgwick Reserve support oak research, agricultural ventures, and even astronomy. (Christopher Woodcock)

At the end of a country road in northern Santa Barbara County, past rolling vineyards, upscale horse stables, and lavender farms, lies the expansive former ranch that is now Sedgwick Reserve. Sedgwick, named for the donor family that traces its lineage back to the Massachusetts Bay Colony and the American Revolution, graces the western escarpment of the San Rafael Mountains in the Santa Ynez Valley. It is among the largest and most diverse protected sites within the NRS, rich in both natural and cultural resources.

Sedgwick Reserve lies midway between what were once the two largest Chumash villages in the Santa Ynez region. While traveling between these two villages, Chumash camped near the confluence of Figueroa and Lisque Creeks, near what is now the reserve's headquarters. The tribe's 800-year occupation of the campsite ended in 1822 when the last of the Chumash in the Santa Ynez Valley were removed from their villages,

SEDGWICK RESERVE

Administering Campus: UC Santa Barbara

Established: 1996

Location: Santa Barbara County, in the Santa Ynez Valley, 35 miles north of the city of Santa Barbara

Size: Approximately 5,900 acres, including an approximately 780-acre agricultural easement in favor of the County of Santa Barbara

Elevation: 950 to 2,600 feet

Average Precipitation: 15 inches per year

Facilities: Overnight accommodations in 4-bedroom ranch house and 2 tent cabins; 49- and 75-person occupancy in 2 wi-fi enabled classrooms; shaded patio area and Platinum LEED-rated Tipton Meeting House serve as a base for researcher housing, laboratory, meeting and teaching facilities; T-1 Internet connection

Databases: Network of meteorological stations; GIS under development; astronomical observatory administered by Las Cumbres Observatory Global Telescope Network

baptized, and brought into missions. This camp remains a place of archeological and cultural significance to the Santa Ynez band of Chumash people.

The Santa Ynez region was included in the 48,000-acre La Laguna Mexican Land Grant of 1845—a vast land holding that stretched from the eastern base of the Figueroa Mountain all the way to the Los Alamos Valley, a distance said to be "a long day's ride on a fresh horse." The land was used for dry land farming and livestock grazing for the next two centuries, changing hands numerous times. Evidence of the site's ranching heritage—wooden corrals, barns, and horse-drawn farm equipment once used to tame the chaparral of eastern Santa Ynez Valley—remain in and around the buildings.

In 1952, Francis Minturn "Duke" Sedgwick and his wife, Alice de Forest Sedgwick, purchased 5,896 acres of the La Laguna de San Francisco landholding and spent the next three decades raising eight children on the ranch. The Sedgwicks—artists, ranchers, philanthropists, and parents of eccentric fashion icon Edie Sedgwick—created a pop culture mystique that imbues the property to this day.

In 1967, just months before Duke's death, the Sedgwicks bequeathed most of the ranch to the University of California. The remaining portion, now the field station, fruit orchard, and hay barn, was acquired in a 1990s campaign led by the Land Trust for Santa Barbara County. In 1997, the land entered the NRS with administrative duties assigned to the University of California, Santa Barbara.

Encompassing nine square miles and two complete watersheds, Sedgwick is well suited for scientific investigations at watershed and landscape scales. Ridges atop the

A valley oak rises through the morning mist at Sedgwick Reserve.
(Christopher Woodcock)

Native wildflowers and coast live oaks overlook the Santa Ynez Valley.
(Nick DiCroce)

reserve's northern border are the origins of Lisque and Figueroa Creeks, which merge to flow through the reserve and continue in a 10-mile, meandering flow, much of it underground, to the Santa Ynez River. Both watersheds are fed by winter rains averaging 15 inches per year. Coastal fog that blankets the reserve intermittently throughout the year adds significant moisture to the system.

Several freshwater springs supply water year round to the upper reaches of Sedgwick, seeping from the ground into "spring boxes" built to collect water for grazing cattle. The reserve is also home to a series of vernal ponds and wetlands that fill with rainwater during spring.

The reserve lies within the wedge-shaped Santa Ynez Valley, which is flanked by the San Rafael Mountains, part of the Coast Ranges, and the Santa Ynez Mountains, part of the Transverse Ranges. The Little Pine Fault marks the boundary between the valley and the San Rafael Mountains, bisecting Sedgwick Reserve. Below the fault, the thick porous surface alluvium of the Paso Robles Formation has eroded over thousands of years into gently undulating hills and flat-bottomed valleys. Above the fault, an uplifted Jurassic-era seafloor forms an escarpment punctuated with serpentine outcrops and colorful chert, greenstone, and blue schists. Soils derived from the serpentine outcrops are rich in magnesium and heavy metals but low in calcium and are prevalent at the reserve. Research interest in serpentine hummocks is high, in part because they are a refuge for many local endemic plants and support relatively few non-native plant species. One such serpentine endemic is the Santa Barbara jewelflower (*Caulanthus amplexicaulis* var. *barbarae*), which occurs in only five locations in the San Rafael Mountains, including the reserve.

Plant communities at Sedgwick are dominated by oak woodlands, hard and soft chaparral, and both perennial and annual grasslands. Keystone species include valley, blue, and coast live oaks (*Quercus lobata, Q. douglasii, Q. agrifolia*), locally restricted wildflowers, and native bunchgrasses. Grassland ecology is a principal research topic at Sedgwick, with dozens of investigators from multiple universities studying the reserve's native bunchgrasses.

Year-round availability of water and a diversity of habitats support a robust assemblage of vertebrate and invertebrate species expected in a Mediterranean-type climate. Bird species include the endangered California condor (*Gymnogyps californianus*) and the yellow-billed magpie (*Pica nuttalli*), found only within the state.

The Byrne Observatory at Sedgwick is the first astronomical facility to be built on an NRS reserve. This observatory allows for exploration of an increasingly rare California resource: clear, dark night skies. The Sedgwick telescope is part of the Las Cumbres Observatory Global Telescope Network, a worldwide network of robotic telescopes that allows for uninterrupted, 24-hour-a-day viewing of the night sky. The solar-powered, 32-inch telescope is designed to document transient astronomical events such as supernovae and gamma ray bursts and to follow objects in space that require long periods of darkness for observation, such as planets outside of our solar system. Privately funded through a long-term lease to the University of California, the telescope is also used as a teaching facility for astrophysics classes.

At Sedgwick, science and education intersect with pastoral uses. Fifteen percent of the reserve's acreage is earmarked for private market agriculture production, in accordance with an agricultural easement that permits ventures including organic row crop

The robotic Byrne Observatory Telescope, part of the Las Cumbres Observatory Global Telescope Network, comes alive at night. (Lobsang Wangdu)

Morning View, 2010, oil on canvas (Marie-Thérèse Brown)

and stone-fruit farming as well as seasonal cattle grazing. These ventures are managed through University of California lease agreements.

A comprehensive public outreach program at Sedgwick Reserve is supported by a volunteer docent program 50 members strong. Docents enable more than a thousand students and adults to visit Sedgwick each year to participate in outdoor education classes, docent-led hikes, workshops, and community events. Volunteers maintain a native plant nursery at the reserve that supports demonstration gardens and restoration projects and contribute hundreds of hours of service annually.

Infrastructure projects continue to improve the reserve's amenities. The most exciting is the Tipton Meeting House. Built to meet the most stringent sustainable design standards, the privately funded administrative center also serves as a lecture hall and viewing center for the Las Cumbres Observatory Global Telescope Network. Restoration projects are under way to renovate three of the reserve's historic structures: a hay barn, the ranch house, and art studio. New visitor housing and laboratory facilities will round out Sedgwick Reserve, making it a world-class research and education site.

SIERRA NEVADA RESEARCH STATION: YOSEMITE FIELD STATION

El Capitan and Bridalveil Fall frame the entrance to spectacular Yosemite Valley. (Daniel Liberti)

Following the ridge which made a gradual descent to the south, I came at length to the brow of that massive cliff that stands between Indian Cañon and Yosemite Falls, and here the far-famed valley came into view throughout almost its whole extent. The noble walls—sculptured into endless variety of domes and gables, spires and battlements and plain mural precipices—all a-tremble with the thunder tones of the falling water. The level bottom seemed to be dressed like a garden—sunny meadows here and there, and groves of Pine and Oak; the river of Mercy sweeping in majesty through the midst of them and flashing back the sunbeams. The great Tissiack, or Half Dome, rising at the upper end of the valley to a height of nearly a mile, is nobly proportioned and life-like, the most impressive of all the rocks, holding the eye in devout admiration, calling it back again and again from falls or meadows, or even the mountains beyond—marvelous cliffs, marvelous in sheer dizzy depth and sculpture, types of endurance. Thousands of years have they stood in the sky exposed to rain, snow, frost, earthquake and avalanche, yet they still wear the bloom of youth.

—JOHN MUIR, *My First Summer in the Sierra* (1911)

SIERRA NEVADA RESEARCH STATION: YOSEMITE FIELD STATION

Administering Campus: UC Merced

Established: 2006; joined NRS 2009

Location: Wawona Village, just inside the south entrance to Yosemite National Park

Size: Field station is inside Yosemite and near the northern border of the Sierra National Forest; it enables access to the largest contiguous roadless wilderness area in the continental United States.

Elevation: 4,000 feet

Average Precipitation: 37 inches per year in Yosemite Valley

Average Temperatures:

Winter average 55°F

Summer average 88°F

Facilities: Offices, laboratory, classroom/meeting room, and guesthouses with beds for up to 40 people. Additional housing is available for rent nearby, including the historic Wawona Hotel.

Databases: Sierra Nevada San Joaquin Hydrologic Observatory, Southern Sierra Critical Zone Observatory, publicly available spatial data for Yosemite National Park and Sequoia-Kings Canyon National Park, publicly available spatial data for neighboring USDA Forest Service land, and plant list

John Muir's descriptions of Yosemite have moved generations to appreciate the spirit of wilderness and the importance of nature conservation. Muir's work to familiarize the public with the glories of the High Sierra continues today within the spectacular national park he helped to preserve. Located in the historic village of Wawona, Yosemite Field Station serves as both a vibrant intellectual center and a gateway that supports field research in the park and beyond.

As an example of the natural marvels the Sierra Nevada has to offer, Yosemite National Park is unrivaled. Its sheer-walled valley and granite peaks were carved by the advance of glaciers over hundreds of thousands of years. Remnants of these massive ice sheets linger in the form of three glaciers atop several of the park's highest peaks. Heavy winter snows melt to spill across the land in the form of myriad lakes, dizzying waterfalls, and tumbling rivers. Habitats across the park range from colorful alpine meadows to snow-fed tarns and great conifer forests to lower elevation oak woodlands and chaparral. This diverse collection of habitats, which spans a vertical range of 11,000 feet, supports a tremendous variety of animals, including the California spotted owl (*Strix occidentalis occidentalis*) and the endangered Sierra Nevada bighorn sheep (*Ovis canadensis sierrae*), 11 species of woodpeckers, and 17 species of bats. This profusion of wildlife in a dramatic geological setting has attracted students of nature from John Muir's time to today.

Snowmelt from park peaks meets a frothy riffle on the Merced River. (Daniel Liberti)

Yosemite Field Station was established in 2006 as a place for those students to rest and exchange ideas. It was conceived as a component of UC Merced's Sierra Nevada Research Institute (SNRI), which promotes use of the Sierra Nevada and San Joaquin Valley as interdisciplinary outdoor laboratories. The field station joined the NRS in 2009 as the first reserve to be administered by the University's newest campus. When the reserve was first established, the facilities provided by the National Park Service included a manager's residence and a historic house and stable refurbished to hold offices, a laboratory, and a classroom/meeting room. While adequate as a modest base for field research, the site lacked sufficient housing for class field trips, workshops, and writing retreats. In the few years since Yosemite Field Station joined the NRS, overnight lodging for up to 40 people has been added. Current emphasis is on expanding the reserve's academic programs and visitor facilities.

The presence of the reserve has helped the National Park Service recruit an ethnically diverse staff that reflects the demographics of today's park visitors. As the administer-

ing campus for Yosemite Field Station, UC Merced has established the Yosemite Leadership Program, an instruction and fieldwork program that also offers internships to UC Merced students. Because the student body of that campus is so diverse, interns who speak Spanish, Hmong, and various other languages are valuable as as bilingual interpreters at the Mariposa Grove of giant sequoias, the largest stand of *Sequoiadendron giganteum* in the park. Many interns are hired on as seasonal rangers. Other interns are helping park staff manage invasive weeds, save lives as part of the Yosemite Search and Rescue Team, and work with nonprofit park partners.

The golden-mantled ground squirrel (*Spermophilus lateralis*) is a common sight in Yosemite National Park. It can be distinguished from chipmunks (*Tamias* spp.) by the lack of stripes along its cheeks. (Max Eissler)

Sierra sulfur butterflies (*Colias behrii*) mate in a subalpine meadow near Mono Pass. These butterflies are found only in the central and southern portions of the Sierra Nevada. (Max Eissler)

Another opportunity for undergraduates is the National Science Foundation's extraordinarily successful program Research Experiences for Undergraduates (REU). This program, in place at Yosemite from 2008 to 2010, allowed college students from across the nation to conduct independent research projects under dedicated academic mentors: scientists at the Yosemite Field Station, the combined UC Merced faculty, US Geological Service researchers from the Western Ecological Research Center, and Yosemite National Park staff. Project topics range from general ecology to geosciences and hydrology to engineering. Such undergraduate programs catalyze research partnerships between the University and the national park.

Yosemite's breathtaking landscapes have long inspired painters, writers, and other artists. Likewise, the field station offers a summer residency inside the park through the SNRI Scientific Visualization Fellowship. Fellows receive a three-month summer residency to create art in all media inspired by nature and science. The program supports work by artists inspired by nature and science or artists exploring new and creative ways to communicate scientific research to a general audience. For example, in 2009, San Francisco Bay Area composer and sound artist Patrick Cress accompanied former reserve director Eric Berlow on research trips to Yosemite's alpine meadows.

A tarn hidden in the granite walls of Lyell Basin. The northern slopes of nearby Mount Lyell support the largest glacier in Yosemite National Park. (Christopher Woodcock)

Using high-quality recording equipment, Cress captured the sounds of the meadows, then sampled, looped, and layered them with saxophone and bass clarinet recordings. The resulting aural art evoked the experience of being in this uniquely Californian wilderness. This melding of art and science allows the public to better understand the concept of wilderness and encourages those beyond the immediate research community to appreciate and steward these protected lands.

VALENTINE EASTERN SIERRA RESERVE:
SIERRA NEVADA AQUATIC RESEARCH LABORATORY

Housing facilities at Sierra Nevada Aquatic Research Laboratory offer researchers a jumping-off point into the Great Basin ecosystems of eastern California. (Christopher Woodcock)

Each spring, streams born in the peaks of the Sierra Nevada tumble east to water the Great Basin. One of those streams, Convict Creek, emerges from the high mountains south of the resort town of Mammoth Lakes to fill and drain eleven alpine lakes. Swollen by melting winter snows, it winds around the base of jagged Mount Morrison to enter the grounds of the Sierra Nevada Aquatic Research Laboratory. Originally conceived as a site for federal fisheries research, the laboratory has since expanded into a world-class center for stream ecosystem studies and a center for environmental research and teaching in eastern California.

Sierra Nevada Aquatic Research Laboratory began in 1935, when the federal Bureau of Sport Fisheries and Wildlife, now the US Fish and Wildlife Service, leased 54 acres from the Los Angeles Department of Water and Power to study fingerling trout survival. The University of California acquired the facilities, assumed the lease, and

VALENTINE EASTERN SIERRA RESERVE:
SIERRA NEVADA AQUATIC RESEARCH LABORATORY

Administering Campus: UC Santa Barbara

Established: 1973

Location: Mono County, eastern slope of Sierra Nevada; 8 miles east of Mammoth Lakes just off US Route 395

Size: Approximately 50 acres

Elevation: Regional elevation is 4,100 to 13,163 feet; site elevation is 7,052 to 7,116 feet

Average Precipitation: 10 to 15 inches per year, mostly as snow

Average Temperatures:

Summer 32°F to 84°F

Winter –10°F to 52°F

Facilities: Experimental stream complex with nine wet labs, controlled-environment room, radioisotope lab, offices, and conference room; dormitory for 25 and 4 houses with room for 20; classroom annex; database center with extensive computer facilities; storage for long-term researchers' equipment; Mammoth Mountain Snow Science Lab located nearby

Databases: Long-term flow/temp records for Convict Creek, climate data, maps, bibliography of on-site research, synoptic collections, aerial photos, regional GIS, flora lists

added the site to the NRS in 1973. The reserve is managed together with a second nearby NRS site, Valentine Camp, as the two components of Valentine Eastern Sierra Reserve.

Research conducted at the Sierra Nevada Aquatic Research Laboratory has focused primarily on Convict Creek, beginning with the Bureau of Fisheries studies on trout, stream ecology, and limnology (e.g., Maciolek and Needham 1951; Jenkins 1969; Herbst et al. 2009; Epanchin et al. 2010). Federal researchers went on to modify this reach of the creek into four experimental stream sections with a series of control structures. Those first replicate stream reaches set the stage for much of the research carried out at the reserve today.

Under the management of the NRS, a second set of channels was constructed in 1991. Built on a separate reach of the creek, the new system has nine matching stream sections with identical patterns of riffles, pools, and meanders. Roughly 3 feet wide and 165 feet long, the channels were designed to be used broadly in many types of experiments, from fisheries research to modeling of landslide effects on rivers. Though constrained by concrete, each channel offers a natural base of cobbles and finer sediments. Still smaller channels have been constructed in a variety of ways and placed in the main body of the creek.

Replicate stream channels at Sierra Nevada Aquatic Research Laboratory allow scientists to examine how different flow conditions affect water quality and other factors. (Kim Kratz)

The reserve also includes a snow science laboratory on the flanks of Mammoth Mountain at an elevation of 9,613 feet. The roughly 10-foot by 23-foot lab is buried partially underground, beneath a platform that sits approximately two stories off the ground. A variety of instruments mounted on the platform transmit data to computers inside the lab. Researchers access the site via a ski lift at Mammoth Mountain Ski Area. Comfortable sleeping and laboratory facilities enable scientists to conduct research in the region for months at a time.

Greater sage-grouse (*Centrocercus urophasianus*) rely on the sagebrush habitat in and around Sierra Nevada Aquatic Research Laboratory for food and shelter. During the spring breeding season, adult males gather to strut about, hoping to be selected by females to mate. (Stephen Ting)

The total area of the reserve is limited, but relationships with the managers of surrounding public lands enable researchers to venture beyond the site's boundaries. The full range of eastern Sierra communities, from alkali scrub to alpine tundra, is located nearby—a region John Muir (1911) described as "a country of wonderful contrasts." This strategic location makes the reserve a gateway to the entire eastern Sierra region and one of the most intensely used sites in the NRS.

Tectonic forces that helped lift and carve the Sierra Nevada are writ large across the reserve's surrounding landscape. Some of the oldest rocks in the Sierra Nevada are visible on the slopes of adjacent Mount Morrison. Five-hundred-million-year-old fossils of

A flattened petiole, or leaf stem, causes quaking aspen foliage to shiver in the slightest breeze. This characteristic is described by its scientific name, *Populus tremuloides*. (Christopher Woodcock)

marine invertebrates are layered in the cliffs above Convict Lake. Movements of glaciers from past ice ages have left two sets of moraines at the reserve's doorstep. Immediately to the north lies Long Valley Caldera, a collapsed volcano 20 miles wide. Underlain by a large magma body, the caldera is both seismically and volcanically active, heating flowing groundwater until it bubbles to the surface in the form of hot springs. The surrounding landscape remains one of the most intensively monitored volcanic areas in the world. Several faults cut through the area, including the Hilton Creek Fault that crosses the reserve's entrance road. Surface waters percolate through these faults to recharge underground aquifers. These highly visible examples of earth forces in action attract geology and geography classes from across North America.

Even within the reserve's relatively small area, natural communities are available for study. High desert riparian woodland lines Convict Creek, with stands of quaking aspen (*Populus tremuloides*), water birch (*Betula occidentalis*), and willows (*Salix exigua, S. lutea*). Riparian meadow vegetation occurs along the creek banks and in the low-lying wet meadows. The upland alluvial soils support Great

The scallop-leaved lousewort (*Pedicularis crenulata*) was believed to be extinct in California for several decades until it was rediscovered in 1980 at Sierra Nevada Aquatic Research Laboratory. (Ann Howald)

Basin sagebrush (*Artemisia tridentata*), rubber rabbitbrush (*Ericameria nauseosa*), and antelope bitterbrush (*Purshia tridentata*). The reserve now supports the only known wild population of this critically rare plant species.

In a region with few museums, science centers, or community colleges, the Sierra Nevada Aquatic Research Laboratory is an important educational resource for residents of the eastern Sierra. Commencing in 1995, reserve education coordinator Leslie Dawson developed a hands-on field curriculum for students from kindergarten through sixth grade. Every year since, thousands of youngsters have come to the laboratory and its sister reserve, Valentine Camp, to learn about aquatic invertebrates, fire ecology, ant behavior, and more. Lessons are aligned with state educational standards to provide a better integrated science program for Inyo and Mono county schools. During the summer, one-week science courses are offered for students in the second through seventh grades. These programs are augmented by public walks, talks, and lectures featuring current research in the region, making the reserve an integral part of community life in this otherwise remote part of California.

VALENTINE EASTERN SIERRA RESERVE: VALENTINE CAMP

The wet meadow at Valentine Camp is fed by underground springs supplied by deep Sierra Nevada snows. (Christopher Woodcock)

The spine of the Sierra Nevada marks the boundary between two worlds. To the west lie craggy peaks and deep snows; to the east stretches a vast desert and slumbering volcanic caldera. An occasional breach in these mountains admits storms from the Pacific Ocean that powder the ski slopes of Mammoth Mountain. A glacier-carved basin between the mountain and the town of Mammoth Lakes encompasses the small jewel of Valentine Camp. Bordered by slopes of chaparral, sagebrush, and conifers, the reserve follows Mammoth Creek as it cuts down through a small canyon. Plunging over a waterfall, the creek then meanders through a riparian corridor and spring-fed meadow on its way to town.

Valentine Camp is a crossroads between the eastern and western Sierra Nevada. Proximity to Mammoth Pass ensures a deep winter snowpack in most years, which feeds extensive seep and spring wetland complexes. Animals of the western Sierra Nevada

VALENTINE EASTERN SIERRA RESERVE: VALENTINE CAMP

Administering Campus: UC Santa Barbara

Established: 1972

Location: Mono County, on the eastern slope of the Sierra Nevada in the town of Mammoth Lakes

Size: Approximately 150 acres

Elevation: 7,994 to 8,545 feet

Average Precipitation: 20 to 25 inches per year

Average Temperatures:

   July maximum 82°F

   January minimum 14°F

Facilities: Housing for 16 in 3 renovated cabins with modern cooking, sleeping, and bathroom facilities; electricity; Internet; spring water; limited parking/storage space; classroom building; supplies available in neighboring Mammoth Lakes; single lab space, dormitory space for class groups (up to 25); and extensive lab facilities available at Sierra Nevada Aquatic Research Laboratory

Databases: Synoptic collections of plants/insects available at SNARL and UC Santa Barbara, bibliography of publications based on on-site research, and aerial photos

use the pass as a corridor into eastern California. The natural bowl shape of the reserve offers a wide range of slope, exposure, soil, and moisture regimes supporting strikingly distinct plant communities.

The reserve was once used by Paiute groups living along the edge of the Great Basin. Obsidian flakes collected from nearby volcanic craters and a grinding stone found on the site indicate Valentine Camp meadow was used as a seasonal campsite. Indeed, Paiutes from the Bishop area camped for the summer just downstream as late as the 1930s. The city of Mammoth Lakes, which began as a mining town in the 1870s, was a ski resort by the 1950s.

Among those who first came to the eastern Sierra for rest and relaxation was Los Angeles real estate magnate and oil entrepreneur William L. Valentine. In 1919, Valentine and five friends purchased a quarter section of land—roughly 160 acres—on either side of scenic Mammoth Creek. In the 1960s, Valentine's son Edward purchased the entire property and with his wife, Carol, made plans to preserve Valentine Camp. After Edward's death in 1972, Carol and the Valentine Foundation donated the land to the NRS, along with a generous endowment to maintain the property in its natural state to support research and teaching.

The Mammoth Lakes region has a tumultuous geological history. Two interconnected magma systems underlie the area: Long Valley Caldera, beneath the Mammoth Basin itself, and Mono-Inyo Craters volcanic chain to the north, beneath Mono Lake. Massive volcanic eruptions first began around 730,000 years ago, building mountains and convulsing the region with earthquakes and ejections of lava, toxic gases, and other volcanic materials. About 20,000 years ago, a glacier advanced down Mammoth Creek, leaving behind a moraine of boulders and gravel. Reserve soils consist of volcanic materials such as pumice and lava, glacial till, and alluvial sediments deposited alongside Mammoth Creek.

The reserve is located in a transition zone between the sagebrush plains of the Great Basin and the conifer forests of the high Sierra. Most widespread is Sierran upper montane forest, dominated by Jeffrey pine (*Pinus jeffreyi*) on sunnier slopes and red fir (*Abies magnifica*) on steeper northeast-facing exposures. Sierran upper montane chaparral featuring greenleaf manzanita (*Arctostaphylos patula*) and mountain whitethorn (*Ceanothus cordulatus*) occurs on drier slopes, while Great Basin sagebrush (*Artemisia tridentata*) sprawls across a glacial moraine in the northeast corner of the reserve. Mammoth Creek supports a wide and intact riparian corridor, but native fish have largely been extirpated by non-native trout.

The heart of Valentine Camp is the large meadow north of Mammoth Creek. Surrounded on three sides by slopes, the meadow's rich soil remains saturated by springs nearly year round. Largely protected from trespass and grazing since 1919, it is almost entirely populated by native species. In summer, this slope wetland complex is covered by a thick mat of perennial grasses and sedges, and brightened by the blooms of corn lily (*Veratrum californicum*), cow parsnip (*Heracleum lanatum*), meadow lupine (*Lupinus polyphyllus*), and meadow paintbrush (*Castilleja miniata* subsp. *miniata*).

A Jeffrey pine shaped by the wind at Valentine Camp. A high-altitude species, it tolerates serpentine soils much better than its close relative the ponderosa pine (*Pinus ponderosa* var. *pacifica*). (Galen Rowell, Mountain Light Photography)

Black bears (*Ursus americanus*) are thought to hibernate at Valentine Camp in winter and can be seen roaming reserve slopes on long summer days. (Max Eissler)

DANIEL DAWSON, DIRECTOR, SIERRA NEVADA AQUATIC RESEARCH LABORATORY AND VALENTINE CAMP

Valentine Eastern Sierra Reserves Director
Daniel R. Dawson (Peter Morning, MMSA)

The Valentine Eastern Sierra Reserves consist of two small sites nestled in a landscape of almost entirely public lands. We're the base of research operations for a very large part of the Sierra Nevada. The bulk of our university-level instruction and much of the research spills out onto public land.

NRS reserves serve as gateways to these public lands. We need to have good relationships with our neighbors, the National Park Service and the Forest Service, and in the Owens Valley, the Bureau of Land Management and Los Angeles Department of Water and Power. When they trust us, we can accomplish quickly the extensive permitting that allows the research to take place.

We've also rolled out a grant program for graduate students working here, which has been overwhelmingly successful. My idea was not only to help students but also to attract students to choose these reserves in the early part of their graduate careers, because once a researcher finds a system they want to work on, they usually keep coming back.

These students and faculty are interacting socially at barbecues and soaking together in the local hot springs, but they are also teaching each other about their research. It's a really great dynamic. Social interactions are a vital part of what happens at field stations.

Sometimes I think that despite all the focus on research and university-level teaching, the work with younger children might be the most significant thing we've done over the past 20 to 30 years. The Owens Valley is an underserved region of the state, in part because there are no large museums or science centers here. We offer the only opportunity in that vein. On average, 2,000 local schoolchildren a year visit our reserves for hands-on science lessons. By the time a local student graduates from the sixth grade, he or she has probably visited here five times. We know our outdoor programs make an indelible impression on them. The kids tell us that when we see them in the supermarket or at the high school. They remember the lessons they had here, so we know we're making a positive, lasting difference in their lives.

Valentine Camp's remarkable plant diversity supports a comparably rich variety of animals. The most visible vertebrates are the lodgepole chipmunk (*Tamias speciosus*) and the Douglas tree squirrel (*Tamiasciurus douglasii*). More secretive is the mountain beaver (*Aplodontia rufa*), not a beaver at all but one of the most primitive living rodents. Almost blind but highly sensitive to touch, the mountain beaver lives in small burrows near active seeps. The birds of Valentine Camp include many species that forage in tree bark, such as sapsuckers (*Sphyrapicus ruber, S. thyroideus*), woodpeckers (*Picoides* spp.), nuthatches (*Sitta* spp.), and kinglets (*Regulus calendula, R. satrapa*). The meadow's many wildflowers attract rufous (*Selasphorus rufus*) and other hummingbirds.

The biological variety and pristine condition of Valentine Camp make it particularly well suited for teaching. Approximately 1,000 elementary school students from Inyo and Mono counties visit the reserve each year, most several times before entering middle school. In summer, a wide variety of weeklong science classes are provided for children from elementary through middle school. Adults also visit the reserve for educational programs on topics such as reserve history, wildflowers, and the ecology of bears. As a link between the community and the natural wonders of the eastern Sierra, Valentine Camp has become an invaluable educational resource for the entire region.

Valentine Camp is visited by nearly all local schoolchildren multiple times in their school careers, providing lessons about their environment that complement textbook learning. (Lisa Anderson)

WHITE MOUNTAIN RESEARCH CENTER

White Mountain Research Center is located on the flanks of the third-highest peak in California. (Christopher Woodcock)

Midway along the angled eastern edge of California, the spare slopes of the White Mountains rise high above the deserts of the Great Basin. Though little known among many Californians, this lofty range is a place best described in superlatives. The west face of the mountains climbs 10,000 feet in seven brief miles. The oldest trees on earth endure the passage of eons rooted to these wind-scoured slopes. At the summit of White Mountain itself, often lashed by hurricane-force winds, stands the highest permanent research station in the lower 48 states. The extreme environment and unspoiled landscapes of these mountains have made this remote range a magnet for research ranging from astronomy to zoology.

The first research outpost in the area was established in 1948 by the US Navy, which constructed a building partway up the mountain for missile testing. The high altitude and low humidity of the Crooked Creek Station began attracting University of California research scientists. One of these was Dr. Nello Pace, a former Navy scientist turned UC Berkeley professor who sought a place to conduct experiments in high-altitude physiology. In 1950, Pace and colleagues arranged for the University to manage Crooked Creek and spearheaded the construction of a Quonset-hut laboratory called Barcroft Station higher up White Mountain. These buildings formed the nucleus of White Mountain

WHITE MOUNTAIN RESEARCH CENTER

Administering Campus: UCLA

Established: 2012

Location: White Mountains and Owens Valley, east of the town of Bishop, Inyo County

Size: Situated on National Forest lands and lands owned by the city of Los Angeles

Elevation: Owens Valley Station: 4,108 feet; Crooked Creek Station: 10,150 feet; Barcroft Station: 12,470 feet; Summit Station: 14,246 feet

Average Precipitation: Owens Valley Station: 5.6 inches per year; Crooked Creek: 12.9 inches per year; Barcroft: 17.9 inches per year; Summit: No data available

Average Temperatures:

> Owens Valley Station: July maximum is 109°F, July minimum is 40°F, July average is 77°F, January maximum is 77°F, January minimum is –7°F, and January average is 37°F

> Crooked Creek Station: July maximum is 79°F, July minimum is 22°F, July average is 52°F, January maximum is 54°F, January minimum is –21°F, and January average is 20°F

> Barcroft Station: July maximum is 72°F, July minimum is 12°F, July average is 47°F, January maximum is 47°F, January minimum is –23°F, and January average is 16°F

> Summit Station (2003–11 only): July maximum is 62.2°F, July minimum is 25°F, July average is 42.4°F, January maximum is 37.7°F, January minimum is –27.3°F, and January average is 8.1°F

Facilities: Owens Valley Station: Dining hall, dormitories, animal care facilities, laboratories, computer room and library, two classrooms, greenhouse, shop, and storage facility; Crooked Creek Station: Classroom, dormitories, computer room, meeting room, laboratories, and shop; Barcroft Station: Dining hall, dormitories, laboratories, animal care facilities, shop, and two observatory domes; Summit Station: Two-room stone hut with no water or power

Databases: Long-term climate records, species lists, publications, historical documents and photographs, geosciences references, and regional and geological maps

Research Station. By the 1980s, White Mountain had blossomed into a multidisciplinary field station that hosted not only high-altitude physiology experiments but also a full palette of research projects in animal ecology and behavior, plant physiology, earth sciences, and archaeology.

The station joined the NRS in 2012, when it was renamed White Mountain Research Center. Today the reserve comprises four facilities: Owens Valley Station (4,108 feet) near the town of Bishop, Crooked Creek Station (10,150 feet), alpine Barcroft Station (12,470 feet), and Summit Station on White Mountain Peak (14,246 feet). Reserve lands

A view of Sheep Pass in summer, named for the Sierra Nevada bighorn sheep that roam White Mountain's rocky slopes. (Jonathan Lamb)

are owned and managed by the Los Angeles Department of Water and Power on the valley floor and the Inyo National Forest elsewhere.

A tour of White Mountain Research Center begins at the Owens Valley Station, situated on the arid scrubland of the Owens River floodplain. The water table here is close enough to the surface to support Fremont cottonwoods (*Populus fremontii* subsp. *fremontii*), willows (e.g., *Salix exigua*, *S. lasiolepis*), and saltgrass (*Distichlis spicata*) meadows. Although unremarkable in appearance, this habitat consists of a diverse assemblage of shadscale (*Atriplex confertifolia*), creosote (*Larrea tridentata*), rubber rabbitbrush (*Ericameria nauseosa*), and other Great Basin species.

The Crooked Creek facility, on the flanks of White Mountain peak, is nestled in a small valley on the granitic Sagehen Flat Pluton. It is surrounded primarily by various sagebrush species (*Artemisia nova*, *A. rothrockii*), with piñon-juniper (*Pinus monophylla*, *Juniperus osteosperma*) woodlands lower down. Higher up, limber pines (*P. flexilis*) alternate with stands of bristlecone pine (*Pinus longaeva*), which grow on exposed soils derived from white, nutrient-poor dolomite. Groves of quaking aspen (*Populus tremuloides*), often dwarfed by the harsh mountain conditions, line nearby canyons.

Barcroft Station is located on another granitic pluton above the tree line. Conditions here are reminiscent of a desert, with high winds, intense solar radiation, and a brief summer growing season. The ground-hugging shape of the plants here are characteristic of alpine environments exposed to strong winds and heavy snows. On White Mountain itself, California's third highest peak, fellfield buckwheat (*Eriogonum ovalifolium* var. *ovalifolium*), cushion phlox (*Phlox condensata*), alpine gentian (*Gentiana*

White Mountain buckwheat (*Eriogonum gracilipes*) grows only on sandstone and granite gravels in and around the southern Sierra Nevada, producing raspberry red flowers a few millimeters in diameter. Stemless mock goldenweed (*Stenotus acaulis*) is a perennial herb that prefers rocky soils on mountains and sagebrush plateaus. (Stephen Ingram)

newberryi), and dwarf lewisia (*Lewisia pygmaea*) are common up to the summit. The jumble of frost-heaved rocks and actively moving soil above the permafrost present physiological challenges for all but the hardiest plant species.

The most famous denizen of White Mountain Research Center is the bristlecone pine. Among the oldest living organisms on earth, some individuals were saplings as far back as 4,800 years ago, when the first pyramids in Egypt and the great stone lintels of Stonehenge were being erected. Edmund Schulman of the University of Arizona's Laboratory of Tree-Ring Research and colleagues pieced together a White Mountain bristlecone chronology spanning the last 8,700 years, making this one of the longest continuous records of ancient climate conditions found to date. Because the annual growth rings of trees reflect local conditions, with relatively wider rings laid down in warmer, wetter years, the bristlecone chronology has enabled scientists to reconstruct ancient climate trends. Analysis of the radiocarbon content of older rings has helped calibrate techniques for dating organic materials.

Other unusual reserve residents include herds of Sierra Nevada bighorn sheep (*Ovis canadensis sierrae*). Found in the White Mountains and few other places, these holdovers from the time of wooly mammoths (*Mammuthus primigenius*) and saber-toothed cats (*Smilodon* spp.) are now among the rarest mammals in North America. Biologist John Wehausen began studying the ecology and conservation of these elusive, hard-to-track animals in 1975. Since then, he has compiled one of the most impressive long-term datasets on the population dynamics of any vertebrate species. Wehausen's work has been instrumental in conserving this symbol of the Wild West and has since been applied

A relative of crows and ravens, Clark's nutcracker (*Nucifraga columbiana*) devours pine nuts at high elevations. (Michael Sulis)

to the management of other protected wildlife (Wehausen 1996, 1999; Epps et al. 2007).

The thin, dry air of the White Mountains was recognized early as an asset for radioastronomy. Using exquisitely heat-sensitive instruments developed and tested at Barcroft Observatory, George Smoot, now a UC Berkeley professor of astronomy, and colleagues discovered tiny fluctuations in the temperature of the radiation produced during the Big Bang. Variations in the cosmic microwave background radiation are considered the beginnings of structure in the universe—the nuclei of future stars and galaxies. In 2006, Smoot received the Nobel Prize for work he began on White Mountain.

With predicted increases in global temperatures, high mountain environments are expected to experience accelerated environmental change. Steep mountain gradients should permit plant and animal species to migrate to higher elevations in search of amenable growing conditions. At the same time, scientists are concerned that species already acclimated to alpine habitats will essentially run out of mountain and go extinct. An international consortium of scientists interested in such changes has established an ecosystem observation network on mountains around the world to document environmental change. White Mountain Research Center is a principal site in this effort, known as the International Global Observation Research Initiative in Alpine Environments (GLORIA). Each August since 2004, researchers of many disciplines have gathered at the reserve to conduct their surveys during what is now known as GLORIA Week.

These and other research projects conducted at White Mountain Research Center have produced more than 1,000 refereed journal articles and more than 100 master's or doctoral dissertations since 1950—a remarkable record for any research facility. As a field station that inspires intellectual creativity, collegiality, and ground-breaking insights into the natural world, White Mountain Research Center has no equal. The future for this most recent NRS reserve appears as bright as the stars above Barcroft Observatory.

YOUNGER LAGOON RESERVE

The mouth of Younger Lagoon opens onto a seasonal sand berm and the waters of Monterey Bay.
(Christopher Woodcock)

Younger Lagoon Reserve protects one of the few remaining, relatively undisturbed wetlands along the central California coast. Located along a marine terrace on the northern edge of the town of Santa Cruz, the reserve supports a surprising array of coastal habitats. Its brackish water lagoon dead-ends into sand dunes and a small beach. A sea stack resembling the tower of a submarine rises just offshore, crowned by coastal bluff flora. The oceanside cliffs are riddled with sea caves, while the tidepools below teem with algae, crabs, and fish. Seasonal ponds and a broad coastal prairie, reclaimed from decades of brussels sprout farming, complete the reserve.

Younger Lagoon Reserve was originally part of a large ranch that has belonged to the Younger family of Santa Cruz for more than a century. Donald and Marion Younger donated 40 ranch acres to the University of California in 1972 for the development of a marine laboratory and for the study and protection of the lagoon environment. The parcel

YOUNGER LAGOON RESERVE

Administering Campus: UC Santa Cruz

Established: 1987

Location: Santa Cruz County, 4.5 miles from main Santa Cruz campus in Westside Santa Cruz; adjacent to the UC Santa Cruz Long Marine Laboratory

Size: Approximately 70 acres

Elevation: 50 feet

Average Temperatures:

    Winter average 54°F

    Summer average 59°F

Average Precipitation: 24 inches per year

Facilities: Observation platform and access trail provide wheelchair access and full view of beach area without disturbance to wildlife or plants (with additional trails and overlooks being planned); no on-site housing or laboratory facilities; site best suited for day use

Databases: Annotated checklist of more than 100 bird species documents; observed/expected lists for vertebrates and plants as well.

included Younger Lagoon, its beach, and an adjoining coastal terrace that is now the site of UC Santa Cruz's Long Marine Laboratory. Younger Lagoon joined the NRS in 1987.

Gumplant (*Grindelia hirsutula*) is a salt-tolerant perennial often found in California's central coast wetlands. Flowers exude a sticky substance, giving this plant its common name. (Lobsang Wangdu)

In 1999 UC Santa Cruz purchased the former farm fields adjacent to Long Marine Lab to expand the marine laboratory facilities. Known as Terrace Point, the property included 47 acres of open land including former cropland, coastal bluffs, and wet coastal prairie. In 2008, these additional acres were incorporated into the reserve to facilitate the restoration of its habitat.

The Santa Cruz coastline consists of a series of marine terraces uplifted from the seafloor. The reserve is part of the lowest and southernmost of these terraces, which emerged from the sea roughly 100,000 years ago. Younger Lagoon is a stream-cut feature across the marine terrace, a relic of the last glacial period when sea level was much lower and the coastline was at the continental shelf break, about

10 miles offshore. The reserve's two sea caves were formed by wave action along joints in the soft mudstone that make up the terrace.

The character of the lagoon changes dramatically over the course of the year. From spring until fall a stable sand berm separates lagoon waters from the sea. As winter storms increase in frequency and strength, lagoon waters rise with rain and runoff from the surrounding terrace lands while high waves overtop the sand berm. Pressure from the accumulated water in the lagoon,, often combined with wave erosion, eventually breaches the lagoon. During breaching events, nearly the entire lagoon drains into the sea over a period of a few hours. The resulting mudflat is often littered with stranded fish that get snapped up by waiting shorebirds. Cold ocean waters inundate the lagoon until waves and littoral drift rebuild the berm, usually within a few tide cycles, allowing the lagoon to fill again with fresh water.

Red-necked grebes (*Podiceps grisegena*) can be found wintering in the calm waters of Younger Lagoon Reserve, diving for fish and picking insects off vegetation. (Donna Dewhurst)

Although small in size, the reserve supports a wide variety of plant communities. The upland arms of the y-shaped lagoon disappear into arroyo willow (*Salix lasiolepis*) thickets. Its steep banks are cloaked in dense coastal scrub. The inland portion of the sand bar features a pickleweed (*Salicornia pacifica*) flat. Non-native annual grassland and native coyote bush (*Baccharis pilularis*) scrubland occupy most of the coastal terrace lands. A nearly pristine coastal strand community thrives on the beach, in large part because the reserve restricts beach access. The prostrate branches and subterranean roots of native perennials such as yellow sand verbena (*Abronia latifolia*) and beach primrose (*Camissonia cheiranthifolia*) capture sand, creating hummocks. Bluff lettuce (*Dudleya farinosa*) thrives on old driftwood littering the dunes and also thrives on the adjacent cliffs. This coastal plant community provides a glimpse of what many central California beaches were like prior to heavy human use.

Younger Lagoon Reserve is prime habitat for many types of wildlife. Striped skunks (*Mephitis mephitis*), brush rabbits (*Sylvilagus bachmanii*), coyote (*Canis latrans*), and bobcat (*Lynx rufus*) are common. The lagoon is a way station for coastal waterfowl such as egrets, herons, and ducks, which are preyed upon by peregrine falcons (*Falco peregrinus*) and other raptors. The beach itself attracts willets (*Tringa semipalmata*), marbled godwits (*Limosa fedoa*), sanderlings (*Calidris alba*), and other shorebirds. Several species of cormorants roost on the adjacent sea cliff. The federally threatened California red-legged

Reserve staff members acquaint students with the aquatic creatures of
Younger Lagoon Reserve. (Tara de Silva)

Student volunteers from nearby UC Santa Cruz have helped replant Younger
Lagoon Reserve with native species. (Sean McStay)

frog (*Rana draytonii*) uses the reserve's seasonal ponds, shrub, and grassland areas as
upland refugia. The most abundant species of fish in the lagoon is the federally endangered tidewater goby (*Eucyclogobius newberryi*). The low oxygen levels and varying salinity
of Younger Lagoon provide an ideal habitat for this fish.

The proximity of this reserve to UC Santa Cruz's Long Marine Laboratory and main
campus permits both faculty and students to visit frequently. Researchers can test field

equipment from nearby laboratories, while classes can practice field research techniques. The reserve's habitat restoration program, which seeks to replace agricultural weeds with native plants, attracts many student interns. Students lend a hand to remove exotic weeds such as iceplant (*Carpobrotus chilensis*) and wild radish (*Raphanus sativus*) and experiment with methods such as light exclusion, solarization, soil scraping, and mulching to kill non-native weed seeds. Interns also nurture native plant seedlings in greenhouses and use them to recreate the original coastal prairie habitat found at the reserve.

The restoration program enjoys popular local support, although this was not always the case. Initially, people accustomed to walking along the terrace edge complained about the removal of iceplant. Reserve staff and student interns in turn began educating the public about the advantages of coastal prairie restoration. With the restoration flourishing, locals have only praise for California's native flora and the importance of ecological restoration.

BOX SPRINGS RESERVE

Box Springs Reserve, adjacent to the city of Riverside, is marked by a concrete letter C representing the University of California. (Christopher Woodcock)

Merely a mile from the UC Riverside campus, Box Springs Reserve lies on a rocky slope along the western crest of Box Springs Mountain. Located atop the highest peak in the Box Springs Mountains, a small range in Riverside County, this boulder-strewn reserve marks a transitional zone between coastal sage scrub and chamise chaparral. A cold spring on adjacent land gives rise to freshwater seeps and an intermittent stream. Decades of urban sprawl have deposited suburban neighborhoods at the foot of the reserve, presenting management challenges common to many protected areas at the urban-wildland interface.

Box Springs Reserve was among the first seven wildland sites placed in the care of the nascent NRS in 1965. UC Riverside biology faculty wanted to incorporate the land into the reserve system because it was largely undisturbed and close enough to visit during a class period. NRS cofounder and UC Riverside Professor Bill Mayhew had already conducted lizard physiology research at Box Springs, and the site had long been

BOX SPRINGS RESERVE

Administering Campus: UC Riverside

Established: 1965

Location: Riverside County, adjacent to Riverside campus on Box Springs Mountain; 2.5 miles east of the city of Riverside

Size: Approximately 150 acres

Elevation: 1,660 to 2,444 feet

Average Precipitation: 11 inches per year

Average Temperatures:

August maximum 95°F

December minimum 42°F

Facilities: None; the site is best suited for day use

Databases: Inventory of vertebrates on the reserve; list of all plants on Box Springs Mountain

a destination for field botany courses. After lengthy negotiations with the federal government, the US Bureau of Land Management turned over 160 acres to the University of California to be used solely for research and educational purposes.

Over the past half century, modern influences have drastically altered the ecological integrity of both the reserve and the Box Springs Mountains. Areas once dense with native coastal sage scrub and chaparral vegetation now harbor invasive grass species and other non-native vegetation. The conversion from native to non-native plant communities had been accelerated by automobile exhaust (Fenn et al. 2003; Rao and Allen 2010).

The Dulzura kangaroo rat (*Dipodomys simulans*) hops about on oversized hind feet, using its long tail as a counterweight. It constructs an elaborate burrow with multiple side branches and food storage chambers. (Mark Chappell)

The low shrubs and open scrub of Box Springs Reserve make ideal nesting areas for the lazuli bunting (*Passerina amoena*). (Dave Menke)

Typical of open grasslands and recently burned areas, delicate cream cups (*Platystemon californicus*) thrive at Box Springs Reserve. (Peggy L. Fiedler)

Prevailing winds draw polluted air from the Los Angeles Basin directly east into Riverside and other inland valleys. Polluted air collects against the mountain slopes, depositing nitrogen compounds that fertilize the soil and promote the growth of invasive plant species at the expense of natives. In fact, many areas of inland southern California have experienced similar vegetation transformations.

The resulting profusion of plant biomass on the mountain far exceeds historic levels. High fuel loads increase the likelihood of wildfire, especially during the dry summer months and during periods of drought. Nearby city streets contain many sources of ignition, including backfiring cars, discarded cigarettes, and sparks from heavy equipment. Wildfires now burn the reserve far more frequently than in the past, perpetuating disturbance in this landscape..

Another management challenge at Box Springs Reserve comes from unauthorized human visitors. Box Springs Mountain is a popular hiking destination for UC students and local residents drawn to the large cement letter C overlooking the city. Students constructed the C on what is now reserve land in 1955. Heavy foot traffic on trails leading up to the C causes topsoil erosion and gully formation. Vandals paint graffiti on rocks along these routes and elsewhere on the mountain. To address these problems, NRS personnel at UC Riverside have met with undergraduate groups to educate students about the environmental impacts of vandalism. Fraternities and sororities have volunteered to clean up the graffiti and patrol the area to prevent additional damage.

Balancing environmental needs with public access remains a struggle at Box Springs and other protected lands near urban centers. As California's population continues to grow, more protected fragments of the state's native landscapes will be overtaken by development, making Box Springs a valuable place to test methods for protecting wild city edges.

PHILIP L. BOYD DEEP CANYON
DESERT RESEARCH CENTER

Cholla cacti, creosote bushes, and ochre-tinged boulders populate the spare landscapes of Philip L. Boyd Deep Canyon Desert Research Center. (Christopher Woodcock)

The Coachella Valley is known to most visitors as a winter playground of swimming pools and palm trees. The desert iguanas and roadrunners that once frequented this sandy floodplain have been displaced by tile-roofed tract houses and golf greens. But the hills that fringe the valley's southern edge still harbor great expanses of near-virgin desert. Studded with century-old barrel cacti and frequented by bighorn sheep, Boyd Deep Canyon Desert Research Center offers a protected venue for field science in an increasingly populated region.

The landscape of Deep Canyon links the broad desert floodplain of the Coachella Valley to the peaks of the Santa Rosa Mountains. The canyon narrows from an open desert studded with creosote bush (*Larrea tridentata*) and palo verde trees (*Parkinsonia florida*) to a steep-walled gorge carved by seasonal torrents. Ocotillo (*Fouquieria splendens* subsp. *splendens*) and teddy bear cholla (*Cylindropuntia bigelovii*) cling to ledges and talus slopes.

PHILIP L. BOYD DEEP CANYON DESERT RESEARCH CENTER

Administering Campus: UC Riverside

Established: 1958 (joined NRS in 1965)

Location: Riverside County, 5 miles south of city of Palm Desert; 2-hour drive from the Riverside campus

Size: Approximately 6,100 acres, and use agreements with the Bureau of Land Management and the USDA Forest Service to access 10,000+ adjacent acres

Elevation: 30 to 8,716 feet within Deep Canyon Transect

Average Precipitation: Annual means range from 6 inches at Boyd Center to 16 inches along the upper plateau

Average Temperatures:

>   January average 51°F
>
>   July average 102°F

Facilities: Two laboratories with basic equipment (balances, etc.), herbarium, small library, housing facilities for 14 researchers, and reserve office at Boyd Center; small four-bunk facility with workspace at Agave Hill (no water on site); and teaching area and campground for classes. Wireless Internet access at Boyd Center and over a broad area of low elevation floodplain.

Databases: Complete herbarium and other synoptic collections, data from six weather stations and ongoing plant/animal monitoring, maps of various scales, and reference library with extensive bibliography of on-site research

A polished stone streambed forms the upper canyon floor. Above the gorge, steep slopes open into a rolling plateau cut through by shallow canyons and ridges. Small stands of native California fan palms (*Washingtonia fififera*) sprout from moist crevices in side canyons. On the exposed plateau, beavertail cactus (*Opuntia basilaris*) and Mojave yucca (*Yucca schidigera*) give way to California juniper trees (*Juniperus californica*) and piñon pines (*Pinus monophylla*) tucked into higher, milder microclimates. From here, the land tilts upward to form Toro Peak, with habitats shifting from evergreen chaparral to coniferous forest. The 8,700-foot elevation range of the Deep Canyon watershed encompasses alluvial fans, sandy washes, rocky slopes, and even montane forest, providing a comprehensive cross-section of Colorado Desert habitats.

Deep Canyon once served as a route for indigenous Cahuilla people traveling between seasonal hunting and gathering sites. Their campsites, roasting pits, and pottery have been found at more than 50 archeological sites across the reserve. As the Coachella Valley was being developed in the early decades of the twentieth century, businessman Philip L. Boyd bought land in and near the canyon in search of a water supply for his valley ranch. After World War II, Boyd became a member of the California State Assembly and later a

The Coachella Valley is considered part of the hot, low-elevation Colorado Desert. (Ansel Adams, UCR/California Museum of Photography, Sweeney/Rubin Ansel Adams Fiat Lux Collection, University of California, Riverside)

UC Regent. He donated his extensive canyon and floodplain property to the University of California for desert research in 1958. The center became one of the seven original sites assigned to the NRS in 1965. Over the years, additional land gifts from the Boyds and the Burns Foundation, as well as other land transfers, have significantly expanded the reserve.

One of the largest NRS reserves at approximately 6,100 acres, Boyd Deep Canyon Desert Research Center is the only protected area within California's Colorado Desert dedicated solely to research and teaching. Adjacent public lands that are protected by state and federal regulations are available for comparative study, as are a variety of protected habitats nearby, including aeolian sand dune systems and the high-elevation Mojave Desert.

Deep Canyon's remote and protected location makes it a suitable site for deploying sensitive environmental monitoring equipment. For example, instrumentation based at the reserve monitors the atmosphere for the low-frequency sound waves produced not only by natural phenomena such as tsunamis, meteors, and earthquakes but also by rocket launches and nuclear bombs. Known as an optical fiber infrasound sensor (OFIS) array, this instrumentation is part of a worldwide network of more than 300 test sites established by the United Nations after the 1996 nuclear test ban treaty. Other long-term climate monitoring equipment at the reserve has recorded temperature and

ALLAN MUTH, DIRECTOR, PHILIP L. BOYD
DEEP CANYON DESERT RESEARCH CENTER

Philip L. Boyd Deep Canyon Desert Research Center Director Allan Muth (Violet Nakayama)

I first went to Deep Canyon in 1974 as a graduate student to work on desert iguanas. Soon after finishing my doctorate, I was hired as the director at Deep Canyon, commencing work in January 1982. My original plan was to stay there for a couple of years, publish a few more papers, and after that get a "real job" as an assistant professor. Soon, however, I became entangled in the biopolitics of the Coachella Valley fringe-toed lizard and have been at Boyd Deep Canyon ever since.

Pursuant to both the US and California Endangered Species Act, the federal government listed the Coachella Valley fringe-toed lizard as a threatened species in 1980. Shortly thereafter, the state of California also listed it as an endangered species. Despite this protection, urban development was occurring in lizard habitat across the desert.

In 1983, when yet another development was planned in the middle of their habitat, I wrote a single-page handwritten letter that completely stopped the development. And within two years, a coalition of conservationists, developers, and local governments prepared a habitat conservation plan that became the model endangered species protection plan for the next 10 years.

A decade later I was part of the core science group that developed the multispecies habitat conservation plan for the Coachella Valley. When finished, the plan included extensive analyses and protection plans for 26 species across one million acres, drawing reasonable boundaries for places to be developed. If you go to the Coachella Valley today, the developments you see in the hills and floodplains surrounding the valley floor are all that will ever be; the remaining lands are protected in conservation areas. I've had a hand in setting aside a significant portion of the Coachella Valley landscape for future generations. I could not have done that, had I not been working at Boyd Deep Canyon Desert Research Center for the NRS.

rainfall records since 1961, and a carbon-flux tower measures the net flow of carbon dioxide between the desert ecosystem and the atmosphere.

Barrel cacti (*Ferocactus cylindraceus*) are a source of food for bighorn sheep, which knock over the spiny tops with their horns and bite off chunks of the succulent interiors. (Peggy L. Fiedler)

The dominant environmental characteristics of Deep Canyon are aridity and heat. As part of the low elevation Colorado Desert, the area routinely attains summer temperatures in excess of 120°F while receiving less than six inches of rain. What precipitation does fall comes mostly in the form of brief, intense summer thunderstorms and longer midwinter storms. In spite of these environmental extremes, the Boyd Deep Canyon region supports a rich flora and fauna. More than 600 species of vascular plants and 334 species of vertebrates are known to occur within the Deep Canyon landscape.

The Deep Canyon watershed drains most of the northern and eastern slopes of the Santa Rosa Mountains—an area of more than 40 square miles. Water from Horsethief and Deep Canyon Creeks percolates readily into the area's fractured rock and gravelly soils, emerging as springs from canyon cliffs. These intermittent streams support amphibians such as the red-spotted toad (*Anaxyrus punctatus*) and the endangered desert slender salamander (*Batrachoseps major aridus*).

The protected lands around Philip L. Boyd Deep Canyon Desert Research Center are among the few places in the Coachella Valley where endangered Peninsular bighorns are still regularly seen. (Mark Chappell)

Male Costa's hummingbirds court females with high-speed aerial swoops, whistles, and close-range hovering. (Mark Chappell)

Despite rapid development in the Coachella Valley, the reserve still supports an intact desert ecosystem. The reserve is a magnet for researchers studying desert ecology. For example, Deep Canyon has been the site of major work on the health and demography of the endangered Peninsular bighorn sheep (*Ovis canadensis nelsoni*), a protected species that requires many acres of open space. Reptiles are conspicuous in the sparse vegetation. Desert iguanas (*Dipsosaurus dorsalis*), the banded gecko (*Coleonyx variegatus*), and even the federally threatened desert tortoise (*Gopherus agassizii*) can be seen on occasion.

Deep Canyon provides respite for both migrating and breeding birds. Cactus wrens (*Campylorhynchus brunneicapillus*) build their nests among the spines of chollas, while phainopeplas (*Phainopepla nitens*) raise their chicks in the green-hued branches of palo verde trees. Avian studies at the reserve focus in part on mechanisms that maintain genetic barriers between closely related species. For example, California quail (*Callipepla californica*) and Gambel's quail (*Callipepla gambelii*) form mixed-species flocks at Deep Canyon. Studies begun in 1997 by Jennifer Gee of UC Riverside have demonstrated that social intermixing makes quail more likely to choose mates of different species. Yet the two species remain distinct elsewhere in California because ecological gradients such as temperature and rainfall separate their ranges (Gee 2003).

The spare slopes of Deep Canyon are frequented by six hummingbird species. Among these are Anna's (*Calypte anna*) and the more numerous Costa's hummingbirds (*C. costae*). Recent research at the reserve has confirmed that though the two are closely related, Anna's hummingbirds learn their songs as juveniles, while Costa's hummingbirds seem to use simpler, innate vocalizations. These findings support the hypothesis that some bird species have lost the ability to learn songs, resulting in the phylogenetically complicated pattern of vocal learning seen in birds today (Clark and Feo 2010).

Boyd is one of several NRS reserves supporting a full-time reserve biologist. Since 1985, biologist Mark Fisher and herpetologist and reserve director Allan Muth have been investigating the population biology of the endangered Coachella Valley fringe-toed lizard (*Uma inornata*). Together, Fisher and Muth have nearly six decades of on-the-ground field experience at Deep Canyon. Their insights into where wildlife is found and what types of environmental conditions to expect help visiting researchers make the most of precious time in the field.

BURNS PIÑON RIDGE RESERVE

The former home of the Burns family now provides accommodations for Burns Piñon Ridge Reserve visitors. (Christopher Woodcock)

Burns Piñon Ridge Reserve is tucked amid the hills and mesas along the western edge of the Mojave Desert. Its boulder-strewn landscape forms a transition zone between the high-elevation ecosystems of the San Bernardino Mountains and those of the lower, hotter Mojave Desert. Here, the outstretched limbs of Joshua trees (*Yucca brevifolia*) give way to piñons (*Pinus monophylla*) and California junipers (*Juniperus californica*). A wetland seep adds further diversity to the reserve's habitats. The reserve draws not only university-level field courses and scientific researchers but also nature writing and poetry classes seeking inspiration and quietude.

The reserve was once the home of Bruce and Jean Burns, who moved to the area in 1947. At the time, electricity in the region was still spotty, homesteaders fortified meals with the occasional "slow elk," and water seekers still used forked sticks to "witch" for wells. Jean Burns recalled these and other tales of local and natural Yucca Valley history

BURNS PIÑON RIDGE RESERVE

Administering Campus: UC Irvine

Established: 1972

Location: San Bernardino County, 1.2 miles north of Yucca Valley

Size: Approximately 300 acres

Elevation: 3,540 to 4,260 feet

Average Precipitation: 10 inches per year

Average Temperatures:

   July maximum 95°F

   January minimum 30°F

Facilities: Burns Reserve Station provides workspace and housing for individuals and small groups; bunk beds sleep 16; primitive campground; continuously operating weather station; locked gates at entrance

Databases: Vascular plant collections vouchering the vascular plant checklist and historic vertebrate surveys; synoptic collection of moths and representative insects

---

in a column she wrote for the *Hi-Desert Star* newspaper in the early 1970s. After spending a lifetime in their high desert home, the couple sold much of their property to the University to become a UC natural reserve site in 1972; the university purchased the remainder in 1990. The Burns family home now provides comfortable accommodations to visiting students and researchers.

Beyond the Burns residence, most of the site is undisturbed. Non-native plant species represent less than 7 percent of the reserve's vascular flora. Even the few roads made by the Burns family over a half century ago are nearly invisible today. US Bureau of Land Management properties abut the reserve on one side, while thousands of acres of other public lands and open space are located within 10 miles, including Joshua Tree National Park, Big Morongo Canyon Preserve, San Gorgonio Wilderness Area, and the Bighorn Mountain Wilderness Area.

Burns Piñon Ridge Reserve has several characteristics common to most areas within the Mojave Desert. As is typical for a desert, where insulating vegetation is scarce, the area experiences wide annual temperature swings of nearly 100°F. The rain shadow of the San Bernardino Mountains makes precipitation scarce, with reserve rainfall averaging less than 10 inches per year. Over millions of years, the rain shadow effect dried and eroded the area's soils, exposing the granitic bedrock below. Additional weathering and thermal spalling produced the granite boulder piles that are characteristic of the Burns landscape. Soils consist primarily of granitic gravel and sand. Although the reserve offers no perennial surface water, it contains a freshwater seep, and its washes and gullies fill with runoff during seasonal episodes of rainfall.

The reserve includes three distinctive examples of native Mojave Desert habitats. The lowest elevation within the reserve is a broad desert wash. Known as Lower Railroad Canyon, the wash supports desert willow (*Chilopsis linearis* subsp. *arcuata*), mesquite (*Prosopis glandulosa* var. *torreyana*), and catclaw (*Senegalia greggii*) along its outfall. A freshwater seep in which a new species of beetle was discovered emerges from a fault along the canyon above Lower Railroad wash. This perennially moist area sustains desert baccharis (*Baccharis sergiloides*), Muller's oak (*Quercus corneliusmulleri*), and three species of rush (*Juncus balticus* subsp. *ater, J. bufonius,* and *J. mexicanus*).

Desert bluebell (*Phacelia campanularia*) is an annual native to the Mojave and Sonoran deserts. (Peggy L. Fiedler)

The northern area of the reserve, which encompasses its facilities, consists of a flat studded with rock piles. Classic Mojave plants such as Joshua trees (*Yucca brevifolia*), Muller's oak, nolina (*Nolina parryi*), ephedra (*Ephedra californica*), and several species of cacti grow here. Gnarled piñon and juniper sprout from the dramatic rock piles and boulder-stacked ridgelines. Green clumps of mistletoe (*Phoradendron californicum, P. bolleanum, P. serotinum* subsp. *tomentosum*) stand out amid the branches of many trees and shrubs. Their seeds support the phainopepla (*Phainopepla nitens*), which flies to higher elevations as summer heat intensifies. Other animals include mountain and Gambel's quail (*Oreortyx*

Also known as evening snow, *Linanthus dichotomus* often grows on serpentine soils in the Southwest. (Robert W. Patterson)

pictus, Callipepla gambelii), which mix within the reserve, while horned lizards (*Phrynosoma blainvillii, P. platyrhinos*) compete for ants and other insects.

In wet years, reserve slopes brighten with spectacular displays of purple phacelia (*Phacelia purpusii*) and the bright orange petals of desert mallow (*Sphaeralcea ambigua*). Mosses, desert dudleya (*Dudleya saxosa* subsp. *aloides*), perennial bunch grasses (*Stipa speciosa, S. hymenoides*), and California cloak fern (*Notholaena californica*) sprout from shady rock crevices, while showier golden cholla (*Cylindropuntia echinocarpa*), beavertail cactus (*Opuntia basilaris*), and other succulents appear throughout the reserve. Colorful

The coachwhip (*Masticophis flagellum*) is a fast-moving snake with good eyesight that hunts lizards, small birds, and rodents. (Peggy L. Fiedler)

lichens appear in mosaics on the granite exposures.

A wide variety of field research occurs at protected Burns Piñon Ridge Reserve. The UC Irvine Earth System Sciences research group has taken measurements of soil carbon levels at the reserve to help calculate California's carbon budget. The Burns Reserve is also one of the test sites for the Salton Seismic Imaging Project, a federal project using sound waves to map the faults and sediments around the San Andreas Fault. A detailed picture of the earth's crust beneath the Imperial and Coachella Valleys will allow scientists to predict ground shaking and how violently the earth will move during a major earthquake. This knowledge will help engineers understand how best to retrofit buildings and highways to resist collapse.

Far from the hectic spin of urban life, Burns Piñon Ridge Reserve is a place of solitude and silence. Only the sounds of nature—quail in the mornings and coyotes in the evenings—break the quiet. The peace of Burns begins at dawn with the pink glow of the granite cliffs opposite the reserve's facilities. The desert's rhythm continues with the early stirrings of birds and jackrabbits, an intense quiet during the midday heat, and the insect bustling of evening as the landscape cools. Here, human dimensions slip into cycles dictated by the topography, habitats, and weather of this isolated desert environment.

DAWSON LOS MONOS CANYON RESERVE

Dawson Los Monos Canyon Reserve follows the course of Agua Hedionda Creek. (Christopher Woodcock)

Agua Hedionda Creek cuts through the western foothills of San Diego County, a twisting line of deep green in a seasonally parched landscape. Five miles from the Pacific Ocean, it cuts through a canyon thick with blooming chaparral. Stands of leafy sycamores (*Platanus racemosa*) and oaks (*Quercus* spp.) shade the canyon floor, which opens to the east onto expansive grassland meadows. Known as Dawson Los Monos Canyon Reserve, this swath of open space became one of the seven founding sites of the NRS in 1965. Since then, the reserve has been surrounded by the rapidly expanding cities of Carlsbad and Vista. It now serves as an increasingly important refuge for native plants and animals in an urbanizing region.

Members of the Luiseño tribe were the primary inhabitants of northern coastal San Diego County for thousands of years before the Spanish invaded. They used Los Monos Canyon primarily as a convenient route between valley and ocean. In autumn, the

DAWSON LOS MONOS CANYON RESERVE

Administering Campus: UC San Diego

Established: 1965

Location: Western San Diego County, within the cities of Carlsbad and Vista; 30 miles north of San Diego; straddles middle reach of Agua Hedionda Creek

Size: Approximately 230 acres

Elevation: 220 to 587 feet

Average Precipitation: 16 inches per year

Average Temperatures:

    Annual high 75°F

    Annual low 49.5°F

    Annual mean 62°F

    August maximum 88°F

    December minimum 39°F

Facilities: Field station includes a trailer for staging and research, a classroom, and short-stay accommodations for up to 4; storage shed; Internet connection and wireless access. Two weather stations offer real-time data accessible over the web.

Databases: Aerial and historic photo archive, plant-recovery records from postfire monitoring since 1982, species lists for vascular plants and vertebrates, reserve-based publications since 1995, preliminary archaeological survey report, extensive data on stream habitat conditions, and benthic macroinvertebrate collection from Agua Hedionda Creek

Luiseño returned to harvest and grind acorns; *manos* and *morteros* scattered about the area are evidence of this traditional practice.

The Spanish who colonized the area in the eighteenth century gave the watershed its name. After camping adjacent to the creek's coastal lagoon in 1769, explorer Gaspar de Portola and his party dubbed it "stinking water." Nearly 75 years later, the canyon passed into private ownership as part of Rancho Agua Hedionda, a Spanish land grant. Juan María Marrón, a former ship captain, received 13,311 acres that extended from the Pacific coast to the inland boundary of the current reserve. Half a century later, when the rancho was split into several parcels, Mary Emma Kelly inherited 650 acres, including Los Monos Canyon. Her daughter, Ida Belle Squires, was born on the property in 1901 and grew up on the land. She and her husband, Clarence Dawson, took charge of the family's cattle and horse ranch in 1944 in Los Monos Canyon. By the 1960s, housing developments and industrial sites had sprung up on surrounding ranchlands. Dawson was an avid naturalist who made it her business to learn the nesting sites of owls, the hunting habits of resident rattlesnakes, and the history of fire in the ecosystem. Determined

The patchwork grey bark and spreading leaves of a California sycamore
shade the banks of Agua Hedionda Creek. (Peggy L. Fiedler)

to save a piece of the countryside for posterity, Ida Belle Dawson began donating portions of her land to the University of California in 1965. By the time of her death in
1996, Dawson had bequeathed a significant portion of the rancho's natural landscape to
the NRS.

Downstream of the reserve lie estuarine and freshwater wetlands associated with
upper Agua Hedionda Lagoon, fish and shellfish hatcheries, and a jetty-protected lagoon
mouth leading to the ocean. This corridor
of protected land and water enables species
to move among coastal and inland habitats,
helping to prevent the reserve from becoming
a biological island.

Dawson Los Monos Canyon Reserve em-
braces several southern California ecosystems
distinguished by terrain, exposure, and land-
use history. Open pasturelands of introduced
grasses are primarily the result of a century
of grazing. Although livestock have been
eliminated within the reserve, the meadows
remain dominated by introduced annual
grasses and forbs. However, native fascicled
tarweed (*Deinandra fasciculata*) and vinegar
weed (*Trichostema lanceolatum*) are still common here in wet years. The large, white flowers of jimson weed (*Datura wrightii*), annual

Western bluebirds (*Sialia mexicana*) feed primarily on
insects and berries. (Jeffery T. Wilcox)

and bush lupines (*Lupinus* spp.), foothill needlegrass (*Stipa lepida*), and pungent coyote gourd (*Cucurbita foetidissima*) vines are among the meadow's native species.

The canyon at its steepest point is flanked by Mount Hinton to the north and Mount Maron to the south. Mount Hinton's south-facing slopes support elements of inland and coastal sage scrub as well as south coast chaparral. Stands of chamise (*Adenostoma fasciculatum*) are interspersed with black sage (*Salvia mellifera*), laurel sumac (*Malosma laurina*), and scrub oak (*Quercus dumosa*). The north-facing slopes of Mount Marron are moister and support chaparral characterized by chaparral lilac (*Ceanothus tomentosus*), mission manzanita (*Xylococcus bicolor*), and bush monkey flower (*Mimulus aurantiacus*). The abundance and composition of flowering annuals on these slopes vary with annual weather patterns and the frequency of wildfire but can include tiny-flowered cryptantha (*Cryptantha intermedia, C. micromeres*), bright pink canchalagua (*Zeltnera venusta*), and California poppy (*Eschscholtzia californica*). Where fire has not occurred for a century or more, slow-growing endemic lichens encrust towering mission manzanita, lemonade-berry (*Rhus integrifolia*), and mountain mahogany (*Cercocarpus betuloides*).

Along Agua Hediona Creek, mature California sycamores, coast live oaks (*Quercus agrifolia*), and large arrow willows (*Salix lasiolepis*) form what may be the last intact riparian forest in urbanized north-coastal San Diego County. The proliferation of pavement and other man-made impervious surfaces in surrounding neighborhoods has increased the pace and volume of local runoff. As a result, higher stream discharge is eroding the banks of Agua Hediona. Fast-growing arroyo willows and California ash (*Fraxinus dipetala*) spring up in the light gaps created by the loss of large coast live oaks along unstable creek banks.

The Virginia opossum (*Didelphis virginiana*), introduced to California from the East Coast, thrives in human environments where it feeds on pet food, rotten fruit, and human garbage. (Tree and J. Hensdill)

Further down the canyon, moisture increases and soils are deeper. Large bracken ferns (*Pteridium aquilinum* var. *pubescens*) grow in a woodland understory that blooms in spring with fuschia-flowered gooseberry (*Ribes speciosum*) and an unusual double-flowered California blackberry (*Rubus ursinus*). The woodland's edge is brightened by yellow cinquefoil (*Drymocallis glandulosa*), while the conical flowers of yerba mansa (*Anemopsis californica*) prefer the wet edges of creek banks.

This varied landscape attracts a surprising diversity of animals. The moist canyon floor harbors a variety of amphibians, including the Pacific chorus frog (*Pseudacris regilla*). Along the drier slopes, southern

Pacific rattlesnakes (*Crotalus oreganus helleri*) and rosy boas (*Lichanura trivergata*) hunt abundant birds and small mammals.

The riparian woodland provides nest sites for birds from the forest canopy to the forest floor. Anna's hummingbirds (*Calypte anna*) nest in the woodland understory and feed upon the nectar of monkeyflower on adjacent dry slopes. Cavities in tree trunks attract hole-nesters such as white-breasted nuthatches (*Sitta carolinensis*) and tree swallows (*Tachycineta bicolor*). Chaparral nesters include wrentits (*Chamaea fasciata*) and snake-hunting greater roadrunners (*Geococcyx californianus*). Small rodents and rabbits provide a steady diet for raptors, coyotes (*Canis latrans*), and bobcats (*Lynx rufus*).

Close proximity to one of the nation's largest urban populations has made Dawson Los Monos Canyon Reserve a vibrant center for local science and education programs. Hundreds of schoolchildren and university students visit regularly to learn about riparian and aquatic ecosystems. Professional consultants, public employees, and community groups also attend courses on streambank stabilization and water quality sampling. Scientists study subjects ranging from the effects of fire on chaparral communities to local insect fauna. All of these groups come to Dawson Los Monos Canyon Reserve to experience a natural world difficult to access in San Diego outside of reserve borders.

ELLIOTT CHAPARRAL RESERVE

Once widespread in San Diego County, open stands of coastal chaparral are now found in only a handful of places, including Elliott Chaparral Reserve. (Christopher Woodcock)

Elliott Chaparral Reserve occupies a narrow ridge and adjacent slopes 10 miles east of UC San Diego. From this ridge, headwaters flow both north and south down seasonally dry arroyos into two distinct major watersheds. The reserve supports an exceptional mixture of natural coastal and desert habitats. Together with its neighbors, the University of California Elliott Field Station and a military air station, the reserve encompasses a broad expanse of contiguous, largely undeveloped land within rapidly urbanizing San Diego.

Lands that make up Elliott Chaparral Reserve once belonged to Mission San Diego de Alcalá. Mission property stretched 20 miles north to the San Dieguito Valley, 50 miles east to Santa Ysabel, and much farther south to El Rosario in Baja California. When the Mexican government confiscated these lands in 1846, Rancho Ex-Mission San Diego was granted to Santiago Arguello, commandante of the San Diego Presidio. Like the rest

ELLIOTT CHAPARRAL RESERVE

Administering Campus: UC San Diego

Established: 1969

Location: San Diego County, 10 miles northeast of San Diego campus; adjacent to Marine Corps Air Station Miramar

Size: Approximately 180 acres

Elevation: 760 to 950 feet

Average Precipitation: 14 inches per year

Average Temperatures:

    Annual high 73°F

    Annual low 55.8°F

    Annual mean 64°F

Facilities: Trailer for staging, research, and short-stay accommodations for up to four; storage container; wireless Internet access; weather station offers real-time data online

Databases: Reserve-based publications since 1995; herbarium (on campus); species lists for birds, reptiles, amphibians, small mammals, and vascular plants

of Alta California, this land grant became part of the United States after the Mexican-American War of 1846–48.

During the military buildup to World War II, the US Marine Corps commandeered 32,000 acres of land in the hills five miles east of what is now UC San Diego. The new outpost was designated Camp Elliott in honor of Major General George F. Elliott, tenth commandant of the US Marine Corps. Nearly a quarter century later, in 1960, Camp Elliott was decommissioned and apportioned between Marine Corps Air Station Miramar and an Atlas missile test facility.

The University of California acquired approximately 500 acres of former Camp Elliott land from the military in 1965. UCLA professor and NRS cofounder Mildred E. Mathias urged that the Kearny Mesa portion of the property be incorporated into the NRS for its unique biological resources. Elliott Chaparral Reserve was created four years later. The adjacent military lands, now called Marine Corps Air Station Miramar, are still used for military training and operational exercises despite the presence of rare claypan vernal pools. However, these seasonally inundated wetlands are available for research use with permission from the federal government.

The rolling topography of Elliott Chaparral Reserve is covered with an unusual mixture of south coastal chaparral community. Stands of nearly pure chamise (*Adenostema fasciculatum*) are intermixed with elements of coastal sage scrub and narrow riparian forests. Chaparral stands at the reserve are more stunted and open than in most other

Quixote yucca is pollinated exclusively by the California yucca moth (*Tegeticula maculata*). The moth collects pollen from one plant and delivers it to the flower of another, where it then lays its eggs. The moth's actions ensure both flower pollination and a source of food in the form of developing seeds for its growing larvae. (Peggy L. Fiedler)

southern California locations because the soils are thin, lack nutrients, and drain rapidly. Demanding growing conditions have helped retain the integrity of the site's plant communities: some 83 percent of the vascular plant species recorded at the reserve are native. Several plant species with restricted distributions, such as scrub oak (*Quercus berberidifolia*), Quixote yucca (*Hesperoyucca whipplei*), ashy spikemoss (*Selaginella bigelovii*), and several species of chaparral lilac (*Ceonothus crassifolius, C. leucodermis, C. tomentosus*), plus many fire-following native annuals, can be found here. Approximately one-third of the reserve supports stands of non-native Tasmanian blue-gum (*Eucalyptus globulus*), primarily along the ridgeline. These fast-growing trees were planted in the late nineteenth and early twentieth centuries to be used as railroad ties and commercial lumber.

Large mammals such as mountain lions (*Puma concolor*), bobcats (*Lynx rufus*), and mule deer (*Odocoileus hemionus*) remain part of the Elliott Chaparral Reserve ecosystem thanks to open military lands to the south. Native birds found at the reserve include the greater roadrunner (*Geococcyx californianus*) and rufous-crowned sparrow (*Aimophila ruficeps*), both of which are sensitive to habitat fragmentation. The reserve also appears to have a particularly rich native ant fauna, including five species of harvester ants (*Pogonomyrmex* spp.) and one ant genus yet to be described.

The dense human population and aridity of San Diego County makes the reserve especially vulnerable to fire. In October 2003, during the driest part of the year, a local citizen lost in the nearby Cleveland National Forest set a fire to signal for help. His blaze ignited a massive firestorm. Fueled by Santa Ana winds, the blaze burned for 10 days before it was fully contained. The largest wildfire recorded in California, the Cedar Fire consumed 280,278 acres, destroyed 2,820 buildings, and killed 15 people.

Ninety-five percent of the Elliott Chaparral Reserve burned in this fire. Within the charred and smoking landscape, scientists saw an opportunity to learn how southern Californian chaparral responds to fire (Keeley and Zedler 2009). Among their discoveries was the fact that different plant species burn with varying intensity. The blaze killed few blue-gum eucalyptus; instead, surviving trunks sprouted shoots with extra vigor. Native woody species also reestablished themselves rapidly, spreading from 45 percent surface cover in the first year to 75 percent in the fifth year. Nearly all the coastal sage scrub oak (*Quercus dumosa*) and mission manzanita (*Xylococcus bicolor*), whose seeds tend to be killed by fire, simply resprouted. Plant species that produce abundant dormant seeds, such as California lilac, rock rose (*Helianthemum scoparium*), and deerweed (*Lotus scoparius*), reappeared in large numbers. Chamise shrubs not only resprouted from root crowns but also produced abundant seedlings.

Wildflowers bloomed with spectacular intensity in the first few years after the burn. Native fire-following annuals such as large-flowered phacelia (*Phacelia grandiflora*), showy penstemon (*Penstemon spectabilis*), and fire poppy (*Papaver californicum*), as well as perennial plants with underground storage organs such as Quixote yucca, mariposa lilies (*Calochortus clavatus, C. splendens, C. weedii*), and goldenstars (*Bloomeria crocea*), flourished in the ashes. Today, Elliott Chaparral Reserve appears even more diverse and vibrant than it did before the burn, a testament to the complex role of fire in Mediterranean-climate ecosystems and to the resilience of nature.

Blaineville's horned lizards (*Phrynosoma blainvillii*) eat a strict diet of native harvester ants (*Pogonomyrmex* spp.). But harvester ants are being displaced across coastal California by invasive Argentine ants (*Linepithema humile*). In research conducted at Elliott Chaparral Reserve, entomologist Andrew Suarez has found that by depriving the horned lizard of its sole food source, the Argentine ant is contributing to this state-threatened reptile's precipitous decline. (Lizard: David Gubernick. Ants: Leslie Saul-Gershenz)

EMERSON OAKS RESERVE

A forest of oaks and coastal sage scrub at Emerson Oaks Reserve supports a wide variety of birds and mammals next to the growing city of Temecula. (Christopher Woodcock)

Located in the Santa Margarita River watershed near the town of Temecula, Emerson Oaks Reserve is clothed in a dense canopy of live oaks, coastal sage scrub, and chaparral. Its position at the convergence of four major climatic zones—mountain, desert, coastal, and interior valley—generates a diverse mix of plant and animal life. Emerson Oaks is the only NRS reserve in southern California devoted to preserving the region's magnificent low-elevation oak woodlands, providing scientists with opportunities to study an ecosystem disappearing from many parts of the state.

The presence of humans in the Santa Margarita watershed dates back at least to the Luiseño people 1,000 years before present. The first recorded landowners of European descent took ownership of the site during the early twentieth century. Harvey and Gertrude "Trudi" Emerson purchased the land in 1948 and established the ranch where they would live for the next 27 years. In the mid-1970s, the Emersons transferred the land

EMERSON OAKS RESERVE

Administering Campus: UC Riverside

Established: 1991

Location: Riverside County, 5 miles southeast of Temecula; 45 miles south of the city of Riverside; 50-minute drive south of Riverside campus; adjacent to Agua Tibia Wilderness

Size: Approximately 240 acres

Elevation: 1,440 to 2,100 feet

Average Precipitation: 11.2 inches

Average Temperatures:

    July maximum 100°F

    December minimum 34°F

Facilities: Small laboratory building; best suited for day use

Databases: Beginning inventory of fungi, vertebrates, and plants

to The Nature Conservancy (TNC), hoping to preserve in perpetuity the natural beauty of their wooded retreat. TNC placed a conservation easement on the land to protect it before donating the property to the University of California in 1991 to form the thirtieth NRS reserve. Trudi Emerson subsequently donated additional lands and funds to the reserve. In 2003, a wildfire destroyed the original Emerson residence and burned much of the reserve's vegetation. A new residence constructed in 2006 now serves as housing for the reserve steward. Most of the vegetation has since returned so that little evidence of the fire exists today.

Emerson Oaks Reserve is situated within the Elsinore Fault Zone at the northern base of the Agua Tibia Mountains. Displacement along the Elsinore Fault uplifted the hills that flank the reserve along three sides. Subsurface rock layers fractured by seismic activity transmit water from the underlying aquifer to the surface at several springs and seeps. Groundwater from these seeps is believed to enable the oaks and their shallow root systems to survive atop reserve hills. Coast live oak (*Quercus agrifolia*) and coastal sage scrub oak (*Quercus dumosa*) dominate the forest community.

True to its name, Emerson Oaks is a popular site to study the natural history of oak trees. Reserve research has generated critical information about new insect pests that threaten oaks and other native trees. One such newcomer is the golden spotted oak borer (*Agrilus coxalis auroguttatus*), which by 2011 had decimated over 21,000 oaks in San Diego County alone. Research by plant pathologist Akif Eskalen of UC Riverside indicates that this Arizona insect is associated with disease-causing fungi (Lynch et al. 2010). Eskalen and his colleagues are currently studying modes of

The western scrub jay (*Aphelocoma californica*) may hide hundreds of acorns each year to eat during lean times and can remember their locations with high accuracy months later. Some jays have been observed stealing acorns from acorn woodpeckers (*Melanerpes formicivorus*) and other jays, looking about for observers before hiding their ill-gotten goods. (Minette Layne)

The acorns of coast live and other oaks feed deer, jays, and woodpeckers today, and once served as a major food source for indigenous Californians. (Lobsang Wangdu)

transmission for the disease—research that will help scientists predict mortality rates for infected oaks and plan for oak mortality in the region.

One factor in oak resistance to disease may be food reserves stored in the form of sugars and starches. UC Irvine scientist Claudia Czimczik and colleagues are analyzing the size, metabolism, and ages of these oak carbon stores (Czimczik et al. 2008). Changes in the extent and usage of these carbon resources may provide a means to monitor oak health in an era of rapid climate change and new diseases.

In addition to live oaks, more than one hundred vascular plant species characteristic of at least five major plant communities have been identified at the reserve. Coastal sage scrub occupies most reserve ridges and washes. Coast live oak woodlands and inland grasslands are more common on the lower, gentler slopes. Higher, more rugged elevations support dense stands of chamise (*Adenostoma fasciculatum*) chaparral. A narrow band of riparian woodland lines the wash located near the center of the reserve and contains California sycamore (*Platanus racemosa*), willow (*Salix* spp.), and a single Fremont cottonwood (*Populus fremontii* subsp. *fremontii*).

Though a relatively small NRS reserve, Emerson Oaks is frequented by some of California's largest predators, including bobcat (*Lynx rufus*), gray fox (*Urocyon cinereoargenteus*), and mountain lion (*Puma concolor*). Wildlife researchers have installed stealth cameras around the reserve to track these predators, taking photographs when movement interrupts the path of an infrared beam. The images are incorporated into a larger study on the movement and range behaviors of

Like many nighttime species, bobcats have a reflective layer of tissue along the retina that reflects visible light. The *tapetum lucidum* increases light available to eye photoreceptors, improving night vision, but also causes the eyes to reflect camera flashes and car headlights. (David Gubernick)

mountain lions in southern California. Persistence of wildlands such as those protected by Emerson Oaks Reserve are considered key to the survival of these apex predators in a densely populated state.

JAMES SAN JACINTO MOUNTAINS RESERVE

A northeastern view of heavily forested James San Jacinto Mountains Reserve; the San Bernardino Mountains can be seen in the distance. (Christopher Woodcock)

The San Jacinto Mountains cast a long shadow over the irrigated playground of the Coachella Valley. Its highest point, San Jacinto Peak, angles sharply upward from sea level to a summit 10,831 feet high. A journey up the mountain moves through the blistering Colorado Desert up to alpine forest and palm oases and into fragrant chaparral. Midway up the mountain's western slopes lies the James San Jacinto Mountains Reserve. Nestled into an alluvial bench amid federally protected Hall Canyon, the reserve is a base for exploring the biological variety and changing moods of this northernmost branch of California's Peninsular Ranges.

The San Jacinto Mountains are the dramatic result of 30 million years of earth movements along the southern San Andreas Fault System. Collisions between the North American Plate and the Pacific Plate uplifted both the San Gorgonio and the San Jacinto Mountain ranges. Due to continual uplift, San Jacinto Peak is the second-highest peak

JAMES SAN JACINTO MOUNTAINS RESERVE

Administering Campus: UC Riverside

Established: 1966

Location: Riverside County, 9 miles north of Idyllwild on State Highway 243; 50 miles east of UC Riverside

Size: Approximately 30 acres, plus an additional 160 acres at satellite reserve Oasis de Los Osos

Elevations: Reserve is 5,325 to 5,550 feet. Black Mountain is 7,772 feet

Average Precipitation: 26.21 inches. January average is 4.41 inches. August average is 0.96 inches

Average Temperatures:

> January 28°F to 54°F
>
> August 51°F to 84°F

Facilities: Trailfinders Lodge dormitory for 28 (kitchen, dining/ meeting room, 2 baths); 2 small cabins for 10 each (kitchen, dining room, bath); 1 large cabin for 20 (kitchen, dining room, bath); tent campground for 10; classroom, campfire circle; outdoor BBQs; data center, electronics workshop, library, herbarium, faunal collections; weather station; Internet-accessible sensor network arrays for climate, soils, phenology, canopy, and avian observations; trail system.

Databases: ArcGIS data library, airborne and satellite imagery for San Jacinto and Santa Rosa Ranges, species database for Hall Canyon and San Jacinto Range, annual bird banding records, bibliography, climate monitoring records including below- and above-ground sensor network, digital image archive, and plant list

in southern California, and its eastern face is one of the steepest in the contiguous United States.

The Cahuilla people are the indigenous inhabitants of the San Jacinto Mountains and Colorado Desert. Mortars carved into bedrock and other artifacts at the reserve indicate they used the site as a seasonal campground for harvesting and milling acorns. Their trails became the basis for present-day hiking routes that link the reserve with public land in the adjacent canyon and wilderness areas. A thriving logging industry inspired the construction of a haul road in the 1870s to transport local timber, but steep terrain saved much of Hall Canyon from the saw and plow. The vast majority of the reserve's trees are second growth, between 40 and 100 years old. The land was also used as an apple orchard for a time; a few remnant apple trees can still be found on the property.

In 1941, educators Harry and Grace James acquired the property as a campsite for The Trailfinders, their school for boys, and built a cabin on the land called Lolomi Lodge. In 1969, the couple sold their land to the University of California to become a UC natural

The only old-growth tree remaining on James San Jacinto Mountains
Reserve land is the 220-foot-tall Champion Ponderosa, estimated at over 500
years old. (Kevin Browne)

reserve. The James Reserve was expanded in 1987 to include a satellite property. Oasis
de los Osos, a 160-acre canyon east of Palm Springs, was a gift from TNC and the US
Bureau of Land Management.

Because the James Reserve lies roughly between 5,300 and 7,800 feet, it experiences
the extremes of all four seasons, from dry summer heat to deep winter snows. Unusual
for balmy southern California, these climate conditions are reflected in the area's mixture
of flora from the Sierra Nevada, Baja California, the Pacific coast, and California deserts.
Deep alluvial soils on the reserve support massive ponderosa pines (*Pinus ponderosa*),
incense cedars (*Calocedrus decurrens*), and Jeffrey pines (*P. jeffreyi*). Conifers grow intermixed with large black oak (*Quercus kelloggii*) and canyon live oak (*Q. chrysolepis*). Mature western rhododendrons (*Rhododendron occidentale*), giant chain fern (*Woodwardia
fimbriata*), and other common riparian species are found along perennial Indian Creek.

The arid slopes of Hall Canyon support two types of chaparral, one dominated by whitebark California lilac (*Ceanothus leucodermis*) and the other by several species of manzanita (*Arctostaphylos glandulosa, A. pringlei* subsp. *drupacea, A. pungens*) mixed with chamise (*Adenostoma fasciculatum*).

The James Reserve is home to 35 species of mammals ranging from mice (*Peromyscus* spp.) and bats (*Myotis californicus*) to mule deer (*Odocoileus hemionus*) and the occasional bobcat (*Lynx rufus*). Amphibians that live in and around Indian Creek include the southern mountain yellow-legged frog (*Rana muscosa*). Captive-raised eggs and tadpoles of this federally endangered species were recently reintroduced to the reserve by the US Geological Survey. The goal of the project is to bolster populations that had declined to as few as 200 wild adult frogs across southern California. The reserve was chosen as a site to reestablish these amphibians because of its high degree of habitat protection and the pristine nature of its stream. Southern mountain yellow-legged frogs historically thrived in Indian Creek until the 1990s, when changing precipitation patterns caused the stream to run dry in summer. But even during droughts, subsurface flows maintain deep streambed pools capable of sustaining these frogs.

Lacking chlorophyll and thus unable to photosynthesize, the snowplant (*Sarcodes sanguinea*) obtains food by tapping into filaments of mycorrhizal fungi that themselves attach to the roots of nearby trees and shrubs. (Becca Fenwick)

Tadpoles of the southern mountain yellow-legged frog were released into the pristine waters of a James San Jacinto Mountains Reserve stream to reestablish wild populations of this endangered species. (Chris Brown, US Geological Survey)

From the late 1990s through the early 2000s, the reserve was used as an outdoor laboratory to test and develop wireless environmental sensors. Though small in size, this reserve is perhaps the most highly instrumented of all NRS sites. Its wireless network cloud gathers and transmits data continuously from the far corners of the property. The information can then be accessed via the Internet from anywhere in the world.

The wireless mesh network at James revolutionize the practice of environmental and ecological research. Its dense array of sensors has enabled field scientists to study the natural world in much greater detail. Automated cameras record phenomena such as the date of tree flowering and the arrival of migrating birds. A carbon-flux tower measures continuous changes in the amount of carbon dioxide leaving the soil and identifies sources of this greenhouse gas. And an automated, underground microscope known as a minirhizotron is shedding light on the complex interactions between vascular plants and associated soil fungi.

The forests of James San Jacinto Mountains Reserve conceal a wide variety of instrumentation, ranging from microphones that capture forest sounds to webcams such as this one. (Christopher Woodcock)

OASIS DE LOS OSOS

The Oasis de los Osos Satellite Reserve is a magical place. Located about five miles north of Palm Springs, on the steep, north-facing escarpment of Mount San Jacinto, it offers a fertile trace of green in a parched environment.

Perennial Lambs Creek flows through the site from high atop the mountain's slopes. At the upper end of the Oasis, the creek cascades over a granite wall into a shallow plunge pool shaded by cottonwoods. After descending into a riparian corridor lined with willows, it travels toward the base of the canyon before disappearing into a broad desert wash. The desert riparian woodland community at the Oasis is one of very few in the Colorado Desert.

The beauty of the Oasis convinced at least one past settler to homestead in this idyllic spot. Remnants of a long-abandoned residence can be seen where the stream enters the wash. A foundation, stairs, a chimney, and a few planted eucalyptus trees and California fan palms (*Washingtonia filifera*) are all that remain; the roadway leading to the historic dwelling has been reclaimed by decades of plant succession.

The Oasis shelters several rare species as well. A healthy population of giant stream orchids (*Epipactis gigantea*) adorns the walls of the plunge pool. Graduate student research has demonstrated that seasonal flooding dislocates these uncommon native orchids and enables them to disperse downstream. The creek's vibrant riparian corridor is one of only a handful of places where the endemic Laguna Mountain springsnail (*Pyrgulopsis californiensis*) is found, alongside a new species of land snail yet to be described. By making space for these organisms to survive, the Oasis is a site of true respite in a relentless desert environment.

Oasis de los Osos, a satellite property of the James San Jacinto Mountains Reserve (Becca Fenwick)

The network enables the observation of resident animals as well. The reserve maintains a network of bird boxes equipped with infrared cameras and microweather stations. Instruments allow researchers as well as the public to watch the nesting progress. During the breeding season, violet-green swallows (*Tachycineta thalassina*), mountain bluebirds (*Sialia currucoides*), and mountain chickadees (*Poecile gambeli*) occupy the nest boxes, while during the rest of the year, Nuttall's woodpeckers (*Picoides nuttallii*) and chipmunks (*Tamias* spp.) frequent these shelters. Additional web cameras and microphones positioned across the reserve record the action at feeding stations and other reserve locations.

By cooperative agreement, visitors to the James Reserve also have access to USDA Forest Service property in Hall Canyon, expanding the reach of this NRS "pocket" reserve to hundreds of acres of mountainous landscape.

KENDALL-FROST MISSION BAY
MARSH RESERVE

Kendall-Frost Mission Bay Reserve protects one of the last remnants of coastal salt marsh in highly urbanized San Diego. (Christopher Woodcock)

The shorelines and waterways of San Diego's Mission Bay have been altered for more than 200 years to meet the needs of local residents. From canals dug in the eighteenth century to the engineered islands of Mission Bay Park, the estuary has experienced continuous change. The salt marshes that once fringed 2,000 acres of the bay have been reduced to a 30-acre remnant along the northern edge of the bay. The majority of this diminished wetland is protected by Kendall-Frost Mission Bay Marsh Reserve; the rest is protected by the city of San Diego's Northern Wildlife Preserve. Together these areas preserve a coastal ecosystem that his now all too rare in southern California.

For thousands of years, the Kumeyaay people lived in small groups around the bay collecting abalone and other shellfish, fishing from reed rafts with woven nets. A Kumeyaay village site can be found along Rose Canyon Creek north of the reserve. European settlement began with the establishment of Mission San Diego along the San

KENDALL-FROST MISSION BAY MARSH RESERVE

Administering Campus: UC San Diego

Established: 1965

Location: San Diego County, on the northern edge of Mission Bay; 7 miles south of San Diego campus

Size: Approximately 20 acres plus use of the contiguous city-owned portion, for a total of approximately 40 acres

Elevation: –2 to +10 feet

Average Precipitation: 12.3 inches per year

Average Temperatures:

    Annual average maximum 67.3°F

    Annual average minimum 55.8°F

    Annual mean 61.6°F

    January minimum 47°F

    August maximum 73°F

Facilities: Observation deck; trailer with utilities (electricity, Internet, hot and cold running water), lab bench, office, living area; overnight accommodations for up to four people

Databases: Plant and bird species lists; bibliography of on-site research, including reserve-based publications since 1995; aerial photos; census of endangered species; long-term data on light-footed clapper rail nesting

The black-crowned night heron (*Nycticorax nycticorax*) is a nocturnal forager that wades into shallow water to spear fish, crustaceans, and small mammals. (Max Eissler)

Diego River. The river historically emptied into either San Diego Bay proper or Mission Bay, depending on the timing and duration of winter rains. But by the middle of the twentieth century, a series of creek and river diversions had severed the bay from the river, its major source of freshwater, leaving Rose and Tecolote Creeks as its only remaining tributaries. After World War II, Mission Bay was dramatically reconfigured to create islands, peninsulas, and deeper water for boaters, a process that destroyed most of the marsh.

The future of the remaining marsh looked dire until 1952, when Lena Kendall and the A. H. Frost estate donated two parcels of the upper marsh. In 1965, Kendall-Frost Mission Bay Marsh Reserve was incorporated into the University's newly established reserve system. Today, the reserve continues a history of educational use begun at the marsh by Scripps Institution of Oceanography in 1942.

Despite major alterations to the surrounding land and water, the wetland remains remarkably productive. Contiguous mudflats, shoals, and open water offer a wide array of habitats for marsh plants and animals. Tides still circulate through the marsh's channels, carrying nutrients to its natural communities. Eelgrass (*Zostera marina*) beds grow within shallow, continuously submerged waters. Mudflats, with their rich communities of microscopic and macroscopic algae, diatoms, and invertebrates, are exposed only at the lowest tides. Algae and bacterial mats also colonize the stems of marsh plants for most of the year, contributing to the wetland's high productivity.

Native to much of the Americas, heliotrope (*Heliotropium curassavicum* var. *oculatum*) can tolerate the salty soils of both coastal and inland wetlands. (James André)

A distinct shift in plant life marks the beginning of the salt marsh at about mean sea level. Cordgrass (*Spartina foliosa*) occurs over more than half of the lower marsh, interspersed with perennial pickleweed (*Salicornia pacifica*). Higher up, a more diverse perennial plant community includes saltwort (*Batis maritima*), saltmarsh daisy (*Jaumea carnosa*), the parasitic saddler's silk (*Cuscuta salina*), and sea lavender (*Limonium californicum*). The highest community, seldom inundated by tides and occupying nearly one quarter of the marsh area, is dominated by rambling sea-blite (*Suaeda californica*), saltgrass (*Distichlis spicata*), alkali heath (*Frankenia salina*), and high marsh pickleweed (*Arthrocnemum subterminalis*). A hypersaline salt panne lacking any plants occurs in the northeastern corner of the marsh.

Not all plants at the reserve are native, however. For example, non-native gray mangrove (*Avicennia marina* var. *australasica*) introduced to the area in 1964 as part of a research project proliferated until they began displacing native vegetation essential for resident marsh birds. Fortunately, restoring native estuarine ecosystems through student and local community projects is an important aspect of the stewardship strategy for this reserve. Since the 1980s, students and community volunteers have removed more than 50,000 mangroves from the marsh. Higher-elevation areas of the reserve were formerly dominated by non-native annuals such as iceplant (*Carpobrotus chilensis*, *C. edulis*), eucalyptus, and acacia trees. Volunteers are gradually replacing these invaders with native coastal sage scrub species.

As one of few remaining coastal wetlands in the area, Mission Bay is a critical habitat for both migrating and resident birds. In winter, large numbers of western (*Larus occidentalis*) and ring-billed gulls (*L. delawarensis*), as well as bufflehead, northern shoveler, and northern pintails (*Bucephala albeola, Anas clypeata, Anas acuta*), are found at the reserve. Black brant (*Branta bernicla*) geese traveling along the Pacific Flyway gather at the lower edge of the marsh to rest and feed. In summer, several hundred Forster's terns (*Sterna forsteri*) nest on the floating rafts of vegetation and debris that collect along the edge of the cordgrass meadow. Endangered California least tern (*S. antillarium browni*) also forage in the marsh channels for small fish to feed young on nearby sandy beaches.

Year-round residents include one of California's rarest birds, the light-footed clapper rail (*Rallus longirostris levipes*). The chicken-sized rail is entirely dependent upon the marsh for food and shelter. Clapper rails weave floating nests for their eggs and forage for crabs, California horn snails (*Cerithidea californica*), arthropods, and small fish among marsh plants and along meandering channels. Though the species was listed as endangered by the federal government in 1970, its population has continued to decline due to the loss of coastal wetlands. In response, the US Fish and Wildlife Service began installing artificial nesting platforms at Kendall-Frost and other wetlands in 1987. These floating platforms are heavily used at the reserve. The most recent rail census tallied at least seven pairs nesting at Kendall-Frost, a small but respectable portion of the fewer

North America's largest sandpiper, the long-billed curlew (*Numenius americanus*), probes mudflats with its long beak in search of crabs and other small invertebrates. (Alan and Elaine Wilson)

than 300 breeding pairs left in the wild between Santa Barbara and the Mexican border. Human activities are restricted to the high marsh for half the year because these birds are sensitive to disturbance.

The marsh's tidal creeks and smaller channels provide habitats for many species of fish: California killifish (*Fundulus parvipinnis*) live in hypersaline pools. Longjaw mudsuckers (*Gillichthys mirabilis*) prey on yellow crabs (*Cancer anthonyi*) and move into crab burrows when newly hatched. Arrow gobies (*Clevelandia ios*) live in mudflat holes, often sharing the burrows with pink ghost shrimp (*Neotrypaea californiensis*). Young Pacific halibut (*Hippoglossus stenolepis*) seek refuge in the marsh before making their way to the open ocean.

The urban setting of the Kendall-Frost reserve demands constant active management. Medium-sized predators such as raccoons (*Procyon lotor*) and striped skunks (*Mephitis mephitis*), as well as non-native Virginia opossums (*Didelphis virginiana*), brown rats (*Rattus norvegicus*), and domestic cats now prey on nesting clapper rails and other marsh birds. One solution being considered is restoring wildlife corridors from the marsh to inland areas. The corridors could provide access for wide-ranging coyotes (*Canis latrans*), which could then assume their natural role as the marsh's apex predator, keeping cats, rats, and raccoon numbers low.

MOTTE RIMROCK RESERVE

The spring wildflower displays at Motte Rimrock Reserve are framed by striking boulder piles. (Christopher Woodcock)

Weathered boulders, indigenous rock art panels, and the rust-brown hue of buckwheat define Motte Rimrock Reserve. Perched on a broad plateau of exposed granite not far from the city of Perris in western Riverside County, the reserve lies midway between two earthquake faults. Shaking generated by these faults is attenuated by the rigidity of the granite, preserving a number of impressively balanced boulders at Motte.

The length of human habitation at the Motte Rimrock Reserve and its environs remains uncertain, but clear evidence exists of occupation from the late prehistoric period beginning 800 to 1,300 years before the present. Both the Luiseño and Cahuilla tribes have strong cultural ties to the area, as evidenced on the reserve by artifacts and cultural sites. A number of elaborate pictograph panels appear to make up a ceremonial complex adjacent to the main habitation area. Motte's rock art reflects at least two

MOTTE RIMROCK RESERVE

Administering Campus: UC Riverside

Established: 1976

Location: Riverside County, 1 mile northwest of Perris; 15 miles south of Riverside campus

Size: Approximately 700 acres

Elevation: 1,580 to 1,985 feet

Average Precipitation: 13 inches per year

Average Temperatures:

> July maximum 98°F
>
> January minimum 36°F

Facilities: On-site housing/kitchen facilities for up to 14 people, campground, wet lab, library/storage area, 642-acre transect grid, bird-banding station, marked trails and dirt roads, and weather-recording station

Databases: Functional geographic information system (GIS), animal records since 1971, synoptic collections, bibliography of on-site research, photographic archive, and users' handbook

distinct episodes: the San Luis Rey style and an earlier Rancho Bernardo style. The paintings are in remarkably good condition and archeologists and rock art specialists generally believe that they range between 250 and 700+ years old.

The most impressive of these rock art panels is colloquially known as Girls Puberty Rock, a possible misnomer because critical analysis suggests that it had multiple cultural functions (Vuncannon 1977). Several of the motifs are relatively detailed and unique; even the brushwork is notable, reflecting mature and purposeful application. Perhaps the most striking of the elements are numerous impression handprints, reflecting the participation of children as well as adults. The pictographs are so well preserved that close inspection of some handprints reveals the fingerprints of their makers.

The NRS established Motte Rimrock Reserve in 1976, following a gift of 300 acres to the University of California and a generous endowment to operate the site by regional landowners Charles and Ottie Motte. Since its establishment, the reserve has grown in size to more than 700 acres through a series of land acquisitions from sources including the US Bureau of Land Management, Riverside County Habitat Conservation Agency, and Eastern Municipal Water District, as well as additional land donated by the Motte family in 2001. Motte Rimrock Reserve is the only protected area in the region devoted primarily to teaching and research.

The pictograph panel at Motte Rimrock Reserve dubbed Puberty Rock. The site is thought to have been used for a variety of cultural purposes. (Steven Freers)

Positioned midway between the warm, dry Colorado Desert and the cool, moist Pacific coast, the reserve is influenced by both climate regimes. As a result, species common to both Mediterranean-type and desert habitats can be found here. For example, the reserve supports stands of coastal sage scrub despite being 40 miles from the Pacific shore. Inland, non-native annual grassland and willow riparian scrub are also present. At Motte, native shrubs such as black and white sage (*Salvia mellifera, S. apiana,* respectively), California sagebrush (*Artemisia californica*), and California buckwheat (*Eriogonum fasciculatum*) dominate the perennial vegetation. Ample winter and spring rains followed by warm temperatures often produce spectacular displays of spring wildflowers.

Like most wild areas in southern California, non-native species, especially red brome (*Bromus madritensis* subsp. *rubens*) and redstem filaree (*Erodium cicutarium*), have colonized areas once occupied by native wildflowers and grasses. Nitrogen deposition from auto emissions in addition to repeated wildfires ignited by humans has made the environment more hospitable to invasive plant species. Research at the reserve has focused on the conservation and restoration of native vegetation communities.

The coastal sage scrub at Motte Rimrock Reserve is home to the federally endangered Stephens's kangaroo rat (*Dipodomys stephensi*). Motte is one of eight core reserves in western Riverside County dedicated to monitoring and conserving this rare mammal. The Riverside County Habitat Conservation Agency established the Stephens's Kangaroo Rat Reserve System in March 1996 as part of the long-term habitat conservation plan for this rodent. Motte biologists conduct quarterly monitoring studies and participate in kangaroo rat ecological and population genetic studies. Much of what is currently known about Stephens's kangaroo rat biology was gained from research conducted on the reserve by UC Riverside biology

A bush monkeyflower bush (*Mimulus aurantiacus*) sprouts from solid rock at
Motte Rimrock Reserve. (Mark Chappell)

professor emerita Mary Price and her colleagues throughout the 1980s and early 1990s
(Price and Kramer 1984; Price et al. 1991; Price et al. 1992). The reserve also harbors
the federally threatened California gnatcatcher (*Polioptila californica*), protected because as
much as 70 to 90 percent of its preferred habitat, southern California coastal sage scrub,
has fallen to development.

Other research conducted at Motte has examined food preferences of the rough harvester ant *Pogonomyrmex rugosus* (Briggs 2009). Ongoing research conducted at Motte and
several other NRS reserves focuses on the strategies ant queens employ to establish new
colonies. More recently, UC Riverside scientists working at the reserve have documented

The Western tanager (*Piranga ludoviciana*) eats both fruits and a wide range of insects caught by foliage gleaning and snapping flying prey from the air. (US Fish and Wildlife Service)

rapid evolutionary change in another insect occurring within just a few generations. UC Riverside scientists compared nonevolving single-clone aphid lineages with dual-clone, evolving lineages both collected from Motte. They found that evolving populations grew much faster and attained much higher densities when exposed to predators and competitors in the wild (Turcotte et al. 2011).

The urban matrix surrounding Motte Rimrock Reserve presents management problems common to protected areas located at the edges of developed landscapes. Rates of vandalism, wildfire, pollution, and introduced species invasions are all greater at the urban/wildland interface. Yet as development intensifies in Riverside County, the need to preserve this singular slice of southern California midway between ocean and desert will only become more acute.

SAN JOAQUIN MARSH RESERVE

A cloak of morning mist returns the view of San Joaquin Marsh Reserve to that of an earlier century. (Christopher Woodcock)

San Joaquin Marsh Reserve is among the last remnants of an extensive wetland mosaic that once fringed California's Orange County coast. Today, the marsh is embedded in a tapestry of anthropogenic disturbance. Dams, modified drainages, flood control measures, and urban development have altered wetland functions to a tremendous degree. Yet the marsh's position adjacent to UC Irvine has made the reserve a locus for environmental learning and research. Years of hard work by marsh stewards and students have transformed a formerly degraded site into an important refuge for locally embattled wildlife.

Around 4,000 years ago, when sea levels were higher, the San Joaquin Marsh ecosystem was a tidally influenced salt marsh. Intensive prehistoric occupation over thousands of years began as early as 5,750 years before present. Local Gabrielino and Juañeno people once used the marsh extensively, as evidenced by shell middens on the coastal bluffs overlooking the extant wetlands.

SAN JOAQUIN MARSH RESERVE

Administering Campus: UC Irvine

Established: 1970

Location: City of Irvine, Orange County; 45 miles southeast of Los Angeles, 20 miles west of the Santa Ana Mountains; 1.25 miles upstream from Upper Newport Bay, adjacent to the Irvine campus

Size: Approximately 200 acres

Elevation: 7 to 10 feet

Average Precipitation: 12 inches per year

Average Temperatures:

> September maximum 86°F
>
> January minimum 40°F
>
> Annual mean 62°F

Facilities: No on-site housing or laboratory facilities, but the reserve is adjacent to the UC Irvine campus

Databases: Herbarium and vascular plant collections vouchering the plant checklist; publications of reserve-based research

Modern hydrologic modifications to the marsh began in the early 1900s. Cienega de las Ranas, a 50,000-acre marshland that once covered this region, was drained to expand farming acreage. Additional development eventually eliminated an estimated 97 percent of the area's riparian habitat. In 1939, a dam built on San Diego Creek filled the lower half of the reserve with sediment before the dam was removed decades later. The dam enabled the creek to recharge the marsh's largest source of water, a subterranean aquifer. But channelizing the waterway also eliminated perennial freshwater flow through the wetland. In the 1950s, the county used an adjacent estuarine embayment and salt marsh as a landfill, which was closed and capped in 1960. Tidal influence was terminated in the early 1960s by a flood control levee built along San Diego Creek. Human activities such as groundwater pumping contributed to the decline of the water table by nearly 20 feet and to over 18 inches of subsidence in the wetlands. San Joaquin Marsh was transformed from a depression fed by groundwater into a wetland dependent upon surface water such as precipitation, runoff, and water diverted from San Diego Creek.

After suffering nearly every disturbance an urban wetland can experience, the marsh has become an ideal canvas for ecological restoration. In 1989 the NRS and UC Irvine established a buffer zone around the upland margin of the reserve. Marsh restoration efforts began in 1990. Since that time, flourishing stands of coastal sage scrub have encircled the wetlands. These uplands are now occupied by nesting

PETER BOWLER, FACULTY MANAGER, SAN JOAQUIN MARSH AND
BURNS PIÑON RIDGE RESERVE, UC IRVINE

San Joaquin Marsh and Burns Piñon Ridge reserves Faculty Manager Peter Bowler (Courtesy Peter Bowler)

I take all my classes to the marsh because it's a perfect template for talking about environmental issues. We start out in the parking lot, the anthropocentric world. I point out all the skyscrapers around us, which I consider "habitat tombstones," and talk about the ecological desert constituted by the city of Irvine. Hardly any of the students have been to a wetland; the closest they've come is the beach.

We then walk to the campus arboretum, where people have created nature for human enjoyment. From the arboretum, we enter the reserve, initially into an area where through restoration humans created naturalness for wildlife, research, and teaching purposes, and where I talk about the California gnatcatchers that live in coastal sage scrub restoration plantings. Then we go into the natural areas of the marsh.

A great deal of habitat destruction occurred in Irvine during the 1990s, due to the building of freeways, development on and around the campus, and so forth. This prompted me to get into ecological restoration. I collected seeds of native plants and began revegetating the adjacent barren bluffs that had been grazed and degraded. Some early pictures of the reserve show not a single plant growing on the bluffs, but today it is coastal sage scrub community with nesting, federally threatened gnatcatchers.

On Sunday mornings from nine till noon, I work to restore the marsh with independent study students and many others who come along just because they like being out there. One year my students grew three species of native bulrush, keeping over individual 3,500 plants alive in the marsh for eventual use in restoration projects. Last week we planted 400 individual plants around the marsh periphery, and we're now planting lots of native cacti to attract the coastal cactus wren.

Doing ecological restoration at the reserve has a significant effect on student environmental attitudes and their behavior toward the environment. They see the value of helping to make the environment healthier. People think restoration is doing good things for nature, but people get a lot out of it for themselves, too. That's one of the beautiful revelations that come to students as they work. They're getting stuck with thorns and are cursing under their breath and suddenly the light comes on. Many return years later to see the fruition of their efforts.

California gnatcatchers (*Polioptila californica*), a federally threatened coastal scrub obligate species, and by California quail (*Callipepla californica*) and greater roadrunner (*Geococcyx californianus*).

Measures to restore the marsh to health have proceeded as restoration money and opportunities have come available. In 1996, a restoration project created new wetland from what had been an abandoned farm field; in 1999, 11 experimental ponds were added to the marsh with California Coastal Conservancy funding. Students have created vernal pools along the marsh periphery that sustain fairy shrimp (*Brachinecta lindahli*) and native vernal pool plants such as the diminutive wooly marbles (*Psilocarphus brevissimus*). In 2009, removal of unneeded roads and dikes made space for three additional acres of brackish marsh habitat. Riparian plantings along the wetland's edge supplement natural populations of native shrubs and trees, primarily black willow (*Salix gooddingii*) and mule fat (*Baccharis salicifolia* subsp. *salicifolia*).

At present, the reserve is configured into five areas with different ecosystem functions. The upper, middle, and lower marsh are wet in the winter and dry by midsummer; these areas are dominated by cattail (*Typha latifolia*). Eddy flux towers in the upper and middle marsh areas allow research into evapotranspiration, gas exchange, and productivity in cattail wetlands. Roughly half of the experimental ponds flood less than a foot deep in the fall; the rest are deeper and typically remain wet year round. The oldest restoration site has been allowed to develop into California bulrush (*Schoenoplectus californicus*) habitat.

In the fall, pond margins are mowed to maintain conditions for bulrush. The experimental ponds are then filled and allowed to dry. Coastal bulrush (*Bolboschoenus robustus*) and Olney's bulrush (*Schoenoplectus americanus*) dominate the shallow shelves, while California bulrush occupies deep channel edges.

An additional seasonal marsh is inundated only in years of heavy precipitation and dries by summer. This area is dominated by mulefat, coastal bulrush, and perennial pickleweed (*Salicornia pacifica*).

Ecological restoration has breathed new life into the reserve. Today, San Joaquin Marsh sustains the largest population of the southwestern

San Joaquin Marsh Reserve attracts a wide variety of wetland wildlife, including the common yellowthroat (*Geothlypis trichas*), which breeds in marshes with dense vegetation. (Daniel Anderson)

Extensive ecosystem restoration has enabled the marsh to sustain a large population of the southwestern pond turtle (*Actinemys marmorata pallida*). (Jeffery T. Wilcox)

Students wade through San Joaquin Marsh Reserve during a practical test in their field freshwater ecology course. (Daniel Anderson)

Pacific pond turtle (*Clemmys marmorata pallida*) in southern California. Over 250 individuals live in the wetland and nest in the upland buffer zone. More than 260 bird species have been recorded in the wetland system since the university purchased the marsh in 1970.

Four sets of paired ponds permit experiments comparing the impacts of different management regimes on vegetation, water chemistry, and insects. The duplicate ponds have proven invaluable for teaching classes such on limnology and freshwater ecology. During the 2009–10 academic year, more than 5,550 user days were recorded for the marsh—remarkable for a small reserve consisting mostly of wetland habitats.

The long-term vision for the reserve is to strengthen ecosystem ties with Upper

Newport Bay estuary and to reestablish the historic tidal influence. As climate change continues and sea levels rise, the lower areas of the marsh will transform into a salt marsh and estuarine habitat. Salt marsh species of Newport Back Bay will relocate here as the ocean inundates their current habitats. This process has begun already, with the first nesting pairs of light-footed clapper rails (*Rallus longirostris levipes*), which have been absent for many decades, fledging young in 2011.

WILLIAM BRETZ, RESERVE MANAGER, SAN JOAQUIN MARSH AND BURNS PIÑON RIDGE RESERVES

San Joaquin Marsh and Burns Piñon Ridge Reserves Manager Bill Bretz (Daniel Anderson)

I like to go on reconnaissance in the marsh early in the mornings to see what's happening. Going routinely to the marsh, you see things in patterns with the vegetation and the water, especially after being there over a long period. There are times that I'm out in the marsh and I feel just like a farmer might. What I'm looking at is the amazing growth of alkali bulrush (*Bolboschoenus maritimus* subsp. *paludosus*), a particular plant species we've encouraged with our management. Sometimes it looks like waving fields of grain, which is a direct result of our management of the marsh's hydrology.

San Joaquin Marsh is one of the most intensively managed places in the reserve system. It remains a wetland because we do all these things that are substituting for natural processes, like mowing and pumping water. It's a bit ironic because one aspect of our mission is to have a desirable place for academic research and study, but the destructive landscape processes humankind has left in the remnants of a once huge, healthy wetland system make it so that you wouldn't have a very desirable place if you left it alone.

We're true believers in the impacts of global climate change, fully expecting the ocean to be flooding the marsh by the end of the century. That will turn it into an intertidal estuarine wetland, which it has been in times past. That's not a great calamity, except so little freshwater marsh remains in urban Orange County. We're making an investment we know is temporary, taking action today for the short-term health of this particular area. The work we're doing now will be literally underwater in a couple of generations.

I feel very fortunate to have stumbled into the NRS so many years ago, and for that I can't possibly contribute enough. The NRS is dedicated to looking after the things that are the most important: the health of the planet and its natural ecosystems.

SCRIPPS COASTAL RESERVE

The ocean view from the top of Sumner Canyon at Scripps Coastal Reserve (Christopher Woodcock)

Scripps Coastal Reserve protects a precipitous slice of San Diego shoreline. Here, a coastal mesa topped by a grassy knoll towers 30 stories above the sea. At mesa's edge, the bluffs plummet down to an open beach. Rollers break across a sandy coastal plain and rocky intertidal zone. Further offshore, submarine Scripps Canyon provides a conduit between the shallow continental shelf and deeper waters offshore. Located at the doorstep of UC San Diego's Scripps Institution of Oceanography, reserve lands are among the longest-studied coastal habitats in California.

Humans have utilized the abundant resources of this coast for thousands of years. Archeological excavations uncovered several flexed human skeletons buried with metates on the bluff just north of the reserve. Estimated at nearly 10,000 years old, they may be the earliest multiple burials yet found in the New World (Kennedy 1983). Artifacts from three prehistoric cultures dated 1,500 to almost 9,000 years old have been found across

SCRIPPS COASTAL RESERVE

Administering Campus: UC San Diego

Established: 1965

Location: San Diego County; upland portion is approximately 0.3 miles west of main campus and 0.6 miles north of Scripps Institution of Oceanography (SIO); marine portion is adjacent to SIO

Size: Approximately 800 acres

Elevation: Elevation below MLLW is 50 feet. Elevation above mean sea level is 370 feet.

Average Precipitation: 9 inches per year

Average Temperatures:

   Air: September maximum 78°F, January minimum 47°F

   Water: August maximum 69°F, February minimum 57°F

Facilities: Scripps Institution of Oceanography and the San Diego campus provide real-time and long-term atmospheric and ocean meteorological data, laboratory and library support, diving facilities, small boats, aquaria, and pier. NRS office can provide field supplies and equipment, including water tanker, flatbed trailer, and small tractor with attachments for rent.

Databases: Collections of marine plants, animals, and sediments at SIO; synoptic vascular plant collection; vertebrate species lists; biological, archaeological, geological reports; site-related research bibliography, including reserve-based publications since 1995; hydrographic and meteorological records available through SIO; long-term monitoring data for rocky intertidal

the undeveloped knoll area. Hundreds of grinding stones near the southern head of the submarine canyon are evidence of human activity during periods of lower sea levels. In the late 1800s, the Kumeyaay people who had lived in the region for thousands of years were displaced by Europeans. The new settlers farmed and grazed cattle on the upland portion of the reserve.

Marine research in the area dates back to 1903, when the Scripps Institution of Oceanography was founded in the sleepy town of La Jolla. Land and funds for the laboratory were donated by newspaper publisher Edward Willis Scripps and his half sister Ellen Browning Scripps, who in 1890 bought a portion of a former Mexican rancho in San Diego and named it Scripps Miramar Ranch. Both Scripps Coastal Reserve and Elliott Chaparral Reserve are located on former Scripps Miramar Ranch lands. The laboratory soon joined the University of California, and the University was granted oversight of intertidal and subtidal lands around the laboratory in 1929. Plants and invertebrates on these lands were granted state protection when the parcel was designated the San Diego Marine Life Refuge in 1957. This complex coastal environment became one of the seven

Scientists ranging from oceanographers to anthropologists for the last 100 years have studied
the lands and waters around Scripps Coastal Reserve (Ansel Adams, UCR/California Museum of
Photography, Sweeney/Rubin Ansel Adams Fiat Lux Collection, University of California, Riverside)

founding sites of the NRS in 1965. Today, additional submerged lands to the immediate
north and west are leased for the reserve from the city of San Diego. Adjacent waters to
the south are part of the city's La Jolla Underwater Ecological Reserve, where fishing and
collecting are prohibited.

The reserve gained upland components in the 1980s. These include a UC-owned coastal
mesa called the Knoll, which is bounded to the north and south by steep canyons descending to the beach. A private parcel in Sumner Canyon, immediately south of the Knoll, is
licensed to the NRS for research and educational uses by Scripps Estates Associates.

The marine riches of Scripps Coastal Reserve are the product of a varied ocean environment. Offshore, cool, nutrient-rich waters from Alaska mix with warmer waters
from the south. Flows are further complicated by currents traveling up and down the

The giant green anemone (*Anthopleura xanthogrammica*) lives among the rocks off Scripps Coastal Reserve Beach. Symbiotic algae living within anemone tissues provide nutrients in exchange for a protected place to live. (Jackie Sones)

submarine canyons. Spring upwelling triggers plankton blooms that form the foundation of the marine food web. Constantly changing ocean conditions, together with bottom conditions that range from canyon rock to shifting sand, support extraordinary biological diversity.

The coastal waters of the reserve shelter the larvae of many intertidal organisms such as gooseneck barnacles (*Pollicepis polymerus*) and sea urchins (*Strongylocentrotus franciscanus, S. purpuratus*). When area waters warm during seasonal and El Niño ocean cycles, species from more southern waters are seen in the reserve, including the jumbo squid (*Dosidicus gigas*).

Underwater, Scripps Coastal Reserve consists largely of a sandy coastal plain. Invertebrates that reside here include a variety of snails, worms, and starfish, while rays, sharks, and flatfish are transient foragers. From the surrounding plain, the narrow mouth of submarine Scripps Canyon opens into vertical rock walls encrusted by stony corals, nudibranchs, and polychaete worms. The canyon, which descends to 650 feet within the reserve, serves as a corridor for large schools of market squid (*Loligo opalescens*) traveling from deep water to spawning grounds. At the upper end of the canyon, mats of cyanobacteria grow on accumulated detritus. These bacterial mats in turn extraordinary densities of crustaceans and the many fish species that prey on them. California sea lions (*Zalophus californianus*) hunt in the canyon and bask in surface waters.

In ancient times, a ribbon of magma from the earth's core rose through sandstone rock fractures near shore. Today this volcanic dike provides a stable anchor for eelgrass (*Zostera marina*) and marine algae. Invertebrates that find shelter within the waving strands include California spiny lobster (*Panulirus interruptus*), giant Pacific octopus

Red diamond rattlesnakes (*Crotalus ruber*) bask atop Scripps Coastal Reserve
Knoll. (Isabelle Kay)

(*Enteroctopus dofleini*), and colorful nudibranchs. Beds of California mussels (*Mytilis californianus*) continue to thrive here while declining further south. Resident fish include opaleye (*Girella nigricans*) and stocky orange garibaldi (*Hypsypops rubicundus*) in deeper waters.

The pilings beneath Scripps Pier teem with schools of anchovy (*Engraulis mordax*) and sardines (*Sardinops sagax*) that swim in densities of thousands per square meter. On occasion, thousands of porpoises can be seen leaping above the water to hunt these schools of bait fish. High tides in spring and summer draw runs of California grunion (*Leuresthes tenuis*), which come ashore en masse to spawn on the beach.

Iceplant (*Carpobrotus edulis*) and other introduced plants now cover large areas of the coastal mesa. Reserve management practices have expanded native coastal sage scrub species such as California sagebrush (*Artemisia californica*) and lemonadeberry (*Rhus integrifolia*). The mesa also supports a breeding population of the federally threatened California gnatcatcher (*Polioptila californica*). Protected mesa canyons shelter coast barrel cactus (*Ferocactus viridescens*), succulent live-forevers (*Dudleya pulverulenta*), and the soil-stabilizing, ground-hugging ashy spike moss (*Selaginella cinerascens*). The reserve's coastal bluffs are a nest site for peregrine falcons (*Falco peregrinus*), which returned in 2005 after an absence of 50 years.

The intimate relationship between the reserve and Scripps Institution of Oceanography has encouraged scientific studies of this coastal ecosystem for nearly a century. Nearby UC San Diego and many other universities use the marine portion of the reserve for undergraduate instruction in earth, marine, and life sciences, while classes in archeology, dance, and ecology take field trips to the Knoll.

A peregrine falcon (*Falco peregrinus*) dives out of the sky to snatch a shorebird in its talons at Scripps Coastal Reserve. The falcon is one of a pair that nested in the face of the bluffs bordering the reserve beach. (Will Sooter)

Unlike most NRS sites, Scripps Coastal Reserve is completely open to the general public. Its waters draw surfers, swimmers, and tidepoolers. On the Knoll, an interpretive trail meanders through the coastal sage scrub, commanding views for 30 miles or more from the edge of the bluffs. A place of tranquility amid California's second-largest city, Scripps Coastal Reserve broadens public appreciation for the glories and benefits of California's natural systems.

STEELE/BURNAND ANZA-BORREGO
DESERT RESEARCH CENTER

Exposed sand and the outstretched arms of ocotillo (*Fouquieria splendens* subsp. *splendens*) give an undersea appearance to this view of Anza-Borrego Desert State Park. (Christopher Woodcock)

Many have written about the ineluctable draw of American deserts, but none have portrayed it with the vividness of Edward Abbey. Author and conservationist, environmental hero and anarchic iconoclast, Abbey (1968) wrote "what draws us into the desert is the search for something intimate in the remote." For those who wish to conduct that search in Anza-Borrego Desert State Park, the NRS's Steele/Burnand Anza-Borrego Desert Research Center provides an ideal staging ground. California's largest park at approximately 615,000 acres, Anza-Borrego offers 500 miles of dirt roads, 12 wilderness areas, and more than 100 miles of trails.

In 2008, the California Department of Parks and Recreation, the Anza-Borrego Foundation and Institute, and the NRS entered into an agreement to establish a new gateway reserve at Anza-Borrego State Park. This agreement authorized the NRS to establish a new reserve in the region and to conduct research and teaching activities within

STEELE/BURNAND ANZA-BORREGO DESERT RESEARCH CENTER

Administering Campus: UC Irvine

Established: 2011

Location: San Diego County, town of Borrego Springs; 2-hour drive from UC San Diego

Size: Approximately 80 acres, in addition to the 615,000 acres of Anza-Borrego Desert State Park

Elevation: Field station is at 597 feet. Anza-Borrego Desert State Park is at 60 to 6,193 feet.

Average Precipitation: 5 to 7 inches per year

Average Temperatures:

   November through March average 75°F

   April and October average 85°F

   May to September average 105°F

   Summer maximum 121°F

Facilities: Researcher and student accommodations, laboratory, and kitchen

Databases: There are no databases accessible at this reserve at present. Any available databases probably would be obtained via the Anza-Borrego Foundation or Anza-Borrego Desert State Park.

Anza-Borrego State Park. A generous gift from a donor with family ties to the area enabled the purchase of a historic country club to serve as a new research hub adjacent to the park.

Anza-Borrego Desert State Park is a study in extremes. A valley surrounded by the Santa Rosa, Vallecito, Pinyon, and Jacumba mountains cuts through one-third of the park. Two erosional badland areas, bone dry today, harbor fossils from a more verdant past. A perennial stream—a rare year-round source of water—provide critical riparian forest habitat in this arid region. Blistering summer heat in the lowlands contrast with cooler, temperate climes atop the mountains. Habitats include Colorado Desert ecosystems, riparian forest, California fan palm oases (*Washingtonia filifera*), piñon-juniper woodlands (*Pinus monophylla–Juniperus californica*), desert shrub forests of redshank (*Adenomostoma sparsifolia*), and even stands of white fir (*Abies concolor*) at high elevations. Cacti and succulents are well represented, as are xeric-adapted lichens and soil crusts.

The park supports many rare and endangered vertebrate species, including the barefoot gecko (*Coleonyx switaki*) and the desert tortoise (*Gopherus agassizii*). Also present are the unusual elephant tree (*Bursera microphylla*), more typical of Baja California, and the largest population of endangered Peninsular bighorn sheep (*Ovis canadensis nelsoni*) in the

The headquarters of the Steele/Burnand Anza-Borrego Desert Research Center are surrounded by open desert. (Daniel Anderson)

United States. Large numbers of migratory birds, together with resident species, make the park an important area for monitoring bird populations. Archeological sites within the park feature petroglyphs, pictographs, and other artifacts left by the Kumeyaay and Cahuilla peoples. Legacies of more recent inhabitants include abandoned mines and remnants of early railroad camps and trestles.

The eroded badlands of the park provide access to a remarkably diverse trove of fossil-bearing sediments laid down over the past seven million years. The over 550 different types of fossilized organisms found here open a window into a vanished world. Petrified shells of marine species and the bones of the extinct imperial walrus (*Valenictus imperialensis*)—laid down when the area was inundated by the warm, tropical waters of the Gulf of California—are replaced by the more recent fossils of mammoths (*Mammuthus* spp.), saber-toothed cats (*Smilodon* spp.), and bathtub-sized tortoises (*Geochelone* sp.). These Pleistocene giants roamed the region when it was an open grassland. An environmental shift toward the more arid climate of today is recorded in the occurrence of fossils from giant ground sloths (order Xenarthra) and giant camels (*Titanotylopus* sp.).

The headquarters of this NRS desert research center is the sleek and airy former Borrego Springs Desert Club. Built in 1949, the club was designed by architect William Kesling, known for his Streamline Moderne-style structures. Developer Alphonse A. Burnand, considered by many the father of the town of Borrego Springs, commissioned the structure. Burnand led an accomplished life, competing in sailing at the 1932 Summer Olympics, founding the Borrego Springs Water Company, and establishing the Alphonse A. Burnand

The brilliant pink blooms of the hedgehog cactus (*Echinocereus engelmannii*) add a grace note to the stark Colorado Desert. (John Rotenberry)

The greater roadrunner (*Geococcyx californianus*) eats mostly insects, fruits, and seeds but supplements its diet by running down lizards and even rattlesnakes at speeds of up to 26 miles per hour. (Joyce Gross)

Medical and Educational Foundation. Burnand hoped the club would become the social hub of Borrego Springs, and for a time, it was a popular nighttime destination for movie stars and locals alike. In the mid-1960s, the Borrego Springs Desert Club was sold and used as an art gallery, then a residence. Burnand's daughter-in-law, Audrey Steele Burnand, donated funds in 2011 to support the purchase, expansion, and establishment of an endowment for the NRS's thirty-seventh reserve.

The reserve will encourage the study of environmental and ecological processes in the region. Already, UC scientists, Anza-Borrego Foundation staff, and affiliated colleagues are conducting research in the park that will be used to inform desert management decisions and conservation planning. For example, climate change models indicate the Sonoran Desert will experience major shifts in water availability, making the area a magnet for global change research. Groundwater pumping from local aquifers is lowering the water table further, attracting the interest of scientists seeking to conduct hydrologic modeling and test remote-sensing equipment. And as predicted increases in temperature drive plant species to higher, cooler habitats, the park's mountains will enable scientists to follow shifts in the annual schedules and ranges of plant species while still within the borders of the park.

The Steele/Burnand Anza-Borrego Desert Research Center will provide scientists, other researchers, and students with a place to sleep, shower, cook, and conduct laboratory work within an extreme desert environment. Proximity to several other NRS desert sites allows students and researchers to use the reserve as a home base while visiting other research sites as well as major geographic features such as the Salton Sea.

The Anza-Borrego Foundation, a nonprofit organization that supports the park and is donating land to the reserve, will provide public outreach programs for adults and schoolchildren at the reserve. The reserve will also provide local and distance learning opportunities. The NRS, California Department of Parks and Recreation, and the Anza-Borrego Foundation, are developing educational materials that will be disseminated from the new research center via satellite to classrooms located elsewhere. These materials will help students in California and beyond appreciate the desert Edward Abbey (1968) brought to life with his words:

> Under the desert sun, in the dogmatic clarity, the fables of theology and the myths of classical philosophy dissolve like mist. The air is clean, the rock cuts cruelly into flesh; shatter the rock and the odor of flint rises to your nostrils, bitter and sharp. Whirlwinds dance across the salt flats, a pillar of dust by day; the thornbush breaks into flame at night. What does it mean? It means nothing. It is as it is and has no need for meaning. The desert lies beneath and soars beyond any possible human qualification. Therefore, sublime.

STUNT RANCH SANTA MONICA MOUNTAINS RESERVE

The Ethel Stunt Oak is named for one of the first European settlers of Stunt Ranch Reserve.
(Christopher Woodcock)

In the midst of the megalopolis of Los Angeles, between the San Fernando Valley to the north and the Los Angeles Basin to the south, rise the green and wild Santa Monica Mountains. An interposition of nature within the state's most populous city, the mountains shelter oak-studded canyons juxtaposed with narrow beaches and chaparral-clad slopes overlooking radiant Pacific sunsets. More than 20 parks and protected areas have been designated within this mountain range, including Stunt Ranch Santa Mountain Mountains Reserve. Located within Cold Creek Canyon, the most pristine and biologically diverse watershed in the Santa Monica Mountains, this NRS reserve is a welcoming place for all students of California natural history.

Humans have occupied the Santa Monica Mountains for at least 10,000 years. Prehistoric artifacts dating from 1,000 to 3,000 years before the present have been found on the reserve itself, including soapstone bowl fragments, hammerstones,

STUNT RANCH SANTA MONICA MOUNTAINS RESERVE

Managing Campus: UC Los Angeles

Established: 1995

Location: Los Angeles County, in Santa Monica Mountains; 4.5 miles north of Malibu; 26 miles by road from UCLA

Size: Approximately 300 acres

Elevation: 1,285 to 1,550 feet

Average Precipitation: 24 inches per year

Average Temperatures:

    High is 90°F, but it can top 105°F

    Low is 40°F, but it can dip to 25°F

Facilities: All destroyed in the 1993 Malibu-Topanga fire; planning is under way for a research/education center

Databases: Maps, aerial photos, geologic surveys; extensive species lists of fungi, vascular plants, and vertebrates

and bedrock mortars. In more recent times, the Gabrielino and the Chumash tribes marked the border between their territories at the eastern ridge of Cold Creek Canyon. Although Spanish colonists settled in nearby Topanga Canyon in the late 1700s, the first Europeans to homestead in the Cold Creek watershed were the Stunt family, who arrived from England in the late 1800s. The Stunts lived and worked in nearby Hollywood during the week, enjoying the ranch on weekends. Over time, the Stunts planted a fruit orchard and built a cabin on the property, located on the north-central flank of the

Santa Monica Mountains between Malibu and Calabasas. In 1937, Harry Stunt and his sister, Ethel, who had worked for many years as head secretary at the British Embassy in Shanghai, both moved to the ranch to live there full time. Ethel, who died in 1971, bequeathed the ranch to Occidental College for field instruction. The state purchased the property seven years later, while the Santa Monica Mountains Conservancy assumed administrative responsibility for the site. The University of California exchanged 395 acres of other lands in the Santa Monica Mountains for Stunt Ranch, which joined the NRS in 1995.

Plummer's mariposa lily (*Calochortus plummerae*), found in Stunt Ranch Reserve chaparral, is endemic to the coast and inland hills of southern California. (Jessica Peak)

The reserve and much of the open space surrounding it lies within the Santa Monica Mountains National Recreation Area, the largest urban park in the National Park system. Administered by the National Park Service in coordination with other jurisdictions, the 123,553-acre recreation area preserves some of the finest examples of Mediterranean-climate ecosystems in the world, despite its proximity to metropolitan Los Angeles.

The Santa Monica Mountains are part of the Transverse Ranges, a group of mountains in southern California oriented east to west against the prevailing north-south axis of most of California's coastal mountains. The unusual orientation of these mountains is due to a southeasterly tending dogleg of the San Andreas Fault. As movement along the fault slides along the margin of the Pacific Plate to the northwest, segments of the plate that encounter the dogleg stall. Pieces of this crust get compressed and uplifted into mountains. To the west, the Santa Monica Mountains extend into the Pacific Ocean, forming the continental anchor of California's four northern Channel Islands.

Perennial Cold Creek provides Stunt Ranch Reserve with year-round fresh water. (Christopher Woodcock)

Stunt Ranch Reserve is centered around Cold Creek, a major tributary of Malibu Creek, the only stream that cuts through the Santa Monica Mountains from north to south. Arising four miles inland from groundwater springs, Cold Creek flows through Stunt Ranch year round. Smaller tributaries provide a well-developed corridor of riparian habitat featuring coast live oak (*Quercus agrifolia*), California bay (*Umbellularia californica*), and arroyo willow (*Salix lasiolepis*).

A mosaic of chaparral communities surrounds the stream. North-facing slopes are dominated by scrub oak (*Quercus berberidifolia*) and other shrubs. Drier, south-facing slopes are cloaked in drought-tolerant chamise (*Adenostoma fasciculatum*), bigpod ceanothus (*Ceanothus megacarpus*), and laurel sumac (*Malosma laurina*). While non-native grasslands grow in areas with heavy clay soils, healthy local populations of native bunchgrasses persist in other areas.

The Santa Monica Mountains harbor a broad range of vertebrate fauna, nearly all of which also occur at Stunt Ranch Reserve. Large carnivores such as mountain lions (*Puma concolor*), bobcats (*Lynx rufus*), coyotes (*Canis latrans*), and badgers (*Taxidea taxus*) continue to have an active presence in the area's extensive protected wildlands. Mule deer (*Odocoileus hemionus*), rodents, and rabbits are all common. More than 380 species of birds have been reported on the range—almost half of those present in the United States—with a third residing and breeding here. Rare reptiles include the ant-eating Blainville's horned lizard (*Phrynosoma blainvillii*) and the San Diego mountain kingsnake (*Lampropeltis zonata pulchra*), which sports vivid rings of red, black, and white.

An island of green amid the nearly 12.8 million people inhabiting the greater Los Angeles area, Stunt Ranch provides an important link between area residents and the natural world. UCLA is less than an hour's drive from the reserve, as are many other colleges and universities. While most of the reserve is open only by appointment, the public can cross the western edge of the Cold Creek watershed via the public Stunt High Trail, which connects to other trails in the mountains.

The side-blotched lizard (*Uta stansburiana*) has a genetically determined system of mating strategies reminiscent of the game of rock, paper, scissors. Males with orange throats are the most aggressive and attempt to control large territories including many females. Males with blue throats are moderately aggressive and control smaller territories, guarding their females closely. Yellow-throated males act like females to sneak into other males' territories to mate. (Ammon Corl)

Although scientists come to the reserve to study topics ranging from lizard mating systems to habitat fragmentation to chaparral fire response, the reserve is perhaps best known for giving city kids a taste of wild California. Stunt Ranch Santa Monica Mountains Reserve is a vital part of the science curriculum for Los Angeles schoolchildren. Since 1977, the Cold Creek Docents, a division of the nonprofit Mountains Restoration Trust, have introduced more than 3,000 elementary students each year to the natural ecology and human history of the Santa Monica Mountains. Students come to Stunt Ranch from dozens of mostly urban elementary and high schools across the Los Angeles Basin. Many are unfamiliar with the living tapestry of a natural landscape when they arrive. But learning about Native American life and natural features including the birds, insects, and native plants while at the reserve sparks an interest in nature and science and an appreciation for the importance of conservation.

JACK AND MARILYN SWEENEY GRANITE MOUNTAINS DESERT RESEARCH CENTER

Eroded granite boulders at Sweeney Granite Mountains Desert Research Center embrace the sandy wash containing the reserve's headquarters. (Christopher Woodcock)

The eastern Mojave Desert is one of North America's most pristine natural landscapes. Its vast open spaces are punctuated by mountain sky islands, sprawling lava flows, booming sand dunes, and saline playas. Broad expanses of creosote bush can be found on alluvial bajadas. This mesmerizing country is home to Sweeney Granite Mountains Desert Research Center, a hub of scientific inquiry and a gateway to the 30 million acres of the greater Mojave Desert.

The reserve lies on the eastern slopes of one of the largest mountain groups in the region. Piñon pine (*Pinus monophylla*) and Utah juniper (*Juniperus osteosperma*) cover ridges that ascend to the highest peak in the Granite Mountains. Large watersheds drop to the north and east into the sandy alluvial valleys of Bighorn Basin, Cottonwood Basin, and Granite Cove. Canyon walls of cleft granite line the lower slopes, interrupted by vertical boulders up to 500 feet high. Near the reserve's eastern

JACK AND MARILYN SWEENEY GRANITE MOUNTAINS DESERT RESEARCH CENTER

Administering Campus: UC Riverside

Established: 1978

Location: East Mojave Desert, San Bernardino County, 80 miles east of Barstow

Size: Approximately 8,600 acres; plus satellite reserves with approximately 265 acres in Old Woman Mountains and approximately 590 acres in Sacramento Mountains

Elevation: Granite Mountains are from 3,700 to 6,796 feet; Sacramento Mountains are from 2,300 to 3,000 feet.

Average Precipitation: 8.9 inches per year at Granite Cove (elevation 4,200 feet)

Average Temperatures:

July maximum 93°F

December minimum 31°F

Facilities: Housing and laboratory with AC electricity, full conveniences for up to 12 researchers; small trailers for long-term researcher housing; cabin with DC electricity for classes of up to 40 persons; campground and conference/lecture room for up to 40

Databases: Vascular plant and cryptogamic herbarium, synoptic collections of animals and rock types, climatological data, aerial photos, maps, library, cultural artifact collection, and bibliography of on-site research

boundary, fractured boulders and exposed pediment give way to densely vegetated washes.

The archaeological resources at the Granite Mountains testify to a long history of human use. Pottery, projectile points, rock art, and habitation sites are scattered throughout the reserve, some dating back 8,000 years. At the time of European contact, the Granite Mountains were inhabited by the Chemehuevi, a Southern Paiute band that had lived in the area for several hundred years. By the late 1800s, disease and conflict with miners and ranchers drove the Chemehuevi from the range.

Ranchers first built homes and corrals within the sheltering rock fins of Granite Cove in the 1920s and tended livestock there for the next 60 years. In the 1940s, General George Patton occupied Granite Cove while conducting US Army training maneuvers in the desert. NRS cofounders Kenneth Norris and Wilbur Mayhew brought field classes to the Granite Mountains in the 1960s, sparking an idea that eventually led to the creation of the NRS. With the help of Norris's brother and fellow UC professor Robert Norris, their dogged persistence and land-acquisition diplomacy led the University to purchase the nucleus of the Granite Mountains Desert Research Center in 1978. In 1994, Jack Sweeney and his wife Marilyn, longtime benefactors of UC Riverside, helped establish an endowment to expand and maintain facilities, support academic programs, and

Rock art panels left by indigenous peoples are scattered throughout Sweeney Granite Mountains Desert Research Center lands. (David Lee)

increase use by researchers and educators. The reserve is named in honor of their gift. The University now owns all formerly private inholdings in the range. Agreements with the US Bureau of Land Management and the National Park Service to access Mojave National Preserve and other surrounding federal lands have expanded the area available to reserve users to nearly 9,000 acres.

The striking formations of the Granite Mountains originated at the edges of an ancient ocean, where a thinner earth's crust enabled magma to flow upward. As the magma cooled, it crystallized into granite. Erosion from wind and water gradually smoothed these granite plutons into the perched boulders, dramatic spires, and rounded cliff faces visible today. Sediments washed from these boulders have accumulated around the flanks of the range in the form of broad bajadas, the product of merged alluvial fans.

The Granite Mountains experience modest seasonal precipitation, broad temperature extremes, and strong winds. Unlike the western Mojave, which is relatively dry in summer, the eastern Mojave Desert receives roughly 25 percent of its annual precipitation during the summer monsoon. Light winter snows are common, and a snowpack may even accumulate across the reserve. Peak summer temperatures at the research center are relatively mild for this harsh desert, with an average high of 94°F.

The Granite Mountains are located in a transition zone between the Sonoran Desert to the south, the Great Basin Desert to the north, the Colorado Plateau to the east, and the western Mojave Desert. Though its flora contains elements from all four arid regions, many of its vascular plants are endemic to the mountains of the eastern Mojave. Only 6 percent of the flora is non-native. Higher elevation ridges harbor open coniferous woodland dominated by single-leaf piñon pine and Utah juniper. Lower alluvial slopes and valleys are dominated by the highest diversity of woody and succulent shrubs in

California, including buckhorn cholla (*Cylindropuntia acanthocarpa* var. *coloradensis*) and Mojave yucca (*Yucca schidigera*). Willows (*Salix* spp.) and Fremont cottonwoods (*Populus fremontii* subsp. *fremontii*) grow in canyons where permanent water is at or near the surface. When watercourses widen into broader sandy washes, a distinct riparian scrub of catclaw (*Senegalia greggii*) and desert willow (*Chilopsis linearis* subsp. *arcuata*) appears. Aeolian deposits from adjacent Kelso Dunes occur along the lower bajadas and support dune-adapted species such as birdcage evening primrose (*Oenothera deltoides*).

Reptiles are abundant throughout the Granite Mountains. The federally threatened desert tortoise (*Gopherus agassizii*) digs burrows into the alluvial soils at the base of the range. Midelevation boulder slopes are inhabited by Great Basin collared lizards (*Crotaphytus bicinctores*) and speckled rattlesnakes (*Crotalus mitchellii*). At higher elevations, striped whipsnakes (*Masticophis lateralis*) and Gilbert's skinks (*Plestiodon gilberti*) take shelter in the boulders and woodlands. By contrast, the red-spotted toad (*Anaxyrus punctatus*) is the only amphibian recorded in the Granite Mountains and throughout most of the Mojave Desert.

The diverse flora of the range and surrounding valleys attracts a diverse array of bird species throughout the year. The cactus wren (*Campylorhynchus brunneicapillus*) prefers open desert scrub, while the mountain quail (*Oreortyx pictus*) and juniper titmouse (*Baeolophus ridgewayi*) remain within piñon-juniper woodland.

Common mammals of the Granite Mountains include eight species of bat, the kit fox (*Vulpes macrotis*), and desert bighorn sheep (*Ovis canadensis nelsoni*). One-third of the

The "Bunny Club," with rooms sheltered by massive boulders, was constructed out of spare parts by brothers and fellow University of California professors Ken and Robert Norris, with help from family, students, and friends. (Christopher Woodcock)

mammal species are restricted to upper elevation habitats; the remainder are widespread generalists found throughout lower desert landscapes.

Invertebrate surveys have identified numerous species that are new to science, including an ant, a beetle, a nematode, a cricket, and two wasps. The limited extent of past invertebrate sampling, combined with the detection of so many new species, suggests the Granite Mountains would be fertile ground for additional discoveries.

The Sweeney Granite Mountains Desert Research Center provides a base of operations for those wishing to investigate a host of nearby desert destinations. The Sacramento Mountains Reserve, a satellite site, features desert pavement and stands of teddy bear cholla (*Cylindropuntia bigelovii*) with spines so numerous they resemble animal fur. Parts of 3 national parks and more than 40 wilderness areas are located nearby. Cinder cone remnants at Cima Volcanic Field and the lava flows of Amboy Crater evoke the area's fiery geologic past. Joshua

A visit to Sweeney Granite Mountains Desert Research Center is unforgettable for university students and researchers alike (John Rotenberry)

trees (*Yucca brevifolia*) raise spiky arms to the sky on Cima Dome, and the singing Kelso Dunes offer lessons in both climate change and the physics of sound production.

The Sweeney Granite Mountains Desert Research Center has been a mecca for university-level instruction and research for more than 40 years. It has hosted more than 50,000 students since opening its doors in the 1970s, as well as more than 500 research projects conducted by scientists from all over the world. For its spectacular natural features and strategic desert location, this reserve is a premier example of the need for outdoor classrooms and living laboratories.

FUTURE DIRECTIONS FOR
THE UC NATURAL RESERVE SYSTEM

The UC Natural Reserve System (NRS) was born of a great idea that took root and blossomed throughout California by the close of the twentieth century. In the twenty-first century, this same great idea has expanded far beyond state borders. The NRS is participating in an increasing number of innovative partnerships created to protect world biodiversity and to understand and manage global climate change. In the process, the NRS operates not only as a collection of related, interlocking parts but also as a cohesive whole whose synergy is far greater than the sum of its parts.

A CLEARER PERSPECTIVE ON GLOBAL CHANGE

The world has become a smaller place in recent decades, thanks to the development of cell phones, global positioning satellites, and wireless networks. Advances in communications technologies have proved a boon to scientists studying the environment. Traditionally, researchers have had to go into the field to obtain weather and other types of data. In the 1990s, the development of wireless mesh networks began to revolutionize the collection of data in real time. These networks consist of communications nodes linked via radio to each other and function in a coordinated fashion to transmit information.

NRS reserves have been at the forefront of developing field sensors to monitor climate and other data. These sensors gather information such as ambient temperature, humidity, and other climatological parameters and pass these data to wireless networks. Miniaturization and mass production of components have made such arrays reliable, durable, relatively inexpensive, and able to withstand extreme conditions in both terrestrial and aquatic ecosystems. Other sensors include video cameras and devices that can read data from rice-sized silicon chips located nearby. Scientists can track animal movements by embedding chips in migrating trout, hunting coyotes, wandering newts, and so on. The NRS has received several National Science Foundation (NSF) grants over the past decade to deploy wireless sensor networks at reserves. The environmental data these networks gather establish baseline climate patterns and permit scientists to identify changes that may be significant in the future.

The NRS is now poised to participate in a national experiment to assess climate change on a continental scale. The $434 million National Ecological Observatory Network (NEON) will collect standardized climate information from field stations in every region of the United States. Because these data are collected in a coordinated, uniform fashion, scientists will be able to monitor and forecast ecological change across the country over many decades. The NRS's Sierra Nevada Aquatic Research Laboratory will be the site of a NEON experiment to gauge the effects of stressors on stream ecosystems. One experiment will add nutrients to the reserve's engineered stream channels. Effects on the food web will be compared against conditions upstream, where the channel has not been manipulated.

Scientists and educators who wish to explore California's natural history are turning

The White Fang rock formation welcomes visitors to Sweeney Granite Mountains Desert Research Center. (Christopher Woodcock)

to the NRS in greater numbers. For several decades, field research on the life history and habitat requirements of single organisms too often has been viewed as lacking in intellectual rigor compared with laboratory research. However, understanding the basic cycles and needs of the state's flora and fauna is becoming more important in efforts to protect rare, threatened, and endangered species.

An example of how renewed interest in natural history research is likely to relate to future biodiversity protection efforts is the Grinnell Resurvey Project, spearheaded by UC Berkeley's Museum of Vertebrate Zoology. The museum's founding director, Joseph Grinnell, built up its specimen collection from more than 700 field sites across California. Museum scientists are now resurveying the vertebrates at these same 700 locations, which include NRS sites such as White Mountain Research Center and Yosemite National Park. By comparing data from the two periods, researchers expect to document changes in animal communities as well as shifts in the relative abundance of individual species. This information will help scientists predict how animals will respond to California's changing landscapes.

Similar efforts are under way at the NRS to track the responses of native plant species to global warming. The California Phenology Project aims to monitor the timing of events such as bud formation, leaf out, flowering, fruit production, and leaf loss in individual California plants. Scientists can model how climate change is affecting entire groups of plants and their ecosystems by observing changes in the timing of when these events occur. Reserve personnel, students, and the public are being trained to conduct these assessments, which will continue over several years. Seven UC natural reserves and several national parks will be among the first sites where phenology data will be collected. Reserve participation dramatically broadens the range of ecosystems and locations being monitored and offers venues where monitored plants are protected from human interference.

One disturbing trend, true not only in California but also throughout the world, is the rapid increase in human population. For example, the population of San Diego County in 2010 was calculated to be approximately 3.2 million residents, but the state of California estimates that by 2050—only two generations later—San Diego County's population will rise to more than 4.5 million people, an increase of 29 percent. UC San Diego's Elliott Chaparral and Dawson Los Monos Canyon reserves lie within the rapidly urbanizing coastal region of this southernmost California county. These and several other NRS sites already are grappling with being located at the urban/wildland interface. Vandalism of infrastructure and research instrumentation, the spread of diseases, invasion of nonnative species, predation by feral pets, and accidental wildfires are but a few such problems. These NRS reserves are in a position to develop the management tools needed to mitigate the consequences of human encroachment on wildlands.

ACCOMPLISHING MORE THROUGH INNOVATIVE PARTNERSHIPS

Protecting California's natural heritage today requires collaboration. One recent example of such a partnership can be seen in the establishment of one of the NRS's newest reserves. The reserve brought the University of California together with the California Department of Parks and Recreation; the Anza Borrego Foundation, a local conservation organization; and Audrey Steele Burnand, a farsighted donor who appreciates the University of California's role in protecting the state's natural heritage. The result of this collaborative effort is Steele/Burnand Anza-Borrego Desert Research Center, a field station that enables users to access the largest state park in California and to collaborate with the Anza-Borrego Foundation, supporting conservation, education, and research in the park. Over its nearly a half-century of operation, the NRS often has worked with private citizens, nonprofit organizations, government agencies, and others to incorporate lands into new reserves. The relationships that produced the Steele/Burnand Anza-Borrego Desert Research Center, which joined the NRS in 2011, are a fine example of the kind of partnerships the NRS will seek to foster while embracing new lands for research, teaching, and public service.

Among the most far reaching of the NRS's projects are its initiatives to protect the fragile ecosystems in the world's five Mediterranean-climatic regions: most of California, the Mediterranean basin, the western cape of South Africa, southwest Western Australia, and central Chile. International Cooperative for the Management of Mediterranean-Climate Ecosystems, established through funding from the NSF, fosters exchanges in research, management, and personnel among Mediterranean-climate ecosystems. The goal is to share conservation strategies and address common problems facing these embattled habitats. This group led to the founding of a Mediterranean-Type Ecosystem Thematic Group (MTEG) within the world's oldest and largest global environmental organization, the International Union for the Conservation of Nature (IUCN). The IUCN is a nonvoting member of the United Nations, composed of more than 11,000 experts from all fields related to biodiversity protection. The IUCN's Commission on Ecosystem Management consists of experts who volunteer their time and expertise to address ecosystem management issues around the world. MTEG is a subset of the commission, providing expert advice to address conservation concerns across the five Mediterranean-climate regions. With these initiatives, the NRS seeks to accelerate information and technology sharing within and beyond California.

To preserve plant species, the NRS has joined the global conservation program of the Royal Botanic Gardens, Kew: the Millennium Seed Bank. This is the largest *ex situ* seed bank storage facility in the world. Begun in 2000, the bank's goal is to save seed from 25 percent of the world's wild plant species by 2020. Partners from more than 50 countries participate in the effort, including botanic gardens, arboreta, government agencies, and universities.

The NRS's role in this conservation effort is to construct a seed bank for native species from NRS lands. Banking seeds from plants on site ensures the preservation of genes adapted to local conditions and helps to ensure future genetic diversity within species. NRS scientists and staff expect to use the banked seeds to restore California's degraded ecosystems and, more broadly, for research into restoration ecology. To date, the NRS's California Seed Bank Project includes partners from the UC Santa Barbara's Vernon and Mary Cheadle Center for Biodiversity and Ecological Restoration, the Santa Barbara Botanic Garden, and the US Bureau of Land Management's Seeds of Success program. The bank itself will be located at the NRS's Sedgwick Reserve. An initiative that ranges from local to global in scope, the seed bank is perfectly aligned with the NRS mission to contribute to the wise stewardship of the earth.

ENSURING THE GROWTH OF UC'S RESERVE SYSTEM

Working under the adage that the entirety of the NRS is greater than the sum of its parts, the reserve system today is on the verge of many new ventures to further its mission of university-level research, education, and public service.

One such project aims to bolster the declining practice of field research. At present, the number of field courses available to students, particularly for undergraduates, continues to shrink. Meanwhile, there is a nearly complete absence of field-based teacher training in graduate-level courses. School administrators with shrinking budgets often deem such coursework expendable, but biologists trained to study natural systems are crucial to creating a secure and sustainable future. As botanist and NRS cofounder Mildred Mathias

Claret cup cactus (*Echinocereus mojavensis*) is widely distributed throughout the Southwest. It is arguably one of the most beautiful members of the cactus family. (Peggy L. Fiedler)

put it, "It is through field studies and training that we produce the future managers of our environment—the planners for land uses of tomorrow, the preserve managers, the citizens with a land ethic" (Mathias 1973). The shift toward laboratory-based learning in the biological sciences has resulted in a diminished appreciation of field-based curricula, a decline in faculty qualified to teach field courses, and a cascade of other consequences such as fewer competent specialists in plant and animal identification and wildlife studies. This is occurring just as humankind is starting to acknowledge the widespread and deleterious environmental changes taking place on planet earth.

The NRS is taking direct measures to reinvigorate the venerable practice of field science at the University of California. The NRS is working with UC faculty to develop new systemwide field courses similar to the Natural History Field Quarter developed and taught by NRS cofounder Ken Norris. The systemwide field courses will feature faculty from multiple University of California campuses, and NRS reserves will serve as field sites for teaching ecological, evolutionary, and conservation principles.

At the same time, the NRS is renewing its commitment to support public service. For many years, the NRS was the University's "best-kept secret" among not only the University community but also the citizens of California. Open houses, lectures, public hikes, and restoration events are becoming popular additions to reserve calendars. Recognizing the importance of staying current in a changing world, the NRS seeks to broaden links to communities beyond the field sciences. Several existing programs at NRS reserves illustrate this wider reach—from the Adventure Risk Challenge program, which brings high school English-language learners to Sagehen Creek Field Station, to the summer residency offered to artists through Yosemite Field Station within Yosemite National Park.

Over the decades, the NRS has become more than the lands it stewards, the flora and fauna these lands support, and the human activities that occur on them. The NRS is also a state of mind that involves awareness of, interest in, and love for the natural world. Those touched by the NRS develop concern for the environment and a sense of humanity's place within it. NRS people are students at heart, studying nature because they love it and loving it more because of what they have learned about it. This love and concern for the natural world has grown into what could be called the NRS ethic, which NRS founder Ken Norris (2010, p. 287) expressed so eloquently:

> We now understand that everything springs from our Earth as it hurries through space, and that she circles in the most delicate equipoise. Clearly, the human race has grappled with its position in the cosmos since travelers first watched stars wheel overhead. In a tumult of change, we are now reshaping our private visions of place, as we come to know more and more about the Earth itself. . . .
>
> Though we humans are probably the first among the animals to perceive these relationships, such knowledge confers no space for arrogance. Quite the opposite. It says, instead, that we must define and live by a world ethic that will surely be more rigorous than any ever conceived throughout our long history of searching. We must come into balance with the Earth.

This is the path that Ken Norris, Mildred Mathias, and Bill Mayhew envisioned generations ago, and that the University of California, in its wisdom and with a will to serve the public good, has sponsored for nearly half a century. Now onto the NRS's next 50 years.

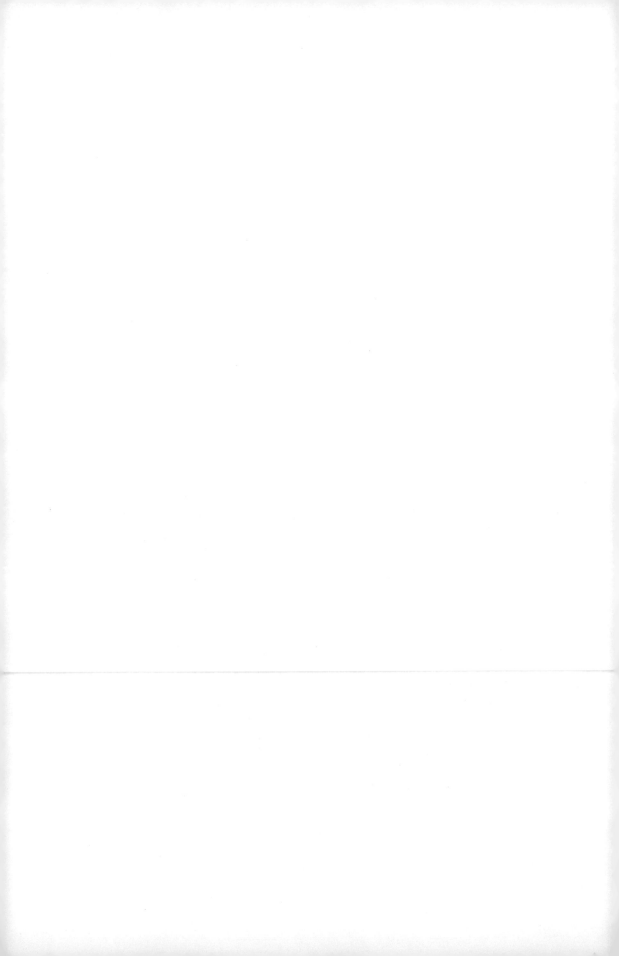

LITERATURE CITED

Editors' note: Included in this section are only those sources cited in the text. A complete set of references consulted in the preparation of this book, as well as a selected listing of research conducted at each of the NRS reserves, can be found at http://www.ucpress .edu/book.php?isbn=9780520272002. The online list includes masters theses, doctoral dissertations, and published research in peer-reviewed journals, books, book chapters, and selected technical reports. These references are not comprehensive but serve to illustrate the range of research that has been, and continues to be, conducted at NRS reserves.

Abbey, E. 1968. *Desert Solitaire: A Season in the Wilderness.* New York: McGraw-Hill.

Alagona, P. S. 2008. Homes on the range: Cooperative conservation and environmental change on California's privately owned hardwood rangelands. *Environmental History* 13: 287–311.

Amundson, R., P. Gersper, A. Schultz, and G. Sposito. 1992. University of California: In memoriam, 1992. Hans Jenny, soils and plant nutrition: Berkeley. http://texts.cdlib.org/ view?docId=hb7c6007sj&chunk.id=div00028&brand=calisphere&doc.view=entire_text.

Anonymous. 1939. Dr. Grinnell, famous U.C. scientist, dies: Ornithologist succumbs to heart attack. *The San Francisco Examiner,* May 30, 1939.

Bakker, E. G., B. Montgomery, T. Nguyen, K. Eide, J. Change, T. C. Mockler, A. Liston, E. W. Seabloom, and E. T. Borer. 2009. Strong population structure characterizes weediness gene evolution in the invasive grass species *Brachypodium distachyon. Molecular Ecology* 18: 2588–601.

Batten, K. M., K. M. Scow, K. F. Davies, and S. P. Harrison. 2006. Two invasive plants alter soil microbial community composition in serpentine grasslands. *Biological Invasions* 8: 217–30.

Block, B. A., I. D. Jonsen, S. J. Jorgensen, A. J. Winship, S. A. Shaffer, S. J. Bograd, E. L. Hazen, D. G. Foley, G. A. Breed, A-L. Harrison, J. E. Ganong, A. Swithenbank, M. Castleton, H. Dewar, B. R. Mate, and D. P. Costa. 2011. Tagging of pacific predators: Tracking apex marine predator movements in a dynamic ocean. *Nature* 475: 86–90.

Boehlert, G. W., D. P. Costa, D. E. Crocker, P. Green, T. O'Brien, S. Levitus, and B. J. Le Boeuf. 2010. Autonomous pinniped environmental samplers: Using instrumented animals as oceanographic data collectors. *Journal of Atmospheric and Oceanic Technology* 18: 1882–93.

Boucher, V. L., and T. H. Nash. 1990. The role of the fruticose lichen *Ramalina menziesii* in the annual turnover of biomass and macronutrients in a blue oak woodland. *Botanical Gazette* 151: 114–18.

Briggs. C. M. 2009. Seed preferences of the harvester ant *Pogonomyrmex rugosus* in coastal sage scrub. Masters thesis, University of California, Riverside.

California Environmental Quality Act, Article 20. Definitions. http://ceres.ca.gov/ceqa/guidelines/art20.html.

California State Department of Education. 2006. *A Master Plan for Higher Education in California, 1960–1975*. Sacramento.

Clark, C. J., and T. J. Feo. 2010. Why do *Calypte* hummingbirds "sing" with both their tail and their syrinx? An apparent example of a sexual sensory bias. *American Naturalist* 175: 27–37.

Czimczik, C. I., K. Druffel-Rodriguez, and S. E. Trumbore. 2008. Concentrations and 14C age of nonstructural carbon in California oaks. American Geophysical Union Meeting, Fall 2008, abstract B23C-0460.

Deveny, A. J., and L. R. Fox. 2006. Indirect interactions between browsers and seed predators affect the seed bank dynamics of a chaparral shrub. *Oecologia* 150: 69–77.

Dickinson, J. L., W. D. Koenig, and F. A. Pitelka. 1996. The fitness consequences of helping behavior in the western bluebird. *Behavioral Ecology* 7: 168–77.

Dickinson, J. L., and W. W. Weathers. 1999. Replacement males in the western bluebird: Opportunity for paternity, chick-feeding rules, and fitness consequences of male parental care. *Behavioral Ecology and Sociobiology* 45: 201–9.

Epanchin, P. N., R. A. Knapp, and S. P. Lawler. 2010. Nonnative trout impact an alpine-nesting bird by altering aquatic-insect subsidies. *Ecology* 91: 2406–15.

Epps, C. W., J. D. Wehausen, V. C. Bleich, S. G. Torres, and J. S. Brashares. 2007. Optimizing dispersal and corridor models using landscape genetics. *Journal of Applied Ecology* 44: 714–24.

Estes, J. A., J. Terborgh, J. S. Brashares, M. E. Power, J. Berger, W. J. Bond, S. R. Carpenter, T. E. Essington, R. D. Holt, J. B. C. Jackson, R. J. Marquis, L. Oksanen, T. Oksanen, R. T. Paine, E. K. Pikitch, W. J. Ripple, S. A. Sandin, M. Scheffer, T. W. Schoener, J. B. Shurin, A. R. E. Sinclair, M. E. Soulé, R. Virtanen, and D. A. Wardle. 2011. Trophic downgrading of planet earth. *Science* 333: 301–6.

Fenn, M. E., J. S. Baron, E. B. Allen, H. M. Rueth, K. R. Nydick, L. Geiser, W. D. Bowman, J. O. Sickman, T. Meixner, D. W. Johnson, and P. Neitlich. 2003. Ecological effects of nitrogen deposition in the Western United States. *BioScience* 53: 404–20.

Gee, J. M. 2003. How a hybrid zone is maintained: Behavioral mechanisms of interbreeding between California and Gambel's quail (*Callipepla californica* and *C. gambelii*). *Evolution* 57: 2407–15.

Gomez-Pompa, A. 1998. Letter nominating Wilbur Mayhew for Chevron Conservation Awards Program. NRS collection.

Harrison, S., C. Hohn, and S. Ratay. 2002. Distribution of exotic plants along roads in a peninsular nature reserve. *Biological Invasions* 4: 425–30.

Henry, B. P. 2005. Monterey pine (*Pinus radiata*) in California: Variation among native forests and health as predictor of tree removal in an urban forest. Masters thesis, Michigan Technological University, Houghton.

Herbst, D. B., E. L. Silldorff, and S. D. Cooper. 2009. The influence of introduced trout on the benthic communities of paired headwater streams in the Sierra Nevada of California. *Freshwater Biology* 54: 1324–42.

Herring, M. 2000. Studying nature in nature: The history of the University of California Natural Reserve System. *Chronicle of the University of California* 3: 65–74.

Holloway, J. M., M. B. Goldhaber, K. M. Scow, and R. E. Drenovsky. 2009. Spatial and seasonal variations in mercury methylation and microbial community structure in a historic mercury mining area, Yolo County, California. *Chemical Geology* 267: 85–95.

Jenkins, T. M., Jr. 1969. Social structure, position choice and microdistribution of two trout species (*Salmo trutta* and *Salmo gairdneri*) resident in mountain streams. *Animal Behavior Monographs* 2: 57–123.

Jenny, H. 1941. *Factors of Soil Formation: A System of Quantitative Pedology.* New York: McGraw-Hill.

Johnson, C. K., M. T Tinker, J. A. Estes, P. A. Conrad, M. Staedler, M. A. Miller, D. A. Jessup, and J. A. K. Mazet. 2009. Prey choice and habitat use drive sea otter pathogen exposure in a resource-limited coastal system. *Proceedings of the National Academy of Sciences USA* 106: 2242–47.

Keeley, J. E., and P. H. Zedler. 2009. Large, high intensity fire events in southern California shrublands: Debunking the fine-grained age-patch model. *Ecological Applications* 19: 69–94.

Kennedy, G. E. 1983. An unusual burial practice in an early California Indian. *Journal of New World Archaeology* 5: 4–6.

Koenig, W. D. 1981a. Space competition in the acorn woodpecker: Power struggles in a cooperative breeder. *Animal Behaviour* 29: 396–409.

———. 1981b. Reproductive success, group size, and evolution of cooperative breeding in the acorn woodpecker. *American Naturalist* 117: 396–409.

Koenig, W. D., and J. L. Dickinson. 2004. *Ecology and Evolution of Cooperative Breeding in Birds.* Cambridge: Cambridge University Press.

Koenig, W. D., and J. M. H. Knops. 2002. The behavioral ecology of masting in oaks. In *Oak Forest Ecosystems,* edited by W. J. McShea and W. M. Healy, 129–48. Baltimore, MD: Johns Hopkins University Press.

Koenig, W. D., A. H. Krakauer, W. B. Monahan, J. Haydock, J. M. H. Knops, and W. J. Carmen. 2009. Mast-producing trees and the geographical ecology of western scrub-jays. *Ecography* 32: 561–70.

Kohler, R. E. 2002. *Landscapes and Labscapes: Exploring the Lab-Field Border in Biology*. Chicago: University of Chicago Press.

Kuris, A. M., and K. D. Lafferty. 1994. Community structure: Larval trematodes in snail hosts. *Annual Review of Ecology and Systematics* 25: 189–217.

Lafferty, K. D. 2001a. Birds at a southern California beach: Seasonality, habitat use and disturbance by human activity. *Biodiversity and Conservation* 10: 1–14.

———. 2001b. Disturbance to wintering western snowy plovers. *Biological Conservation* 10: 315–25.

Lafferty, K. D., A. P. Dobson, and A. M. Kuris. 2006. Parasites dominate food web links. *Proceedings of the National Academy of Sciences USA* 103: 11211–16.

Lafferty, K. D., and A. K. Morris. 1996. Altered behavior of parasitized killifish increases susceptibility to predation by bird final hosts. *Ecology* 77: 1390–97.

Lafferty, K. D., D. T. Sammond, and A. M. Kuris. 1994. Analysis of larval trematode communities. *Ecology* 75: 2275–85.

Le Boeuf, B. J., D. E. Crocker, D. P. Costa, S. B. Blackwell, P. M. Webb, and D. S. Houser. 2000. Foraging ecology of northern elephant seals. *Ecological Monographs* 70: 353–82.

Lynch, S. C., A. Eskalen, P. Zambino, and T. Scott. 2010. First report of bot canker caused by *Diplodia corticola* on coast live oak (*Quercus agrifolia*) in California. *Plant Disease* 94: 1510. doi: 10.1094/PDIS-04-10-0266.

Mabry, K. E. 2008. Searching for a new home: Decision making by dispersing brush mice. *American Naturalist* 172: 625–34

Mabry, K. E., and J. A. Stamps. 2008. Dispersing brush mice prefer habitat like home. *Proceedings of the Royal Society B* 275: 543–48.

Maciolek, J. A., and P. R. Needham. 1951. Ecological effects of winter conditions on trout and trout foods in Convict Creek, California. *Transactions of the American Fisheries Society* 81: 202–17.

Mathias, M. 1970. Natural Land and Water Reserves System of the University of California. *Biological Conservation* 2: 4.

———. 1973. The value of natural areas. *Fremontia* 1: 3–6.

———. 1982. Among the plants of the earth oral history transcript. Interview by Mary Terrall in 1978 and 1979. Oral History Program, UCLA.

Matthes-Sears, U., and T. H. Nash. 1986. A mathematical description of the net photosynthetic response to thallus water content in the lichen *Ramalina menziesii*. *Photosynthetica* 20: 377–84.

Mayhew, W. W. 1998. Transcription of oral history interview with Wilbur W. Mayhew, August 10, 1998, UC Riverside. http://ucrhistory.ucr.edu/mayhew.htm.

Mazor, R. D., A. H. Purcell, and V. H. Resh. 2009. Long-term variability in bioassessments: A twenty-year study from two northern California streams. *Environmental Management* 43: 1269–86.

Muir, J. 1911. *My First Summer in the Sierra*. Boston: Houghton Mifflin Company.

———. 1918. Letter dated Salt Lake, July 1877. Printed as an essay entitled "Mormon Lilies" in *Steep Trails: California-Utah-Nevada-Washington-Oregon-The Grand Canyon*, edited by William Frederick Bade. Boston: Houghton.

Mumme, R. L., W. D. Koenig, and F. L. W. Ratnieks. 1989. Helping behavior, reproductive value, and the future component of indirect fitness. *Animal Behaviour* 38: 331–43.

Nieto, N. C., E. A. Holmes, and J. Foley 2010. Survival rates of immature *Ixodes pacificus* (Acari: Ixodidae) ticks estimated using field-placed enclosures. *Journal of Vector Ecology* 35: 43–49.

Norris, K. S. 1963. Letter to Clark Kerr, June 4, 1963. NRS collection.

———. 1966. The use of natural land and water reserve land. February 11, 1966. NRS collection.

———. 1997. Letter of support for Bill Mayhew to Chevron Conservation Awards, March 23, 1997. NRS collection.

———. 1999. *Kenneth S. Norris, Naturalist, Cetologist and Conservationist, 1924–1998: An Oral History Biography.* Santa Cruz: University of California Press.

———. 2010. *Mountain Time: Reflections on the Natural World and Our Place in It.* Raleigh, NC: Lulu Press.

Oftedal, O. T., K. Ralls, M. T. Tinker, and A. Green. 2007. Nutritional constraints on the southern sea otter in the Monterey Bay National Marine Sanctuary and a comparison to sea otter populations at San Nicolas Island, California, and Glacier Bay, Alaska. Joint final report to the Monterey Bay National Marine Sanctuary, Monterey, CA, and the Marine Mammal Commission, Washington, DC. ftp://brd1.ucsc.edu/Otter/Nutrition/Otter Nutrition Final Report.pdf.

Ogden, J. A. E., and M. Rejmánek. 2005. Recovery of native plant communities after the control of a dominant invasive plant species, *Foeniculum vulgare*: Implications for management. *Biological Conservation* 125: 427–39.

Padman, L., D. P. Costa, S. T. Bolmer, M. E. Goebel, L. A. Huckstadt, A. Jenkins, B. I. McDonald, and D. R. Shoosmith. 2010. Seals map bathymetry of the Antarctic continental shelf. *Geophysical Research Letters* 37: L21601. doi: 10.1029/2010GL044921.

Power, M. E. 1990. Effects of fish in river food webs. *Science* 250: 411–15.

Power, M. E., M. S. Parker, and W. E. Dietrich. 2008. Seasonal reassembly of river food webs under a Mediterranean hydrologic regime: Floods, droughts, and impacts of fish. *Ecological Monographs* 78: 263–82.

Price, M. V., P. A. Kelly, and R. L. Goldingay. 1992. Distinguishing the endangered Stephens' kangaroo rat *Dipodomys stephensi* from the Pacific kangaroo rat *Dipodomys agilis*. *Bulletin of the Southern California Academy of Sciences* 913: 126–36.

Price, M. V., and K. A. Kramer. 1984. On measuring micro-habitat affinities with special reference to small mammals. *Oikos* 423: 349–54.

Price, M. V., W. S. Longland, and R. L. Goldingay. 1991. Niche relationships of *Dipodomys agilis* and *D. stephensi*: Two sympatric kangaroo rats of similar size. *American Midland Naturalist* 126: 172–86.

Rao, L. E., and E. B. Allen. 2010. Nitrogen mineralization across an atmospheric nitrogen deposition gradient in southern California deserts. *Journal of Arid Environments* 73: 920–30.

Roemer, G. W., T. Coonan, D. Garcelon, J. Bascompte, and L. Laughrin. 2001. Feral pigs facilitate hyperpredation by golden eagles and indirectly cause the decline of the island fox. *Animal Conservation* 4: 307–18.

Roemer, G. W., C. J. Donlan, and F. Courchamp. 2002. Golden eagles, feral pigs, and insular carnivores: How exotic species turn native predators into prey. *Proceedings of the National Academy of Science USA* 99: 791–96

Santa Cruz Island Foundation. 2011. Oral history with Lyndal Laughrin, Channel Islands National Park, Santa Cruz Island Foundation, Santa Barbara, May 2011.

Shaffer, H. B., and P. C. Trenham. 2005. *Ambystoma californiense* (Gray, 1853) California tiger salamander. In *Amphibian Declines. The Conservation Status of United States Species*, edited by M. J. Lannoo, 605–8. Berkeley: University of California Press.

Smith, M. L. 1987. *Pacific Visions: California Scientists and the Environment, 1850–1915*. New Haven: Yale University Press.

Sproul, R. G. 1956. Letter to Mrs. Russell P. Hastings, September 5, 1956. University archives, University of California, Berkeley, CU–5, series 3, box 15, folder 7.

Star, S. L., and J. Griesemer. 1989. Institutional ecology, "translations" and boundary objects: Amateurs and professionals in Berkeley's Museum of Vertebrate Zoology. *Social Studies of Science* 19: 387–420.

Stegner, W. 1992. *The Sense of Place*. New York: Random House.

Stromberg, M. R., and J. R. Griffin. 1996. Long-term patterns in coastal California grasslands in relation to cultivation, gophers and grazing. *Ecological Applications* 6: 1189–211.

Stromberg, M. R., P. Kephart, and V. Yadon. 2002. Composition, invasibility, and diversity in coastal California grasslands. *Madroño* 48: 236–52.

Suttle, K. B., M. A. Thomsen, and M. E. Power. 2007. Species interactions reverse grassland responses to changing climate. *Science* 315: 640–42.

Trenham, P. C., and H. B. Shaffer. 2005. Amphibian upland habitat use and its consequences for population viability. *Ecological Applications* 15: 1158–68.

Turcotte, M., D. Reznick, and J. Hare. 2011. The impact of rapid evolution on population dynamics in the wild: Experimental test of eco-evolutionary dynamics. *Ecology Letters* 14: 1084–92

University of California. 1965. Regents Committee on Educational Policy recommendation, approved and adopted by The Board of Regents on January 22, 1965.

University of California, Davis, Natural Reserve System. 2004. *Natural History of the Quail Ridge Reserve, Napa County, California*. Davis: University of California Press.

University of California, Natural Land and Water Reserves System. 1978. Systemwide academic plan. November 14, 1978.

University of California, Natural Reserve System. http://nrs.ucop.edu/index.htm.

———. 1985. *Natural Reserve System: The First Twenty Years*. Oakland, CA: Author.

———. 1999. *Reserve Use Guildelines*. Oakland, CA: Author.

———. 2003. *Acquisition Guidelines*. Oakland, CA: Author.

———. 2004. *Administrative Handbook*. Oakland, CA: Author.

———. 2008. *Special Research Projects: National Centers and Other Landscape-Scale Projects That Utilize NRS Reserves*. Oakland, CA: Author.

———. 2009. *UC Courses Hosted by UC Natural Reserves*. Oakland, CA: Author.

University of California, Oral History Program. 1982. Among the plants of the earth: Transcript 1978–1979. Mildred Ester Mathias, Harlan Lewis, and Mary Terrall. Los Angeles: UCLA.

University of California, Santa Cruz. Natural history field quarter information and application. http://envs.ucsc.edu/undergraduate/courses/nat-his-field-quarter.html.

Vuncannon, D. H. 1977. Do diamond chain patterns found on the high-desert indicate puberty practices? *American Indian Rock Art* 3: 96–101.

Wehausen, J. D. 1996. Effects of mountain lion predation on bighorn sheep in the Sierra Nevada and Granite Mountains of California. *Wildlife Society Bulletin* 24: 471–79.

———. 1999. Rapid extinction of mountain sheep revisited. *Conservation Biology* 13: 378–84.

Westman, W. E. 1975. Edaphic climax pattern of the pygmy forest region of California. *Ecological Monographs* 45: 109–35.

———. 1978. Patterns of nutrient flow in the pygmy forest region of northern California. *Vegetatio* 35: 1–15.

Westman, W. E., and R. H. Whittaker. 1975. The pygmy forest region of northern California: Studies on biomass and primary productivity. *Journal of Ecology* 63: 493–520.

White, K. L. 1966. Structure and composition of foothill woodland in central coastal California. *Ecology* 47: 229–37.

Wootton, J. T., M. S. Parker, and M. E. Power. 1996. The effect of disturbance on river food webs. *Science* 273: 1558–60.

Wright, S. A., J. R. Tucker, A. M. Donohue, M. B. Castro, K. L. Kelley, M. G. Novak, and P. A. Macedo. 2011. Avian hosts of *Ixodes pacificus* (Acari: Ixodidae) and the detection of *Borrelia burgdorferi* in larvae feeding on the Oregon junco. *Journal of Medical Entomology* 48: 852–59.

Wu, D., P. Gupta, and P. Mohapatral. 2007. Quail Ridge Reserve wireless mesh network: Experiences, challenges, and findings. *Proceedings of the International Conference on Testbeds and Research Infrastructures for the Development of Network and Communication (Trident-Com) 2007*: 1–6.

Wu, D., and P. Mohapatra. 2011. QuRiNet: A wide-area wireless mesh testbed for research and experimental evaluations. *Proceedings of the Communication Systems and Networks (COMSNETS) 2010*: 1–10.

INDEX

Fung, Inez, 34, 36
fuschia-flowered gooseberry, 174

Gabrielino people, 201, 219
Gamboa Point Property, 107
garibaldi, 211
gateway reserves, 21
Gee, Jennifer, 166
Gentiana newberryi. See alpine gentian
Geochelone sp. *See* tortoise
Geococcyx californianus. See greater
    roadrunner
Geothlypis trichas. See common
    yellowthroat
giant bison, 88
giant camel, 214
giant chain fern, 186
giant coreopsis, 120
giant green anemone, 210
giant ground sloth, 215
giant Pacific octopus, 210–11
giant sequoia, 133
Gilbert's skink, 226
Gilia tenuiflora. See sandmat gilia
Gillichthys mirabilis. See longjaw
    mudsucker
Girella nigricans. See opaleye
Girls Puberty Rock, 197, 198
glaciation, 47, 118
glaciers, 67, 139
Gliessman, Steve, 26
gold, 55, 56, 65
golden cholla, 169
golden-mantled ground squirrel, 133
golden spotted oak borer, 181
golden star, 179
goldfield, 52
Goleta Slough, 88
gooseneck barnacle, 39, 210
Gopherus agassizii. See desert tortoise
Granite Cove, 223
Granite Mountains, 223, 224, 225, 226,
    227
Grant, Joseph D., 83

gray fox, 121, 182
gray mangrove, 193
gray whale, 41, 80, 111
Great Basin, 136, 142, 143, 146
Great Basin collared lizard, 226
Great Basin Desert, 225
Great Basin sagebrush, 140, 143
great blue heron, 90
greater roadrunner, 175, 178, 204, 216
greater sage-grouse, 137
great white shark, 41, 80, 81
Griffin, Jim, 104
Grindelia hirsutula. See gumplant
Grinnell, Joseph, 9, 11, 13, 102, 231
Grinnell Resurvey Project, 231
grizzly bear, 70
Gulo gulo. See wolverine
gumplant, 152
Gymnogyps californianus. See California
    condor

Habronattus americanus. See jumping
    spider
Haematocarpus bachmani. See black
    oystercatcher
Haliaeetus leucocephalus. See bald eagle
Haliotis rufescens. See red abalone
Hall Canyon, 185, 187, 190
Hamilton, Michael P., 86
harbor seal, 41, 77, 79, 111
harvester ant, 100, 178, 179
Hastings, Frances, 102, 103
[Frances Simes] Hastings Natural
    History Reservation, 7, 10, 11, 13,
    22, 27, 101–5
Hastings, Russell, 102, 103
Hawaiian spinner dolphin, 12
Hearst, George, 115
hedgehog cactus, 216
Helfer's blind weevil, 49
Helianthemum scoparium. See rock rose
heliotrope, 193
Heliotropium curassavicum var. *oculatum.*
    See heliotrope

[W. M.] Keck HydroWatch Center, 34

Kelly, Mary Emma, 172

kelp, 24, 39, 106, 108, 111, 112, 115, 116, 119, 166

Kelso Dunes, 226, 227

Kendall, Lena, 192

Kendall-Frost Mission Bay Marsh Reserve, 7, 23

Kerr, Clark, 6, 12

Kesling, William, 215

kinglet, 145

kit fox, 226

Klamath Mountains, 60

Knoll, 209, 211, 212

Koeleria macrantha. See june grass

Koenig, Walter, 22, 102

Kumeyaay people, 191, 208, 215

Kuris, Armand, 90

Laboratory of Tree-Ring Research, University of Arizona, 149

lace lichen, 99, 105

Lafferty, Kevin, 90–91, 94

Laguna Mountain springsnail, 189

La Jolla, 208

La Jolla Underwater Ecological Reserve, 208

Lake Berryessa, 61, 70

Lake County, 56

Lampropeltis zonata pulchra. See San Diego mountain kingsnake

Landels, Edward, 107

Landels-Hill Big Creek Reserve, 7, 19, 20, 21, 24, 106–12

Land Trust for Santa Barbara County, 126

Land Trust of Napa County. *See* Napa County Land Trust

large-flowered phacelia, 179

larkspur, 57

Larrea tridentata. See creosote

Larus delawarensis. See ring-billed gull

Larus occidentalis. See western gull

Las Cumbres Observatory Global Telescope Network, 126, 128, 129, 130

Lasthenia spp. *See* goldfield

Latrodectus hesperus. See black-widow spider

Laughrin, Lyndal, 122–23

laurel sumac, 174, 221

Layia platyglossa. See tidy tips

Laytonville, 33

lazuli bunting, 160

Le Boeuf, Burney, 80

Leiter, Nancy, 93

lemonade berry, 174, 211

leopard shark, 40

Leopold, Aldo, 66

Leopold, A. Starker, 12, 66

Lepidurus packardi. See vernal pool tadpole shrimp

Leptosyne gigantea. See giant coreopsis

Leuresthes tenuis. See California grunion

Lewisia pygmaea. See dwarf lewisia

light-footed clapper rail, 88, 192, 194, 206

Limacia cockerelli, 38

Limnanthes douglasii subsp. *rosea. See* meadowfoam

Limonium californicum. See sea lavender

Limosa fedoa. See marbled godwit

Linanthus dichotomus. See evening snow

Lincoln, Abraham, 110

lingcod, 39

Linsdale, Jean M., 102

Lisque Creek, 125, 127

Little Pine Fault, 128

liveforever, 211

Loki's chiton, 116

Loligo opalescens. See market squid

long-billed curlew, 90, 194

longjaw mudsucker, 195

Long Marine Laboratory, 26

Long Valley Caldera, 139, 142

Pogonomyrmex rugosus. See rough
  harvester ant
Pogonomyrmex spp. *See* harvester ant
Point Año Nuevo, 77
Point Conception, 87, 113
poison oak, 72, 98
Polioptila californica. See California
  gnatcatcher
Pollicipes polymerus. See gooseneck
  barnacle
popcorn flower, 52
poppy, 55
Populus fremontii subsp. *fremontii. See*
  Fremont cottonwood
Populus tremuloides. See quaking aspen
Power, Mary E., 34, 35
Price, Mary, 199
Prisoner's Harbor, 118
Procyon lotor. See raccoon
pronghorn, 51
Prosopis glandulosa var. *torreyana. See*
  mesquite
Pseudacris regilla. See Pacific chorus
  frog
Pseudotsuga menziesii var. *menziesii. See*
  Douglas-fir
Psilocarphus brevissimus. See wooly
  marbles
Pteridium aquilinum var. *pubescens. See*
  bracken fern
Puma concolor. See mountain lion
purple needlegrass, 53, 62, 85
purple phacelia, 169
Purshia tridentata. See antelope
  bitterbrush
Putah Creek, 60, 61, 70
pygmy blue butterfly, 90
pygmy cypress, 49
pygmy forest, 47, 48
Pyrgulopsis californiensis. See Laguna
  Mountain springsnail

quail
  California, 61, 166, 204
  Gambel's, 166, 169
  mountain, 169, 226
Quail Ridge Reserve, 7, 23, 60–64
Quail Ridge Reserve Wireless Mesh
  Network (QuRiNet), 23, 63–64
Quail Ridge Wilderness Conservancy, 62
quaking aspen, 139, 148
Quercus spp., 171
  Q. agrifolia. See oak, coast live
  Q. berberidifolia. See oak, scrub
  Q. chrysolepis. See canyon live oak
  Q. cornelius-mulleri. See Muller's oak
  Q. douglasii. See oak, blue
  Q. dumosa. See coastal sage scrub
  Q. kelloggii. See oak, black
  Q. lobata. See oak, valley
  Q. wislizenii. See oak, interior live
Quixote yucca, 108, 178, 179

raccoon, 195
radio telemetry, 64, 86
Rallus longirostris levipes. See light-footed
  clapper rail
Ramalina menziesii. See lace lichen
rambling sea-blight, 193
Ramona lilac, 174
Rana boylii. See foothill yellow-legged
  frog
Rana draytonii. See California red-legged
  frog
Rana muscosa. See southern mountain
  yellow-legged frog
Rancho Agua Hedionda, 172
Rancho Ex-Mission San Diego, 176
Rancho Piedra Blanca, 115
Rancho San Simeon, 115
Rancho Santa Rosa, 115
Raphanus sativus. See wild radish
rattlesnake
  northern Pacific, 85, 86
  red diamond, 211
  southern Pacific, 174, 175
  speckled, 226
Rattus norvegicus. See brown rat